GEOFF HAMILTON

COTTAGE GARDENS

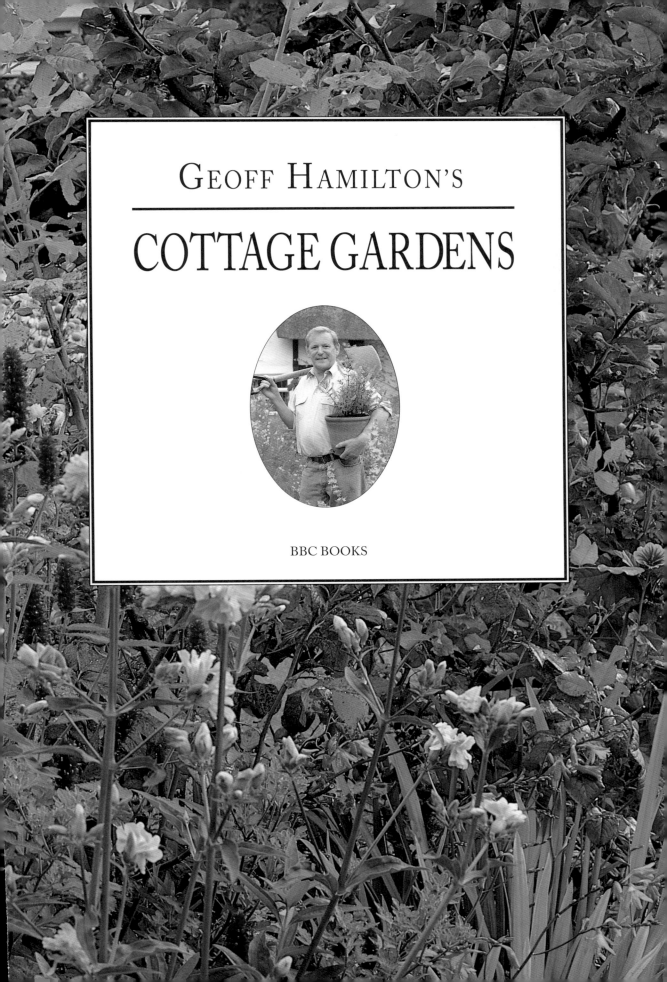

GEOFF HAMILTON'S
COTTAGE GARDENS

BBC BOOKS

*M*y thanks for adding greatly to my knowledge of cottage gardening and to my enjoyment of the pleasant task of making the television series go to the following participants in the programmes, many of whom also allowed us to photograph their beautiful gardens for the book: Arthur Robinson of The Ancient Society of York Florists; Hannah Hutchinson, Owl Cottage, Isle of Wight; Anne Liverman, Dove Cottage, Derbyshire; Malcolm and Carol Skinner, Eastgrove Cottage Nursery, Worcestershire; Peter Herbert and Lindsay Shurvell, Gravetye Manor, West Sussex; George Flatt, Thatch Cottage, Suffolk; Alex Pankhurst, Malt Cottage, Essex; Roger and Margaret Pickering, Barwell, Leicestershire; Leslie Holmes, Camp Cottage, Gloucestershire; Rose Goodacre, Upton, Cambridgeshire; Pat Mansey, East Lode, Norfolk; The National Trust, Blaize Hamlet, Bristol, and Moseley Old Hall, Wolverhampton; Lynne Raynor, The Herb Garden, Derbyshire; Kim Hirst, The Cottage Herbery, Worcestershire; Richard Palethorpe and Bob Holman, The Weald and Downland Museum, West Sussex; John Scarman, Cottage Garden Roses, Staffordshire; Elizabeth Braimbridge, Langley Boxwood Nursery, Hampshire; Dina Penrose, Northfield, Birmingham; Yvonne Bell, Peterborough, Cambridgeshire; Ron Racket, Isle of Wight; Tom Pope, Haddon Hall, Derbyshire.

For helping me find some of the gardens used in the book and the series, my thanks to Pat Taylor and Clive Lane of the Cottage Garden Society and particular thanks too, to Anne Jennings of the Museum of Garden History who went to a great deal of trouble on my behalf

My thanks also to my son Stephen who has surprised me again with his terrific photography, and to Nicky Copeland, Ruth Baldwin and Sarah Amit from BBC Books. I always expect a superb job and they always surpass expectations.

Finally, though they're nothing to do with the book, I'm not going to let this opportunity pass without thanking the crew who made the television series (my baby) come alive. To cameraman John Couzins, sound men John Gilbert and Andrew Chorlton, production manager Sarah Greene and our brilliant director Andrew Gosling, my admiration and gratitude. I don't care what anyone says - they still do it best at the BBC.

❀

PRECEDING PAGES *The cottage garden 'style' was not invented; it simply evolved. So you can just step into that process of evolution to make a traditional, romantic cottage garden – wherever you live.*

❀

Published by BBC Books, an imprint of BBC Worldwide Publishing,
BBC Worldwide Ltd, Woodlands, 80 Wood Lane, London W12 0TT

First published 1995
Reprinted 1995 (eight times), 1996
First published in paperback 1996
Reprinted 1997 (four times)

© Geoff Hamilton 1995
The moral right of the author has been asserted

ISBN 0 563 36985 X (hardback)
ISBN 0 563 38348 8 (paperback)

Illustrations by Gill Tomblin
Diagrams by Hilary Coulthard

Set in Caslon
Printed and bound in Great Britain by Butler & Tanner Ltd, Frome, Somerset
Colour separations by Radstock Reproductions Ltd, Midsomer Norton
Jacket printed by Lawrence Allen Ltd, Weston-super-Mare
Cover printed by Belmont Press, Northampton

Contents

Introduction

The cottage garden style has endured in one form or another in England since the Middle Ages. Even before then, of course, country cottages had gardens, but they were very different from the romantic image conjured up in our minds today. That was to come much later.

What all cottage gardens have in common is that they were there to be *used* – a need which, I think, still exists.

In times gone by, that precious plot of land was home to the pig and a few chickens and also had to raise enough food to feed them, plus something left over for the kitchen. And it was used to raise herbs, mainly for the country medicine chest and to mask much stronger household odours than we're used to today. An aesthetic design was simply not considered at first; but later, when the style was adopted and adapted by wealthier craftsmen and the gentry, the simpler cottage gardeners must have been influenced. They too will have aspired to growing flowers to lift the spirits and to decorate their houses. Nonetheless, inevitably, their designs were very simple.

Well, these days there's no need for medicinal herbs (though many country gardeners do still use them), and a pig or two would drive the neighbours into fits of apoplexy! But gardens are just as necessary now as ever they were.

We live in stressful times and the medical profession is quite clear that stress is a major cause of modern health problems. You only have to spend half an hour in the garden after a day battling with the telephone, the word processor and the rush-hour traffic to appreciate its value as a calming influence.

I suppose there's no real need these days to grow your own vegetables and fruit. It's much more convenient to buy them ready-washed and neatly shrink-wrapped in plastic, even ready-cooked. But just grow one row of fresh lettuce in your own garden and the difference in the quality of your life will shoot through the ceiling, while the cost of it plummets.

Just as important, the garden allows you to use your skill, your artistry and your creative talents to make a thing of beauty. I'm convinced that we all need that. The reasons may be different, but gardens are just as important to a fulfilled life as ever they were.

You may feel that the cottage garden style, with roses round the door and tall hollyhocks lording it over marigolds and violets, is old hat. Yet the style perfectly fits modern gardens and lifestyles. Just ask yourself how and why the cottage tradition arose. Country cottagers long ago had three restrictions: they had little space, less time and no money. And those are precisely the restrictions that many of us face today.

These days, however, we can make much *better* cottage gardens than ever before. With improved varieties of flowers, fruit and vegetables, better materials and techniques and, let's be honest, a bit more time and a lot more money to spend, we can *all* bring a breath of fresh country air into our gardens wherever they are. And that's what this book is all about.

Many old cottages have now been refurbished and brought up to twentieth-century standards. However, where conversions and improvements have been done sensitively, using traditional materials and techniques, they retain their rural charm.

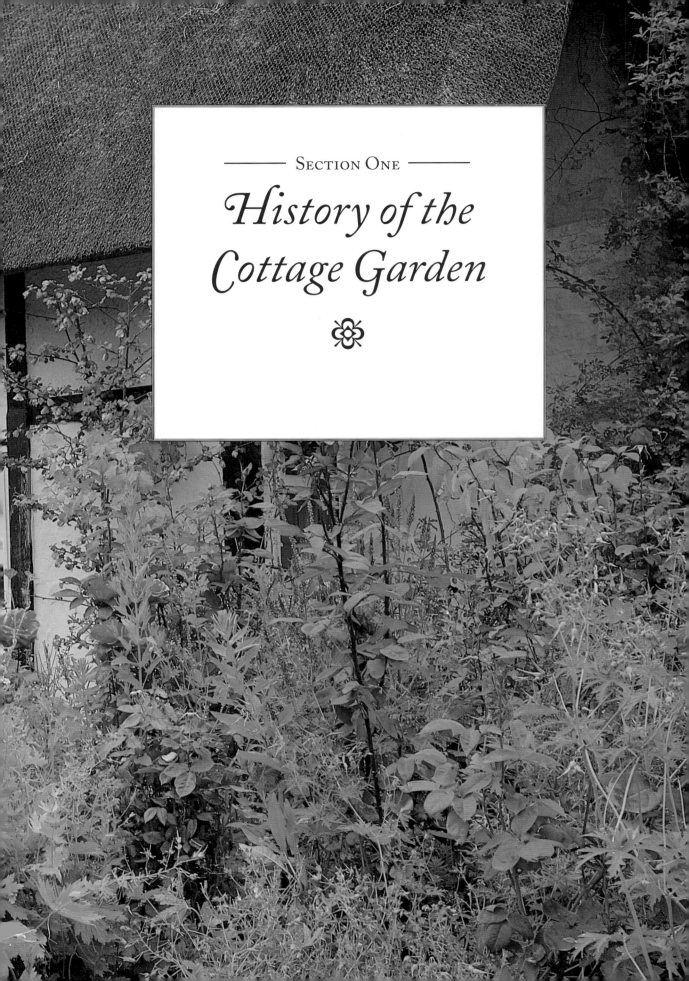

History of the Cottage Garden

*T*HE COTTAGE GARDEN style was never deliberately devised. It has grown over the years from medieval times to the present day, evolving and developing according to need and changing fashion. Though billions of chocolate-box tops have tended to give the impression of a romantic, rural idyll, it certainly didn't start out that way.

The Middle Ages

In the Middle Ages (500–1400) the labouring classes, who made up the vast majority of the population of the countryside, lived in relative

ABOVE *The pig was the mainstay of the medieval cottager's diet and shared the family's facilities.*

PAGES 8–9 *Thatched cottages with wattle-and-daub walls remain, but modern materials and techniques have made them far more comfortable than the originals.*

OPPOSITE *A fine stand of fennel (*Foeniculum vulgare*), backed by the purple spikes of* Agastache foeniculum *with roses in the background, illustrates how plants can be mixed in true cottage garden fashion to produce dramatic effects.*

squalor. Their primitive hovels were made mainly of timber faced with wattle and daub, with leaky thatched roofs, damp walls and wet floors. If they owned animals, these would have shared the space *en famille*, with all the muck and smells, noise and 'wildlife' associated with livestock. At least they provided a primitive sort of central heating.

In such conditions the 'art' of the garden and the thought of improving living conditions with things like flowers in the living room simply weren't considered. Survival was the name of the game.

A bit further up the social strata came the rural craftsmen like the blacksmith and wheelwright and the small farmers. They were important people in the village economy and their comparative wealth and social status reflected that position. They would have lived in slightly more substantial houses, still thatched in the main, but probably drier, warmer and with a separate barn for the animals. Even at this elevated level, however, gardening as we know it hardly existed.

Vegetables certainly were grown, but many of these were used to feed a pig and a few chickens. However, the really poor existed on a diet of cabbages, kale, leeks, onions, turnips and perhaps a few peas and beans plus whatever game they could trap. Meat and cheese were looked upon as luxuries, and a 'pottage' – a sort of thick soup – of dried peas and beans, with the addition of whatever fresh vegetables were available at the time, was much more common.

The wealthier English, on the other hand, have always been great meat eaters. If people could get beef, bacon, mutton or game, they scorned vegetables completely. Indeed, the theory that King Henry VIII (1491–1547) died of malnutrition as a result of an exclusively carnivorous diet does seem to carry some weight. Even as late as the nineteenth century William Cobbett (1763–1835) was proudly proclaiming his good fortune in never having to eat potatoes.

Fruit was quite widely grown, mostly apples, pears, plums, damsons and cherries, with a few wild strawberries dug from the hedgerows, but storage through the winter would have been a problem. No doubt a few morsels were dried and, since bee-keeping was also common, some kind of preserving, making use of the honey, probably existed, but the winter months in particular must have been pretty bleak.

Medieval Medicine

Before the dissolution of the monasteries by Henry VIII in 1536, religious orders were largely responsible for dispensing herbal medicines. And, when villagers visited them for help, they would very likely have gleaned information on cultivation techniques and the uses of herbal remedies.

When the monasteries disappeared, however, this early form of healthcare went with them. The cottagers then had to rely on what they had

Medieval cottages were spartan in the extreme. The walls may have been made of wattle and daub or, if stone was locally available, it would have been used instead. Windows had wooden shutters instead of glass panes and there would have been a fire in the centre of the single living room. Without a chimney the smoke circulated before escaping through a hole in the gable end. With none of today's creature comforts, it's easy to understand why life was lived mostly outside.

been taught by the monks and nuns and grow their own. Almost certainly they would have raided the abandoned monastery gardens for herbs, fruit and decorative plants for their own gardens too.

Inevitably, without the learning and religious discipline of the monks, a generous degree of folklore, superstition and witchcraft crept in.

Some of the properties bestowed upon herbs beggar belief. But perhaps belief was what it was all about – a kind of psychosomatic faith healing process. Valerian is a good case in point: according to Thomas Hill, writing in 1577, it 'provoketh sweat and urine, amendeth stitches, killeth mice, moveth the termes, prevaileth against the plague, helpeth the straightness of breath, the headache, fluxes and Shingles, procureth clearness of sight and healeth the piles'.

Astrology was, in those days, a well respected science and was the basis of what now seems to us the incredible theory behind the 'Doctrine of Signatures'. It was thought that the shape, colour

The small area of land around the cottage was used to house a pig or two and a few chickens and perhaps ducks. The garden grew mainly herbs for medicines and for flavouring stews and soups, plus a few vegetables to feed the livestock and the family. Wheat and more vegetables were grown in strips of land outside the cottage and some wild plants and game would have been hunted in the woods. There would also have been common grazing rights in surrounding woods and on grassland on the common.

and markings of plants indicated their usefulness. Pulmonaria, for example, with its heart-shaped leaves spotted with silver, resembled a diseased lung and was therefore considered to be useful as a cure for consumption; hence its common name of lungwort. Red roses cured nose-bleeding and the fine hairs on the quince made it a sure-fire cure for baldness! My favourite example of early lateral thinking, though, is Thomas Hill's assertion that lentils, famed for causing flatulence, should therefore be sown in exposed gardens to reduce damage from wind!

Primitive Pleasure Gardens

There's a possibility that, even in the deprived conditions under which many of them existed, a small desire for beauty continued to beat in the hearts of some of the less brutalized country folk. Plants would have been collected from the wild and it's quite likely that some small corner of the garden was home to a few violets, primroses and cowslips, perhaps a dog rose and a wild honeysuckle. It's good to think that we still grow all these plants in our gardens today.

Cultivation techniques were primitive but in principle not a million miles from modern methods. The vegetable patch was no doubt rotated: the animals would be penned in with willow or hazel hurdles to muck a piece of land and then moved on, after which the manured area would be used for vegetables and herbs. Fertility came from the proceeds of the privy too. Four centuries ago Thomas Tusser (*c.* 1520–80) in his *Five Hundred Points of Good Husbandry*, an extraordinary instruction manual for small farmers and cottagers, written in doggerel, has this advice for what to do in November:

Foule privies are now to be cleansed and fide [purified],
Let night be appointed such baggage to hide:
Which buried in gardens in trenches alowe,
shall make very many things better to growe.

In fact, of course, this method of fertilizing the soil persisted up to about fifty years ago. In some more remote areas I'm sure it still does.

My own garden is no more than a hundred and fifty years old, yet it's easy to see even now the effect of what was, from the very beginning of man's cultivation of the soil right up to the Victorian age, the *only* method of fertilizing the land. In most of the garden, the soil is light brown in colour and quite heavy clay, except in what was known as the 'crew yard'. Here the pigs and chickens roamed free and I have no doubt that there were a few privy-loads buried there too. The soil is jet-black and it still grows wonderful crops!

In this enlightened age we couldn't contemplate such heathen practices, so we pollute the sea instead. Our plant food is, in the main, put on out of a bag, but the principle is just the same.

Wherever possible, the modern cottage gardener would do well to adopt the traditional methods of manuring and fertilizing with animal wastes just as our ancestors have always done.

The Elizabethan Age

The enlightened era of Queen Elizabeth I (1533-1603) saw the first real improvement in the lot of the peasant. For the times, these were comparatively settled years, with relatively stable government, success in battle and a great surge of exploration. Wealth rolled into England and, because everything relied on manpower, it 'trickled down' even to the labouring classes. There was a marked improvement in working conditions, housing and diet, and even a little spare time to enjoy leisure. This was a golden age for England when even a small farmer, by dint of hard work and a little luck with the weather, could better his standard of living beyond the wildest dreams of his precedessors.

There was no sentiment about preserving history in those days. Here, at last, was a chance for the peasant to improve his living conditions and the energetic Elizabethans seized it with both hands. Whole villages were torn down, probably 'disinfected' with fire and rebuilt. All society, both rich and poor, began to take a pride in its appearance.

The gentry and the richer farmers were now being influenced greatly by the outside world. Many a gentle household would employ a cook from France, Belgium or Italy, so the cuisine became much more varied. At last vegetables and herbs began to assume a more important part in the daily diet.

Revolutionary garden styles and new plants were also imported from the Continent and even from the New World across the Atlantic. It might not be strictly true to say that gardening started in this period, because there were certainly gardens here in Roman times, but a horticultural renaissance had definitely begun. Naturally the innovative styles that became fashionable with the wealthier classes were copied by the peasantry too and cottage gardens began to have a designed shape and form. Most plants would still have been collected from the wild, but it's likely that seeds and cuttings from wealthier gardens found their way into cottages too.

In 1557 Thomas Tusser gives us a good insight into the way in which various plants were spread among the people in the villages:

The Elizabethan era saw major progress in living conditions. Building methods improved and many new plants were imported from abroad.

New garden styles were imported from the Continent to the big houses of the gentry and would certainly have been copied on a much smaller scale by cottage gardeners. This knot garden at Hatfield House is much as it was in the sixteenth century.

Good huswifes in sommer will save their owne seedes
against the next yeere, as occasion needes.
One seede for another to make an exchange,
with fellowlie neighbourhood seemeth not strange.

That's still pretty good advice and widely practised today among gardening friends.

Tusser also provides a quite comprehensive list of herbs and flowers, many of which survive in cottage gardens to this day. Corn marigold, eglantine (sweet briar), campion and heartsease (viola) would probably have been collected from the wild, but clove carnations, lavender and love-lies-bleeding must have come from cultivation.

Vegetables included the protein-rich 'runcivall' peas (to our everlasting shame we seem to have lost this wonderful name and now call them 'marrowfat' or, worse still, 'mushy' peas!) and beans, though he doesn't specify what type the latter were. There were plenty of root vegetables, of course, like carrots and turnips, and even artichokes and pumpkins as well as many kinds of salad crops including endive.

Fruit-growing also expanded greatly. Some gardens now included vines, probably taken from the abandoned monasteries and used to make wine, as well as gooseberries, strawberries and even peaches to add to the apples, pears, plums and cherries.

Apart from the vines to produce wine, Tusser implies that cottage gardeners, or at least small farmers, also grew hops on quite a scale. Certainly we know that ale was consumed in quantity at the time.

In larger gardens, designs from the Continent became fashionable and it's certain that some elements of them were taken and used in humbler gardens too. Formal patterns were all the rage, so the cottager's 'huswife' would have grown vegetables, herbs and flowers in rectangular beds and would probably have planted roses and honeysuckle to grow over a simple form of rustic arch. The cottage garden as we know it was beginning to emerge.

The First Gardening Book

Twenty years after Tusser's rustic doggerel came Thomas Hill's book *The Gardener's Labyrinth*. This was no doubt written with the educated upper classes in mind and the advice is a little more sophisticated. The plans for gardens and parts of gardens are on the grand scale too, but he gives us a very good idea of what was grown.

Comparing Hill's list with Tusser's shows that cottage gardeners grew much the same plants.

Vegetables included 'parsnep, radish, pease, scallions [shallots], lettice, turneps, beanes, cabbage, leekes and onyons' as well as the less usual 'garlike, cucumber, mellion and artechoke'. There's also mention of some vegetables, like 'skerrot' (skirret), that are no longer commonly grown. Among the flowers Hill recommends are marigolds, 'dazie', columbine, sweet John (like sweet Williams), carnations, 'pincks' and, of course, roses. Many of the plants he lists still bring joy to modern cottage gardeners.

In Hill's book, designs are also very formal and, interestingly, there seems to be no distinction made between types of plants. So lettices grow among the gillieflowers, 'parcely' with the 'lupines' and 'ruberb' with the 'musk mellions' – just as in cottage gardens through the ages.

Hill's designs for knot gardens (formal plantings generally of box set out in symmetrical patterns) are fantastically complicated. In fact they're very reminiscent of Moorish designs that can be seen today on the walls of the Alhambra in Granada in Spain, a clear indication of the

The Elizabethans were fond of the formal style and much of their gardening was done in rectangular beds, mixing flowers with vegetables and herbs.

Continental influence on English gardening. The Elizabethans were also great ornamenters, so their garden buildings, arches and even plant supports were elaborately carved and painted, and this could well have also been due to foreign influences.

It's evident that many plants were grown in pots and large containers. Flowers like carnations, which need very good drainage, were suited to this kind of cultivation where the soil would have been lightened with grit and animal manure. Pots were used to grow such fruit as peaches, oranges and lemons too. They were put into a frost-free building in cold weather and brought out again when the danger of frost had passed.

These then, were comparatively comfortable times for cottage gardeners, but they were not destined to continue forever.

Enthusiasms

Inside every gardener there beats the heart and soul of a craftsman. We all know the great personal satisfaction to be had from growing a fine border, a good crop of vegetables or even a superb specimen of a single plant. Cottage gardeners through the centuries have been no exception.

Gardening was a relatively cheap pastime so, from as early as the sixteenth century, the growing of 'special' plants was an occupation keenly espoused by artisans and cottagers.

Gardening has always been enriched by people with special enthusiasms. Nowadays there's enormous competition to see who can grow the biggest pot leek or the heaviest onion. There are coveted prizes for specialist plants like chrysanthemums and dahlias and every village has its annual show where local gardeners vie with each other in friendly competition. It's a tradition that has been handed down through centuries.

It's generally thought that when, towards the end of the sixteenth century, Huguenot weavers arrived in England from France, they brought with them the auricula, a member of the *Primula* family with flowers so perfect in geometry and delicacy of markings that they could almost be hand-painted. This was a plant well suited to the cottage artisan's life: it needed a great deal of minute attention but was hardy, asking only protection from rain, wind and snow. Since the weavers and lace-makers worked at home, their precious plants could be put outside within easy reach in case of a sudden rainstorm.

The cultivation and breeding of auriculas was therefore centred round weaving towns, but elsewhere other plants were enthusiastically bred with the aim of producing perfect flowers. By the eighteenth century eight species were predominant: anemone, auricula, carnation, hyacinth, pinks, polyanthus, ranunculus and tulip. The art of growing and breeding them became known as 'floristry' (nothing to do with the modern usage of the word for the selling of flowers). And, as

The aim of amateur auricula breeders was to grow a perfectly round, almost geometric flower with unusual and delicate markings. It became the speciality of cottage weavers.

plants were exchanged and ideas passed from one enthusiast to another, the logical progression was the formation of florist's societies. They were the forerunners of our modern specialist societies and the grandfathers of today's horticultural societies and garden clubs. Later they also attracted the attention of the gentry, and great feasts were held before each show, with the accent more on food and drink than on plants. Indeed, some of today's enthusiasts blame the eventual demise of most of the societies on this over-indulgence.

Why it is that some plants should have fired the imagination of generations of gardeners is hard to say. The gooseberry, for example, may seem to the gardening philistine a rather mundane sort of a plant. Yet its history is as intriguing as the development of the most exotic orchid.

The gooseberry was adopted by cottage gardeners in the industrial Midlands and the North. Though first recorded in England in 1275, it seems to have been hardly grown until the sixteenth century. But by the nineteenth century there were over 2000 varieties available.

ABOVE *Florist's tulips were highly bred with the aim of producing perfect stripes in unusual colours, again with the rounded shape.*
BELOW *When wealthier plant-lovers took over the florist's movement, they turned their meetings into important social occasions and much food and wine was consumed.*

It was a good plant for cottagers because it could be raised from seed without difficulty, it was small, hardy and easy to grow. Again, competition was the spur to the breeding of such variety. Clubs were formed and, in late July and August, members would bring along their prize berries to be weighed. The 'weigh-ins' were occasions of great jollity and friendship and fierce and serious rivalry. It's a tribute to the humble gooseberry that those very societies still exist today and the friendly rivalry continues.

Topiary

Another abiding passion of the cottage gardener was topiary. The art of clipping plants into various shapes has been practised since Roman times and it became very popular in England in the sixteenth century. Box, yew, rosemary, hyssop, myrtle and holly were among many plants used to

Topiary was in high fashion in the sixteenth century and many examples can still be seen in the gardens of large, old houses.

Cottage gardeners enthusiastically copied the trend for topiary, often with great art and a fine sense of humour. The tradition still exists, as is shown by this locomotive in yew outside a Leicestershire cottage.

form living sculptures. The same plants were also planted to make dwarf hedges around flower and vegetable beds and elaborate knots and parterres in larger gardens.

Often there was a strong religious message expressed in 'foot-mazes' which were planted with low-growing box. They were intended to symbolize man's tortuous passage through life.

The style was eagerly hijacked by cottage gardeners, who often used the faster-growing privet to make all kinds of shapes and figures. Even today it's possible to find cottage entrances dominated by peacocks, chickens, aeroplanes, railway engines and all kinds of human figures.

However, just like the much-maligned leylandii today, topiary was considered in Victorian times to be 'vulgar', and gardens containing it to be over-planted, and many fine specimens were pulled out or cut down in the name of fashion. Fortunately some survived to become an inspiration for the modern renaissance of the art.

Social Division

The eighteenth century and the beginning of the nineteenth were very difficult times for working people. Power was vested solely in the upper classes where corruption was rife. Intent on maintaining the established order, they used their power mercilessly.

First came Enclosure which took away the peasant's right to put his animals on common land. It had been going on continuously since the seventeenth century, and in the eighteenth it gathered pace with 1631 Acts enclosing nearly three and a half million acres.

Without their traditional communal grazing and strips of land outside their gardens, many peasants were unable to feed their stock and were forced to live on home-grown vegetables and whatever their meagre wages could provide. It wasn't much.

Model Villages

The power of the upper classes over the poor was nothing short of savage and I'm afraid that the passion for gardening had a marked effect. Much common land was enclosed simply to provide parks and gardens for the gentry, regardless of the effect it had on their tenants.

The fashion of the day, influenced by designers like 'Capability' Brown (1716-83) and Humphry Repton (1725-1818), was to turn cultivated gardens into agricultural 'parks'. In grand houses, the paved terrace was divided from the park with a stone balustrade and from then on looked out on to rolling pastures. They even went as far as to import cattle, not for any economic reason but purely to provided a 'living landscape'.

Many of their ideas designed for the distraction of the gentry seem outrageous today. Repton, for example, suggested that, at a suitable distance only, the peasantry should be allowed to enter the park for their Sunday stroll, to provide entertainment for the gentry who would be viewing them from the comfort of their opulent salons.

At this time whole villages considered to be 'eyesores' were removed and their tenants thrown out to fend for themselves as best they could. Often they were reduced to roaming the countryside or were sent to the dreaded workhouse. In some cases, though, houses were rebuilt to form 'model' villages. The motive was often less than philanthropic – simply a desire to improve the landscape with a contrived 'rural idyll'. Many were placed where visitors would pass by on their way to the big house to be impressed by the philanthropy of the landlord.

Whatever the reasons behind the construction of model villages, the housing was generally better and the tenants far happier. Naturally this had an effect on their gardens and was later to 'gentrify' the cottage style. Many such villages remain today, though others have almost disappeared in a welter of modern development. In examples like Harlaxton near Grantham in Lincolnshire, stylized thatched country cottages stand cheek by jowl with dwellings built throughout this century. But in Blaize Hamlet near Bristol, they remain unadulterated.

Blaize Hamlet was built in 1810 by a Bristol tycoon, J. S. Harford, to house old retainers. Harford's estate had been designed by Repton in about 1797 and included such indulgences as a vernacular woodman's cottage and a Marie Antoinette-like dairy attached to the house. Later Harford's enthusiasm for the 'traditional' style prompted him to commission John Nash to design Blaize Hamlet. It consisted of a group of cottages built around the village green opposite the estate entrance. There were ten of them, all different and all incredibly ornate. Some had thatched roofs, some slated, some were given

dovecote fascias at the front and all had fantastic Elizabethan chimneys. Today it looks like a Disney theme-park, but then it was much admired and set the pattern for other model villages all over the country.

Developments like this no doubt contributed to the popular view that the peasants were the ones living the good, simple, country life, which was later to encourage the wealthy to follow their 'example'. Meanwhile for the real cottagers life continued to deteriorate.

Despair and Revolt

In 1804 the Corn Laws were introduced. They forbade the import of cheap foreign grain so that British farmers could keep prices high. Larger farmers benefited greatly, but labourers and

ABOVE *When their cottages were demolished to 'improve the view', families were often simply thrown out to tramp the roads in search of work and shelter.*

LEFT *One of ten cottages designed by John Nash for J.S.Harford at Blaize Hamlet near Bristol to house his old retainers. All were self-consciously different and incredibly ornate. They are now owned by the National Trust.*

artisans could no longer afford to buy bread and starvation was common. The effect this had on gardens was not, in fact, to encourage harder work and greater productivity. So miserable were the conditions of the labouring classes that they simply became discouraged and took to crime and the demon drink. It seems hard to believe today that men should be transported and even hanged for the crime of poaching a rabbit or two to feed their starving families. It's even more incredible that their desperation was such that they were driven to take that risk.

Such was the gulf between rich and poor that many of the gentry had no conception of the privations of rural life. From the safe distance of the road they saw the countryman's thatched cottage with neat rows of vegetables and flowers, the housewife contentedly working at her tub while half a dozen grubby children romped around her feet. In reality the thatch leaked, the vegetables were all that made up the family's meagre diet, the far-from-contented housewife took in washing to earn a crust and the 'grubby' children were ragged and ingrained with filth almost from birth.

Yet, despite all the evidence, there was a craving among the upper classes for the simplicity of rural life. Many of them, often recently 'impoverished' (though by no means really poor), built 'cottages' far bigger and more luxurious than the average peasant would dare to dream of and surrounded them with a romantic interpretation of a cottage garden. It was now that the 'chocolate-box' style began to evolve. However, far from being content with the plants the true cottagers grew, mostly collected from the wild, they filled their plots with many of the same plants that were becoming fashionable in the huge houses of the country estates. There were dahlias from Mexico, tulips from eastern Europe and the most sought-after roses from China.

Reform

The end of the eighteenth century saw the birth of a philanthropic movement, strongly resisted by the 'establishment', whose aim was to improve the lot of the rural poor. Men of influence like William Cobbett and John Claudius Loudon (1783–1843) took up their cause. Loudon was a professional gardening journalist and writer and an architect to boot and, perhaps because he seems to have been more tactful and diplomatic than Cobbett, had a great though undramatic influence on political thinking. His influence on horticulture, however, was immense.

Loudon wrote books on every conceivable horticultural subject from hothouses to cemeteries and churchyards, including advice for cottage gardeners. And he still found time to edit the most influential gardening magazine of its time, *The Gardener's Magazine*.

Cobbett, on the other hand, was a man of overweening self-confidence and astonishing lack of tact. He said what he meant and he said it loud and clear in a succession of pamphlets and his own publication, the *Political Register*. By the standards of the day he achieved enormous publicity for his reformist views – so much so that he spent two years in Newgate Prison and two periods of self-imposed exile in America to avoid trouble at home. He eventually became MP for Oldham in the first Reform Parliament.

By the middle of the nineteenth century, reform was irresistible. The Corn Laws were repealed in 1846 and there was a generally more tolerant attitude towards the poor. But the beginnings of the Victorian era brought a morality which we would see today as patronizing and sickly, and even that showed in the gardens of the day.

For some 'philanthropists' the provision of picturesque cottages set around a green, with neat gardens enclosed by hedges and stuffed with flowers, was enough. Surround the poor with the

The romantic, 'chocolate-box' style of cottage gardening really began in the nineteenth century. Malt Cottage in Essex is a weatherboard house typical of the area.

beauty of nature and they would automatically become civilized and educated. Fortunately others, like Cobbett and Loudon, were more realistic. They realized that the single most important factor for a stable life was security of tenure. So they suggested that rural workers should aspire to the freehold of their houses, or at least an absolute guarantee that they would no longer risk being thrown out at a moment's notice at the whim of their landlords – a great idea, but one that has only recently been achieved.

Many of the reformers devised plans for self-sufficiency. Some believed that the cottager should have up to an acre of land, but Loudon felt that an eighth of an acre was all that was needed. Rather optimistically he suggested that this would support a family of four or five. It would house a pig, chickens, rabbits and ducks plus all-year-round vegetables and soft fruit, with apples and pears trained against the house. And he still found space for an enclosing hedge of quickthorn or, better still, varieties of apple to be grafted on wild crab apple roots dug from the woods, and cherries, plums and pears similarly grafted on to their wild counterparts. (This was, of course, before the days of modern rootstocks.) The cultivated food would be supplemented by whatever could be culled from the wild.

Loudon knew that self-sufficiency in home-grown food was vital for many poor country dwellers, but he was essentially an artistic gardener, so no cottage garden, however small it was, should be without its flowers. Few of us today could disagree with his sentiment that 'a few Brompton or ten-week stocks, carnations, picotees, pinks and other flowers ought never to be omitted: they are the means of pure and constant gratification which Providence has afforded alike to the rich and the poor'. Through his writing, Loudon did much to encourage cottagers to take pride in their gardens again.

Evolution of the Typical Cottage Garden

All this encouragement naturally resulted in a general quickening of enthusiasm for gardening and, gradually, what you and I see as a 'typical' cottage garden began to evolve.

Gardening, as you will know if you're a gardener, is a great leveller. A consuming passion for growing plants transcends social differences, and it did so even in those divided days. Then, as now, gardeners began to exchange ideas and, of course, plants. In this way many cottage gardens owned by farmworkers, too poor even to think of spending money on luxuries like plants, became stocked with exotica previously reserved only for the 'big house'. I'm quite sure that many plants were also distributed throughout the village by gardeners to the rich in the form of collected seeds and cuttings snipped off when no one was looking.

Now many cottage gardeners were able to grow dahlias, improved hollyhocks, large-flowered delphiniums, and new, larger-flowered sweet peas. There would have been many more roses available, including the newly introduced hybrid teas and a much wider variety of pinks and border carnations.

Wild clematis had probably always been grown in gardens, but now new, far superior varieties, like 'Jackmanii', were beginning to appear. Crown imperial fritillaries and the cottage lily (*Lilium candidum*) were introduced way back in the mists of time and were grown widely. By the end of the nineteenth century, however, a much wider range of species and varieties started to become available.

Geraniums were among the most popular bedding and windowsill plants, and every Victorian cottage garden would certainly have

In the late eighteenth century the encouragement of writers and artists filtered down to working cottagers who began to take great pride in their gardens. Apart from the addition of a few modern annuals, this row of cottages has changed little and looks today much as it would have done then.

been perfumed by mignonette, which was another well established favourite.

It's hard to say exactly what made a 'cottage garden' plant. There seems little doubt that genuine cottage gardeners would grow almost anything they could get their hands on provided it was easy to grow and propagate, and not so big or rampant that it would overwhelm the plot. Personally I'd go along with the description used by the great Victorian garden writer William Robinson (of whom more later), who suggested that they should be 'unpretentious'.

The Victorians and Beyond

For me there's something rather odious about the Victorian era. All that preaching of morality while sending starving kids up chimneys does not sit easily. But this book is not about politics and I mention it only to put the evolution of the cottage garden into perspective, because the maudlin romanticism of the period did have a bearing on the development of gardens.

In an age where every chimney in every industrial town belched black smoke and covered gardens in soot and sulphur, the cottage garden was an escape to the simple life. Now, more than ever, the rural worker was looked upon as a model of simple happiness. Ignorance was bliss and the blind eye was almost universal.

The change from the worship of wealth and opulence to the idealization of the simple life was largely brought about by artists. Bear in mind that painting, drawing and wood engraving, as well as writing, formed the Victorian equivalent of watching television. Magazines, newspapers and pamphlets gained huge readerships and had enormous power to influence contemporary thinking.

Painters like Myles Birket Foster (1825-99) and Helen Allingham (1848-1926) interpreted cottage life to make it appear ever idyllic. The sun always shone, the flowers never stopped blooming, the housewife was rosy-cheeked and smiling and the children spotless and well-fed. The typhoid, cholera, tuberculosis and diphtheria brought about by insanitary living conditions and appalling diet were rarely, if ever, depicted. With a few honourable exceptions, writers too 'bent' realism somewhat allowing wealthy consciences to be salved. Many gardens painted in the Birket Foster and an Allingham style were recreated by the wealthy, the middle classes, and even by artisans and labourers

But gardening in the mid-nineteenth century was strangely polarized. On the one hand there were the old romantic cottage gardens; on the other there was the new fashion for carpet bedding. Bright annuals were raised every year in the huge, cheaply heated glasshouses of the wealthy and planted out by an army of cheap labour. And, just as plants and ideas from the big house had filtered through to the cottager, so did carpet bedding. Somehow greenhouses and frames must have been afforded, country cottage borders were ripped out and replanted with the bright colours of annuals. In those days, of course, there were no F1 hybrids, so seed could be collected from one year to another and the costs would not therefore have been too hard to bear. The style persisted in many cottage gardens and indeed is still popular today – but only over the dead body of a most influential gardener and garden writer.

A school of romantic artists portrayed the cottager's life as idyllic. They influenced many of the wealthier classes to try to capture the rural dream in the form of flowery cottage gardens.

William Robinson

William Robinson (1838-1935) was a practical gardener first in his native Ireland and then in England, where he was herbaceous foreman at Regent's Park. He later became a prolific journalist, writing for *The Times*, among other publications. In 1871 he founded a magazine, *The Garden*, but his most enduring work was undoubtedly his book *The English Flower Garden*, published in 1883.

Robinson was first and foremost a plantsman

RIGHT AND BELOW *William Robinson was one of the most influential gardeners of his time. His own house at Gravetye Manor, in West Sussex, is now a hotel, but the garden faithfully reflects his love of cottage garden planting.*

and he was much disturbed by what he considered to be the artificial and pretentious fashion that persisted at the time. He disliked carpet bedding and railed against it. He abhorred topiary and all kinds of formal garden design, and he said so loud and clear. For him it was plants that made a garden and he loved the simplicity of real, 'pre-bedding' cottage gardening. To my mind his explanation of the 'secret' of cottage gardening – not an easy thing to define – was perfect.

Cottage gardeners are good to their plots, and in the course of years they make them fertile, and the shelter of the little house and hedge favours the flowers. But there is something more and it is the absence of any pretentious 'plan', which lets the flowers tell their story to the heart.

Robinson brought Gravetye Manor, a large house with 200 acres near East Grinstead in Sussex, and, during the fifty years he lived there, made his ideal garden. The house is how a hotel, but fortunately the owner is also a keen gardener and has restored the garden to its former splendour.

Because of the influence of artists and plantsmen like Robinson, the cottage garden had become something of an art form. And in the 'genuine' cottages of country workers, another important development was to affect the style of the nineteenth century.

Allotments

Agricultural workers were still very badly paid and lived constantly on the edge of starvation, but now they perceived a way out. Many of them,

George Flatt, a retired Suffolk farmworker, now has running water in his cottage, but he remembers tougher times when he had to draw his supplies from the well. Working as a farm horseman in the early part of this century meant that growing his own vegetables, fruit and herbs was an absolute necessity. And, because the hours were long, he often had to dig his half-acre of vegetable garden by the light of the 'parish lantern' – the moon!

fed up and disillusioned with the grinding poverty, poor housing conditions and constant toil of rural life, opted to seek work in the new industrial towns and cities. Farmworkers left the land in droves and, partly to help to retain the remainder and – let's be generous – partly because of an increasing feeling of unease among the wealthier classes about their dire conditions, the allotment movement was conceived.

It started slowly at the beginning of the nineteenth century, but by the end there were many pieces of land rented to agricultural workers to grow vegetables and fruit and to keep a few animals. Vegetables were still grown at home, but now the housewife, who rarely worked on the allotment, had a little more room for her herbs and flowers.

Into the Twentieth Century

A contemporary of Robinson was the great Gertrude Jekyll (1843-1932) who was to have a profound effect on garden design that's still apparent. She too was fascinated by the cottage garden style, but here I tend to disagree with the experts. Her influence, and that of other great gardeners of her time and a little later, while masquerading as 'cottage gardening', in my view missed the essence.

She was, of course, a great gardener with a sensitive and artistic eye. Indeed she started out as a painter, but was forced to give that up because of failing eyesight. She turned instead to gardening and used her undoubted sense of colour to create stunning and original schemes in herbaceous and mixed borders. Her renowned collaboration with the architect Edwin Lutyens (1869-1944) resulted in a number of quite superb gardens that are still an education in the art of colour combination.

Miss Jekyll was followed by other wonderful gardeners of much the same style who must have been inspired by her. Vita Sackville-West (1892-1962), for example, created the amazing garden at Sissinghurst in Kent, complete with a 'white border' that is the model for many imitations.

Great gardeners, talented artists and original plantswomen they certainly were, but were they really cottage gardeners? For me the answer has to be no – the cottage garden is an *artisan's* creation, not an artist's. I agree with William Robinson that simplicity is at its very heart. As soon as the style begins to take on a degree of sophistication, the essence of it is lost. The charm of cottage gardening is its naivety, its honesty if you like. No fancy designs, no coordinated colour schemes, no elaborate statues: just the heart and soul of a simple creator working with nature.

Gertrude Jekyll's garden at Munstead Wood in Surrey shows a strong cottage garden influence. But her interpretation displayed an artistry of planting that would not have existed in genuine cottage gardens.

The cottage garden at Sissinghurst in Kent has also been 'artistically' planted with great thought and care and is the inspiration for countless others.

In the last fifty years society has changed more dramatically than in the previous four hundred. Farmworkers are few and far between now and those that are left often live in their own houses or at least with full security of tenure. And they have a standard of living that would have been inconceivable only a century ago. In fact most of us, wherever we work, whether we're in the town or the country, live in 'cottages' – smallish houses with gardens which may be tiny but which still, albeit for different reasons, are an essential part of our lives. In a frenetic, stressful world we *need* our 'rural idyll' more than ever. We need to surround ourselves with the calming influence and the inspiration of flowers and to indulge our senses in the simple pleasure of growing plants. Cottage gardening is due for another, gentle change in its evolution.

With diligence and application, patience and, yes, a little cash, we can *all* do it and we can make just as good a job of it as our country ancestors.

Of course, that doesn't mean that you should

avoid equipping yourself with as much knowledge as possible about plants and gardening. Certainly we should draw from the experience that has been accumulated over the five centuries that cottage gardening has been around – then we can avoid repeating mistakes that have been made along the way. But it's real folly to allow the ideas of other gardeners, however great, however successful, to submerge your own flair and imagination. Gather together the basic precepts, learn as much as you can about the plants in particular, and then do your own thing.

You'll find that you make mistakes. You'll put sun-lovers in the shade, you'll plant some things too close together and you'll create colour clashes you can't live with. No problem. Provided you realize your errors before too many seasons have passed by, you can do what the old cottagers did. Simply pour a bucket of water over a wrongly positioned plant, lift it, replant it and give it another good drink. Most will never look back.

Remember above all that the great rule in cottage gardening is to avoid the pretentious. Bear in mind the advice of William Robinson and 'Just be good to your plot, make it fertile and let the flowers tell their story to the heart'.

The romantic style suits modern 'cottages' perfectly, as this house in Norfolk shows. You don't need a thatched roof to create a traditional 'rural idyll'.

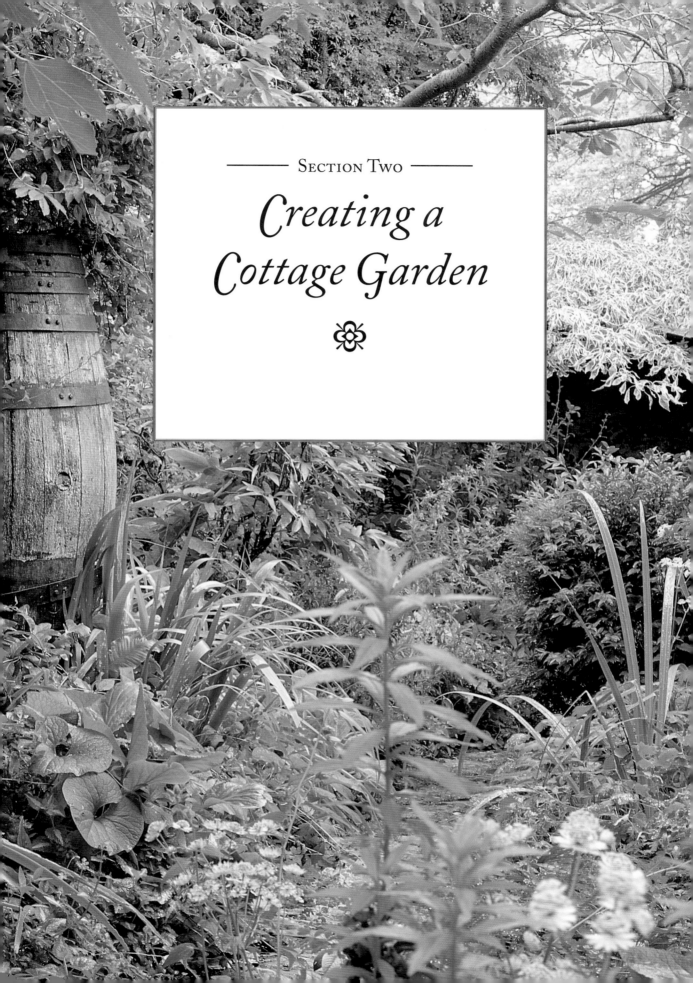

SECTION TWO

Creating a Cottage Garden

❀

*M*Y BRIEF GLANCE through cottage history indicates that there were really two distinct types of cottage garden. The original was definitely a work place, used to feed the cottager's family and, though it gradually evolved to include many ornamental features, it remained a working garden.

Then there was the stylized cottage garden which developed from the enthusiastic espousal of the rustic ideal by more comfortably-off gentlemen and women. There may have been some attempt to grow a few vegetables but it wasn't strictly necessary as it was for the real cottagers. Cottage flowers evoking the romantic rural idyll were the thing.

And, if you detect a note of criticism there, it certainly isn't intended. My own view is that gardens are just as important to refresh and sustain the spirit as they are to feed the body. So a concentration on flowers in Victorian times, for example, when half the country was covered in the soot and grime of the Industrial Revolution, was understandable.

These days, most of us who own or rent a garden can afford to feed our families without the absolute necessity of growing our own. Admittedly there are many allotment gardeners who grow prodigious amounts of food but, unlike the cottagers of old, there aren't many who'd actually starve if they didn't. Having said that, more and more young people in particular, are growing their own, purely because they feel they can produce healthier food, untainted by pesticides. The need is still there.

But the most important function of a garden these days is for relaxation and the restorative value of getting close to the soil and the natural world. Some gardeners, of course, will be able to afford simply to buy their gardens complete. These days, many house owners bring in a designer and a landscaper and have the job done for them. I think they miss a lot.

Others will be able to afford expensive materials that they'll install themselves. But most of us will have to do it ourselves and buy materials as the budget allows. That's *real* cottage gardening and I believe that the creative enjoyment it produces is of the greatest benefit.

But while a young family may not be able to afford all they'd like immediately, things nearly always improve. The kids grow up and leave home, a job promotion generally means more money and, some fine day, most of us actually pay off the mortgage. Then we may want to improve the garden and have the money to do so.

So, I've designed and built two gardens: the first I call the *Artisan's Garden* and it's unashamedly a poor man's garden, just like the originals. Everything is home-made or bought second-hand, and all at low cost.

The second is the *Gentleman's Garden* which has been built with no regard for budget at all. It felt rather grand to be able to order exactly what I liked, regardless of cost. I even began to develop a bit of a swagger! But the funny thing is that I enjoyed doing-it-myself in the poor man's garden much, much more.

I hope that you'll be able to mix and match, with a bit from this garden and a bit from that. Perhaps starting out with beaten earth and gravel paths until brick paving becomes affordable. Or knocking up a coldframe when you start as the teaboy and then buying a greenhouse when you become managing director.

I do urge you, however, to do as much as you can, even if you don't actually have to. You'll have much more fun if you do.

PAGES 34–5 *Even mundane artifacts like the water butt become beautiful when they're surrounded by plants.*
OPPOSITE *These days, when the pace of life is hectic, the garden earns its keep as a place of relaxation and restoration.*

The Artisan's Garden

HERE AND THERE, all over the British Isles, there are old country cottages. Most of them have been got at.

In these days of relative affluence few of us want to live like medieval peasants, so it's hard now to find a cottage with no running water, with damp walls and leaky thatch and tiny windows designed to let in a little light but to retain as much warmth as possible. Nowadays you have to visit a rural museum to see the real thing.

Many old country cottages have had the roof stripped of thatch and replaced with tiles or slates. Most have central heating and nearly always a television aerial or even, horror of horrors, a *dish* on the roof. We mustn't turn up our noses at such improvements. All the owners have done is what the Elizabethans did, for example, during their period of affluence. We are, after all, as much a part of history as they are.

Nonetheless there are quite a few cottages that have retained the *spirit* of their origins. The history of these places is unmistakably impregnated into the walls and in the soil outside. That may sound a little romantic and fanciful but it's not quite so far-fetched as it seems. Most people who buy a country cottage do so because they have an interest in and an empathy with the way of life it's bound to entail. Bear in mind that there will often be much time and expense necessary to 'do it up' and you simply don't buy an old place unless you're interested in doing the job sympathetically.

The modern artisan's cottage garden, like this one built at Barnsdale, suits present-day architecture and building materials but captures all the rural spirit of the old days, and at surprisingly little cost.

Most people, then, would set about discovering the history of their 'dream cottage'. And, because the house is old, it'll be on your side and give you a helping hand. In other words, luck will nearly always be with you, because anyone who has ever lived in the house will inevitably have left bits and pieces lying around waiting to be discovered.

My own house, for example, though only about 170 years old and extensively changed throughout the years, has yielded quite a few clues to the previous inhabitants. In one corner of the garden is the old privy. It's built of brick with a slate roof, which was in a very bad state of repair. To put it right I had to take the roof off, replace the timbers and then put back the slates. In doing so, I made a discovery. Lodged inside, between the top of the wall and the slope of the roof, was an old clay pipe. It had obviously been there since at least the turn of the century, because pipes like that have not been made since then. I like to imagine the old farm labourer creeping in there for a quiet sit-down and a smoke while he rested his weary back in a snatched moment of peace and quiet.

The soil, too, has been a treasure trove. I've dug up horseshoes by the dozen, some of them obviously cart-horse size, bits of old tools and machinery and even the end board of a cart, complete with Victorian sign-writing. All are now carefully preserved.

Plants, of course, are a bit more perishable, but old gardens will often be graced by an ancient gnarled apple tree, a pear or a plum of some unknown variety now rarely grown.

Cottage gardens bought by gardeners are often lovingly re-created in the style that fits the age of the building. Many of these works of art are open to the public and collectively form a superb museum of ancient gardening practice. They can certainly provide enormous inspiration for new cottage gardeners. So, if you can bear the suspense, before you do anything to your own plot, get out and about to have a look at as many good cottage garden re-creations as you can. Quite a few sell plants too which, since they'll have been propagated from the garden, will naturally suit you own new cottage garden.

The Principles

Gathering inspiration from old cottage gardens will improve your knowledge and enthusiasm and greatly benefit your own garden. But to imitate them exactly could be disastrous: it depends on the setting. Naturally, if you're the lucky owner of an old thatched cottage in the country, you couldn't do better than to get hold of a chocolate box or two for your research. But for a brand-new cottage you'd finish up with something twee and pretentious and William Robinson would do another turn in his grave. Let the old chap rest in peace.

I think it's exciting to realize that we're involving ourselves in the next step in the evolution of the cottage garden style. It's been developing for centuries and there's no reason why we should stop now.

You can create a wonderful cottage garden for today's equivalent house. A brand-new semi on an estate may not, at first sight, look like a rural idyll, but by the time your planting has grown a little, you'll swear you can hear the clip-clop of the ploughman's horse as he slowly wends his way! Your cottage doesn't even have to be in the country. Remember the weavers and the spinners, many of whom, in days gone by, lived and worked in the towns. They produced cottage

The inspired gardeners at this cottage in Leicestershire have created a cottage garden that's perfectly in tune with the modern style of their house.

gardens every bit as attractive as their country cousins, albeit with some differences in design. You can do it too, wherever you live. The thing to avoid is pretension.

If your house is modern, don't fill the garden with old cartwheels painted white and pseudo plastic carriage-lamps. Modern materials are often just as attractive in the right setting as older ones, and sometimes quite a lot better.

The Layout

Landscape architects and historians, far cleverer than me, can dissect, analyse and explain classic garden design from the Greeks to Geoffrey

Top AND ABOVE *The design of the demonstration artisan's garden couldn't be simpler: just four main beds and a straight border round the edges. Yet, in its first summer, it really begins to look the part.*

Jellicoe. But the trouble with cottage garden design is that it simply doesn't exist. At most, cottagers of old would have copied the stark, businesslike layouts of the monastery gardens and divided their gardens into rectangles.

Country front gardens are a perfect example of unpretentious simplicity that really *works*. Nearly always the front path runs straight from the gate to the door, but that's no artistic design principle: it's very simply the shortest distance between two points.

That also tells you that the layout can be infinitely variable. If you have, say, an existing tree between gate and door, the path will have to bend round it or, if you simply *prefer* a curve, then that's what you make.

Mind you, I appreciate that, if you're torturing your brain with your first garden design, all this airy-fairy stuff is not a lot of use to you. It's all very well letting your imagination run riot, but where do you start?

Well, you start by firmly establishing that the garden is there to be *used* and that the most important feature has to be the plants.

Then it helps – though it's not entirely necessary – to draw a plan of the garden. The drawing needn't be anything fancy, but you'll find that it has the effect of crystallizing your ideas and reminding you where your imagination has brought you. That's important because, by the time you've drawn and rubbed out your twentieth idea, you'll need a break and you don't want to have to start again because you can't remember what went before.

Above all, keep reminding yourself that this is nothing more or less than a rough, working plan. You're making an artisan's garden, not an artist's, so you'll no doubt change things here and there on the ground once you start work outside. That's how it was always done and no cottager ever got paranoid about 'line, balance or impact'. That stuff's strictly for the birds.

It also helps to make a list of what you need. You may have more special requirements if, for example, you have children or grandchildren who visit, but here's a typical list:

Sitting-out area
Path to gate
Table and bench
Shady arbour
Space for dustbins
Washing line
Compost bins
Somewhere to store tools
Coldframe
Plants, plants, plants and more plants

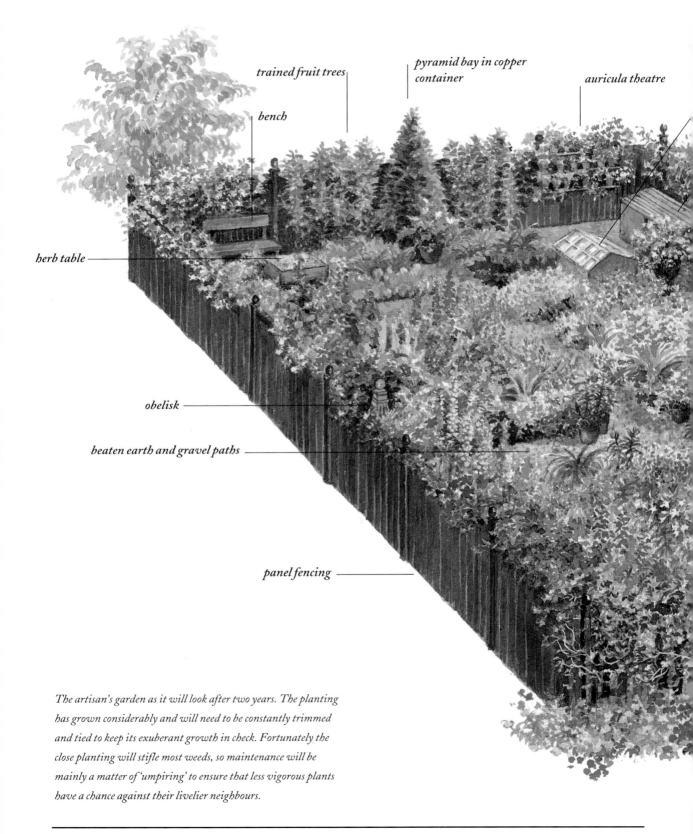

trained fruit trees

pyramid bay in copper
container

auricula theatre

bench

herb table

obelisk

beaten earth and gravel paths

panel fencing

The artisan's garden as it will look after two years. The planting
has grown considerably and will need to be constantly trimmed
and tied to keep its exuberant growth in check. Fortunately the
close planting will stifle most weeds, so maintenance will be
mainly a matter of 'umpiring' to ensure that less vigorous plants
have a chance against their livelier neighbours.

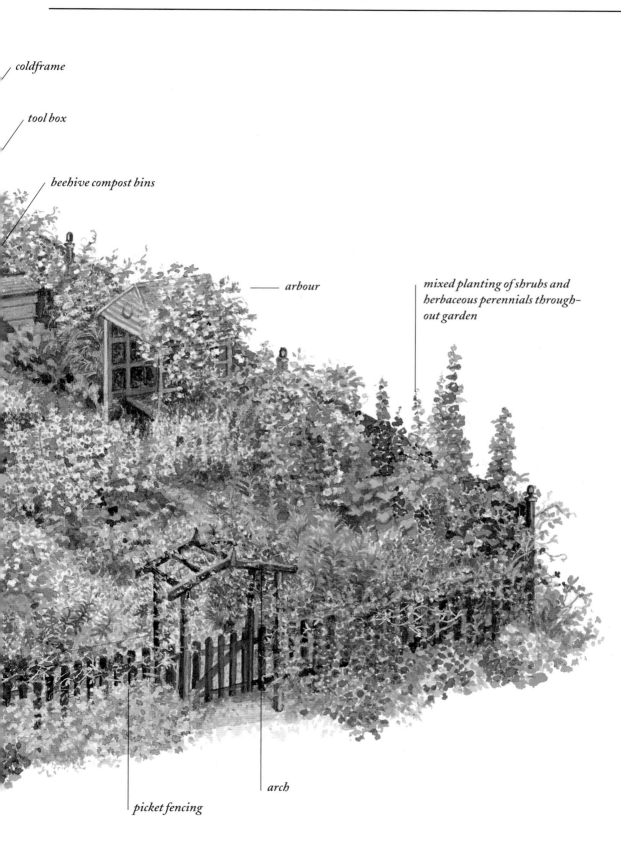

coldframe

tool box

beehive compost bins

arbour

mixed planting of shrubs and herbaceous perennials throughout garden

arch

picket fencing

The final item is undoubtedly the most important, so put it right to the front of your mind all the time. Apart from the obvious fact that plants are really what the garden's all about, they have the great advantage of being able to hide the unsavoury things you might not want to see. However, I believe that *everything* in the garden should be made to be attractive – yes, even the compost bins – but more of that later.

Designing Step-by-step

First of all decide where you want your main essentials. If you take the illustrated garden as an example, you would first ascertain the position of the path. That has to go from one end to the other, and in this case it seems sensible to make it straight. Don't ever worry that straight lines are boring, because the plants will quickly spill over the edges and remove all signs of rigidity.

For maximum convenience the sitting-out and eating area should go near the house, so that can be roughly positioned. I know I want a utility area somewhere near the house too, because it's where the dustbins will be, so that can be roughly drawn in too.

I would dearly love a west-facing seat to catch the evening sun and that should naturally be surrounded by fragrant plants. There's really only one place to put it and there must be a path to get to it too.

I don't want a lawn, so the rest of the garden simply consists of spaces for plants. Suddenly it all begins to take shape.

I obviously need beds along the fences, because those are valuable vertical growing areas for climbing plants, wall shrubs and trained fruit, and I intend to pinch a little extra growing space outside my paling fence too. Those beds will also need narrow access paths to them.

All in all, with only the simple addition of

1 Start by putting in the necessary path (A) from the gate to the house door.

2 The sitting-out area (B) and the utility area (C) should be positioned near the house.

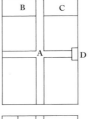

3 There's only one logical place for the west-facing seat (D) and that too needs an access path.

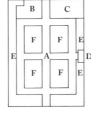

4 With beds at the sides (E) and in the centres (F), plus their access paths, the garden has effectively designed itself.

rectangular flower beds, the garden has virtually designed itself. True, it looks blindingly simple and that's exactly what cottage gardens should be. But don't judge it by the straight lines on paper. Just wait till you see it planted.

Different Shapes

If your garden is exactly the same size and shape as mine, you're in luck and you can skip the next few pages. But the chances are it won't be, so you'll have to fiddle the design around a bit. It's really quite easy if you stick to the idea of modules.

For example, if your garden's wider than it is long, it's easy to create exactly the same garden by simply moving everything around. The only other factor you really must take into consideration is the position of the sun. If your house faces north, say, you won't want to put the eating-out area near the door where you'll never see the sunshine. But – in small gardens especially – there's no reason why it shouldn't be at the other end of the garden in the warm.

It goes without saying that the sun's position is also going to affect which plants go where. At this stage, however, there's no need to worry about that.

Not every garden is as conveniently shaped as my example, and thank goodness for it. I get as excited about gardens with odd shapes and levels as I do about old houses with nooks and crannies. A bit of individuality gives a lot of scope for ideas. Obviously the permutations of shapes and sizes are endless, but with the module method of design, it's easy to work round each and every devious alternative. What could differ more is

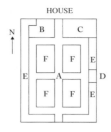

1 In the original design, the house is situated at the end of a rectangular, south-facing garden.

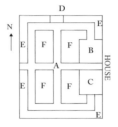

2 If the house is on the east side, the garden is short and wide, so simply move the components about.

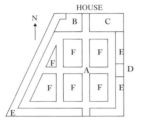

3 A couple of extra beds and access paths cope with an irregularly shaped plot.

Of course, paths need not be straight. At Eastgrove Cottage in Worcestershire irregular brick paths make an attractive foil for the plants spilling over the edges.

your own personal taste. Again, thank goodness for that. You may want curves, you may decide that grass is essential, you perhaps need more space for vegetables: use the modular idea, but simply change the shapes. Circles, semi-circles and ovals fit the modular scheme well too, but keep the shapes simple, strong and not too fiddly.

But, please, treat my examples purely as a basis for your own imagination. Go outside, walk around viewing the garden from every possible angle and imagine yourself sitting on your bench in the sunshine or in the perfumed arbour on a still summer evening. Imagine what you'd like to see around you as you sit there and make sure you realize that absolutely nothing is impossible given a bit of time and patience.

If the garden's small, 'borrow' from next door by hiding your fences with plants so that all you see are the neighbour's trees. They'll look for all the world as if they're in your garden.

If you budget's tight, don't worry. The great beauty of cottage gardening is that it's designed to be painless. All the plants are easily propagated from seed or cuttings which you can collect from friends' plants or buy cheaply and gradually. And provided you're prepared to put in a little effort, the construction materials are not expensive. Looking out for second-hand materials is also great fun and could save you a considerable amount of money.

Don't even worry about the effort. In the artisan's cottage garden you can do a small amount at a time, and I'll give you a cast-iron guarantee that, come rain, shine, snow or heat-wave, you'll *love* every minute.

RIGHT *A mixed hedge with clematis and roses growing through it makes an impenetrable barrier and a superb show of colour throughout the spring and summer.*
OPPOSITE *A rose-covered arch set into a cottage hedge makes a fine welcome for visitors.*

Building the Garden

❁

Hedges

'The most commendable inclosure for every Garden plot is a quick-set hedge, made with brambles and white thorn.' Thomas Hill's advice of 1577 still holds good today, but only if you have the space. A country hedge made with quickthorn (*Crataegus monogyna*) set 30 cm (1 ft) apart in a well-prepared trench will grow fast, can be closely clipped and looks superb. What's more, if it's well looked after to keep it tight and well-furnished at the bottom, it makes an impenetrable barrier against animal and human intruders. It's regarded mostly as a field hedge, but close and regular trimming turns it into a wonderful green wall, ideal for gardens.

If you have enough room to let it grow in a slightly more unkempt way, you could grow wild and eglantine roses through it, planting one at every 6 m (20 ft) or so, to transform it into high

If you have the space, an informal hedge of shrubs makes an excellent boundary and a fine background for the borders. This hedge of Berberis darwinii *produces bright orange flowers over a long period in spring.*

romance. And you'll find that it'll become home to thousands of insects and dozens of birds.

There are other plants you could use, like holly, some of the berberis varieties (such as *Berberis darwinii, B. stenophylla* and *B. thunbergii*) and perhaps beech or hornbeam, but avoid the much-too-hungry privet and most conifers except, of course, for yew. This most perfect of hedges can be clipped to form a green, living wall but it's expensive and more suited to the gentleman's garden. In some gardens I'm not at all averse to the ubiquitous leylandii which, with regular attention, can form an excellent, close-clipped hedge. But for our simpler, rural artisan's garden, hawthorn is definitely the thing.

Another alternative is to grow a mixed hedge, often seen in the countryside where plants that happen to have been growing there have been trimmed to form the hedge. Plants like black-thorn or sloe (*Prunus spinosa*), guelder rose (*Viburnum opulus*), damson (*Prunus institia*), elderberry (*Sambucus nigra*) and hazel (*Corylus avellana*) can be brightened up with the dog rose (*Rosa canina*), the blackberry (*Rubus fruticosus*) and the eglantine rose (*Rosa eglanteria*).

If you plant something like holly here and there along the hedge, you could let it grow above the hedge line and involve yourself in the cottage art of topiary (see page 203).

When you plant a hedge, you'll want to achieve fast growth, so make sure that the soil is really well prepared beforehand. Dig a strip at least 1 m (3 ft) wide and preferably two spades deep, and use plenty of bulky organic matter plus about a handful of organic fertilizer per plant or, if you're planting in winter, bonemeal only.

To achieve a really dense hedge right from the base, some plants need to be cut back hard after planting. Hawthorn, privet, sloe and hazel should all be pruned to within about 15 cm (6 in) of the ground. But don't prune beech, hornbeam or any conifer until it has exceeded the required height by 15 cm (6 in).

Then mulch around the plants with a thick layer of manure, compost or bark to deter weeds and retain moisture. The following year the hedge should again be trimmed quite hard, but allow a little more growth this time.

This is one job where you need a lot of patience to achieve the desired result. Take advice from Thomas Bernhard who, in 1797, published a pamphlet describing in glowing terms the cottage garden of a farmworker, one Britton Abbott, who lived near Tadcaster in Yorkshire. He remarks that the fine quickthorn hedge surrounding his garden was cut down *six years running* after

*Hawthorn (*Crataegus monogyna*) is the traditional hedging plant of cottage gardens. It produces white flowers in spring – the well-known 'May blossom' – followed by red berries, and it has good thorns too.*

planting to produce a very fine, dense hedge.

Unfortunately, you'll need to allow a width of at least 1 m (3 ft) for most hedges to grow to maturity and, in a tiny garden, that's just too much. In any garden under about 10 m (33 ft) wide, you'll have to settle for a solid barrier which takes up less space.

If you happen to have existing walls in stone or brick, praise the Lord and get planting. The extra heat retained by a wall that faces any direction but north will enable you to grow a wonderful range of plants you would never have been able to grow otherwise.

If you don't have one, forget it. Building walled gardens is now, alas, the prerogative of the very rich and not for the likes of us poor artisans! Fencing is the next best thing.

Panel Fencing

The intricacies of putting up fences are dealt with in other books, but there are a few main points that bear repeating.

The first concerns your choice of timber. Cottage gardeners of old would have had one great advantage over us. Because timber was cheap and plentiful, they would have used solid, seasoned English oak for their posts. Today it not only costs too much to be an economic proposition, but is also normally kiln-dried, which means that it'll warp and twist all over the place as it ages. I've seen oak posts with a knot half-way up, which have bent at 45 degrees. And that, of course, both looks bad and destroys the connecting panels.

I would therefore always recommend softwood posts, though here we can get our own back. The old cottagers could never have heard of 'tanalizing'. In this process the timber is treated under pressure with preservative, which is forced into the pores of the wood, right the way through, guaranteeing it more or less for life. If you want to take advantage of this bit of technology (and in my opinion it's crazy not to), give the timber merchant a few days to get it done and expect to pay a little more. It's well worth it.

For me concrete is the only really permanent way to secure posts, but it has one big disadvantage. Unless they're properly pressure treated beforehand (and I have to say that most fencing posts aren't), they'll fairly quickly rot at ground level. You can buy metal sockets that are driven into the ground to take the posts and keep them above the soil, but it's virtually impossible to get them in exactly straight and square, especially in stony ground, and they always finish up wobbling. The good old English compromise gives the best of both worlds: you can also buy metal sockets that concrete into the ground, and

If you have no space for a hedge, at least you can make the fence hedge-coloured by painting it with matt-finish, dark green wood preservative.

these are much the best bet. Fix them to the posts before you concrete them in and they'll last more or less forever.

One other aspect of modern fencing worries me too. Nearly all panel fences are sold in a ghastly orange colour. In small gardens especially they stand out like a sore thumb and make you feel as though you're living in a matchbox. My solution is to paint them green. You can actually buy green panels now, but the preservative used is too pale for my taste, so I use it as an undercoat and paint on top with a dark green matt finish. They look great, but I have to admit that painting does put the price up quite a bit.

Finally, and most important, when you're putting up panel fencing, it's *essential* to build the whole thing, posts and panels, as you go along. Never be tempted to put the posts in first and hope to fit the panels later because they have a nasty habit of shrinking or stretching just enough not to fit! Put in the first post, then measure and dig the hole for the second. Nail the panel to the first and then nail the other end of it to the second before you concrete it in.

Plant Supports

All the fences will be used to grow fruiting plants and climbers, so some means of support is necessary. At all costs avoid plastic trellis which is expensive and looks forever like plastic trellis. Much cheaper and a million times better is galvanized wire stretched between the posts and simply nailed to each with staples. Space the wires about 30 cm (1 ft) apart. To wire walls, use vine-eyes, which are galvanized steel tags you simply hammer in, or drill holes and plug them.

For fruit trees, briar fruits or roses, that's all you need, but if you want to grow twining plants like clematis, you'll have to make a mesh with some vertical wires too. Use thin-gauge wire and simply twist it round the horizontals.

Paling Fences

Look at any Victorian painting of a cottage garden and it's obvious that a paling fence in the front garden was more or less obligatory. Right in the middle was the mandatory wicket gate, often slightly cock-eyed on its rusting hinges and the sort of nuisance no cottager worth his salt would have tolerated for long, although visually it added greatly to the charm of the scene.

There's no doubt that a paling fence does characterize the cottage garden and it certainly looks lovely. If you can arrange to plant cottage flowers either side of the fence, it makes a wonderful welcome to the garden. In small gardens a paling fence defines the boundary without completely cutting off the view, so there's no claustrophobic effect. That's perfect for the front garden but, because of the lack of privacy, often not ideal for the back.

It's possible to buy paling fences in ready-to-erect sections, and they're very easy to put up. It's also not difficult and very much cheaper to make your own. If you do decide to do it yourself, the

Picket fencing can be bought as 1.8 m (6 ft) panels, but it's also very easy to make yourself. The effect is greatly enhanced by growing plants through it. In fact, if you pinch a little border outside your fence, the local authority will rarely object since the effect is so attractive.

posts can be set in first, though it's wise to measure them fairly accurately and, again, put them into metal sockets before concreting them in. They need to be about 2.4 m (8 ft) apart. Leave the concrete to harden for a few days before fixing the horizontal bars and the palings.

The horizontals are made from 75 x 25 mm (3 x 1 in) timber and the palings from 75 x 20 mm (3 x ¾ in). Make sure that it's all pressure-treated with preservative before you start. Then it's just a case of drilling the horizontals and fixing them to the posts with coach screws and nailing on the palings with about 5 cm (2 in) between them.

Gates

You can buy gates ready-made and, unless you're pretty proficient with saw and hammer, that's the best way. However, it is possible to make your own.

The one piece of equipment you might not have is a bevel square. It's an invaluable tool for quite a few jobs where it's necessary to cut angles. If you're going to build, say, a porch, an arbour or compost bins, you'll need one for those too, so it's worth the investment.

A paling gate obviously sets off a similar fence best of all, but if your garden is bounded by a hedge or another type of fence, you may prefer a

A paling or 'wicket' gate is the traditional entrance to old cottage gardens. It's easy to make your own from the same materials used for the fence, or of course you can buy one ready-made.

different type of gate. There are lots of designs and materials that could be suitable, depending on the existing boundary, varying from rustic through to solid, close-board gates, though the more sophisticated they are, the more skilled you'll have to be to make one. The one gate I think I would draw the line at for a cottage garden would be modern wrought iron, but if you could pick up an old iron farm wicket gate, that would be just the job.

Arches

It's likely that the cottage garden arch was an imitation of the common church lychgate where the coffin stood to await the attention of the clergyman. There are no such macabre connections with cottage gardens, though! It's almost obligatory to have an arch spanning the front gate at least, and arches can also be used to good effect in the garden. Covered with roses or honeysuckle, they add instant height and a waft of perfume every time you walk through.

You can buy all kinds of arches from those made of willow withies to plastic-covered metal, and your choice will depend on the garden and, to a large extent, the budget. In one of the cottage gardens I built I used ready-made willow arches down the middle of the garden and these were joined together with a cross-bar of willow too. The cross-bar was made by binding willow shoots around a metal rod normally used for reinforcing concrete (available from builders' merchants).

Roses were planted at the base to train over the arch and along the cross-bar to make a very attractive effect. Ramblers rather than climbing roses are probably the best bet here, since they're more vigorous. They do have the disadvantage of flowering only once with perhaps a smaller second flush later, so a late-summer-flowering

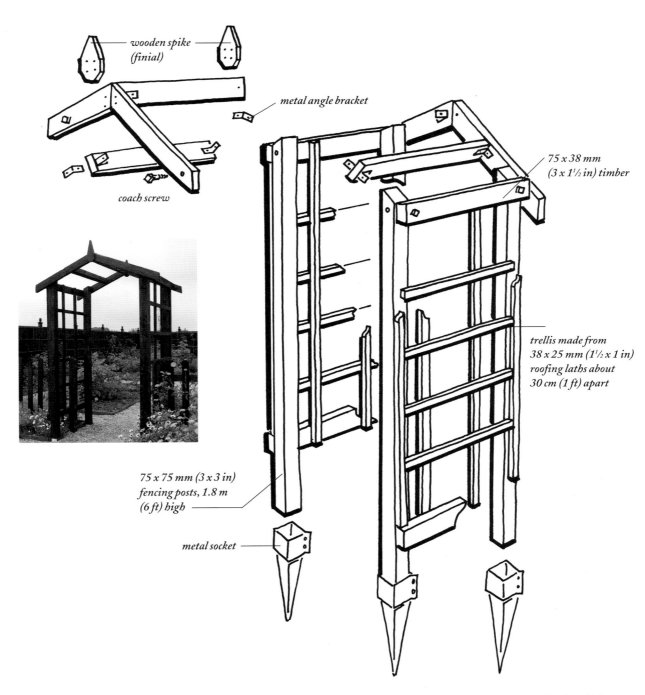

wooden spike
(finial)

metal angle bracket

coach screw

75 x 38 mm
(3 x 1½ in) timber

trellis made from
38 x 25 mm (1½ x 1 in)
roofing laths about
30 cm (1 ft) apart

75 x 75 mm (3 x 3 in)
fencing posts, 1.8 m
(6 ft) high

metal socket

The arch for the artisan's garden is made with four 1.8 m (6 ft) fencing posts set in metal sockets. These can be the type that is hammered into the ground. The cross-beams are fixed to the uprights with coach screws which are turned in with a spanner, except for the three on the top of the arch which are held with metal angle brackets.

The trellis is made from roofing laths and is simply nailed on. As with all the timber used in the garden, make sure it's tanalized first to preserve it for life. The width and depth of the arch is variable depending on your gate and your fancy. As a guide, the Barnsdale artisan's garden arch was 114 cm (3 ft 9 in) wide and 90 cm (3 ft) deep.

clematis was also planted to twine through the roses and give another flowering from August to October.

However, willow arches are not cheap, so in the artisan's garden I have opted for a home-made wooden job. They're not at all difficult to make if you follow the drawings. As with fence posts, set the uprights in metal sockets concreted into the ground or else use those that can be simply hammered in.

Note that the arch is embellished with two wooden spikes (finials). They may be the most difficult part of the job since they need to be fashioned with a plane or a spokeshave. Persevere, though, because they are actually the most important part of the garden. They prevent the Devil sitting on the archway.

TOP LEFT *Metal arches are readily avalable, but can look a little stark to start with. No worry: as soon as the plants start to cover them, they'll be transformed.*

LEFT *It's possible to buy attractive arches made with willow withies woven on to a metal frame. They're simply pushed into the soil and secured by driving a short post into the ground at each leg and wiring the frame to it. Two or more can be connected with a length of metal rod wrapped with withies and wired on.*

Paths

It isn't absolutely necessary to edge the paths in the cottage garden, but it'll certainly make them look a lot neater and it has one other great advantage. When you move into a new house, there's rarely much money left over for the garden. Certainly the modern artisan won't be able to afford thousands. So you need to look for ways of offsetting the costs by making do early on with a view to improving things at a later date. Paths are a perfect example of how this can be done.

Your ideal may be to lay attractive paving slabs or, better still, brick paviors as I've done in the much more expensive gentleman's garden. You may not be able to run to it straight away, but once you've got over buying the curtains and the new cooker and the carpets and the cat flap, you may decide to upgrade the garden.

In the meantime create a hard, dry surface with gravel. It makes an excellent path and it's certainly the most sympathetic material for the artisan's garden. In the old days they would probably have put up with plain beaten earth, and from Victorian times right up to now many gardeners simply spread the ashes from the fire to make a good, dry surface. I wouldn't mind betting that you grow to love your gravel, so you never do actually change, but just to be on the safe side it's a good idea to edge the borders.

If you make the top of the edging boards finish 7.5 cm (3 in) above the level of the path, you'll have space later on to lay the bricks or paving in the easiest possible way. When you decide to do this, all you need do is just work a little dry cement powder into the gravel with a shovel or two of sharp sand and you'll have a ready-made, hard base for the bricks which can be placed straight on top with the minimum of fuss and bother.

Several materials can be used to edge the

Bricks and cobbles make an attractive and durable path, but they may be too expensive to start with.

borders and, over the years, many different types have been employed. If you have, for example, a source of old bricks, they could be sunk about a third into the ground either upright or at an angle of about 45 degrees for a more decorative effect. Only harder stock or engineering bricks which will withstand frost are suitable in this situation. Fletton or common bricks will flake when they freeze, and they'll look very tatty indeed.

The Victorians made special edging tiles with scrolled or scalloped tops and they're still available today. Realistically, however, both bricks and tiles, even second-hand, are too expensive for this garden, though I've used them in the gentleman's garden.

Timber edging 75 mm (3 in) wide and 25 mm (1 in) thick is much cheaper. It looks good; if it's tanalized it lasts a long time; and it's very easy to install. You may wish to stain the timber, which should naturally be done before fixing. I stained mine dark green to match the fencing.

Start by setting out the garden with string lines. If the site's level, there's no need to dig out because the boards should be installed on top of

ABOVE Gravel laid straight on to consolidated soil is certainly the cheapest way to make a very attractive, traditional, cottage garden path. The plants can spill over on to it and many will seed into the gravel too, to create a very informal effect.

the soil. In practice this generally means a certain amount of scraping and filling to ensure that they lie straight.

If the garden slopes slightly, the paths can follow the slope, reducing the amount of soil that has to be re-graded. Simply set the line for the first edging board in the correct place and put a house brick on edge under the line, one at each end. This will raise the line 7.5 cm (3 in) above the ground and all you have to do is to ensure that the tops of the boards comply with the line.

Fix them in position by nailing them to pegs made with the same 75 x 25 mm (3 x 1 in) timber banged in about 30 cm (1 ft) so that they finish just below the top of the board and are effectively hidden. Naturally the pegs should go on the bed side of the edging rather than on the path side. When nailing, put a sledge hammer behind the

Victorian edging tiles make an attractive and authentic edging for paths. They're still available and are even sometimes made in the identical moulds used since the end of the last century. They can also be bought second-hand, though not necessarily at lower cost.

In this old garden there's a grass path, so the plants have to be restrained from growing over it with low hazel hurdles. Hazel has been widely used since medieval times for making similar hurdles to pen animals and for wind-breaks. They're still available.

peg and use nails slightly longer than the width of the peg and board together so that they turn over against the sledge hammer when driven fully home. With two nails to each peg, the boards will never move. (See the photographs on page 58.)

When the first board is in position, set the line up on the other side of the path for the second one, and when you're installing it, check with a spirit level from time to time to ensure that it's going in level with the first one.

In the artisan's garden I made an octagon at the intersection of the two main paths. This was just to add a bit of interest and to create space for a few decorative pots. I made it the final job, after setting the edgings of all four beds. Then I simply marked a circle on the ground and cut the boards *in situ*. It looks complicated but it really is quite difficult to go wrong.

With the edgings in, it's easy to see any high or low spots in the path and these should be levelled off. Generally, since there will be no vehicular traffic on the paths, all that's necessary is to tread the soil down firmly with your weight on your

heels, paying special attention to the edges. If the soil is particularly light or it's an organic soil like peat, it's a wise precaution to cultivate the top 5 cm (2 in) and to rake in some cement powder. Once trodden firm, it'll harden off perfectly. After firming, all that's necessary is to spread small gravel (pea-shingle) over the top for a very attractive effect.

There are three problems with gravel. First, weeds seed in it and must be controlled by hand weeding. You could, of course, use a path weed-killer, but that's hardly in the spirit of the cottage garden and you'll also kill everything – which would be a shame because many flowers will seed in the gravel too. You'll find things like small violas and erigerons coming up in places where you don't walk and adding greatly to the natural, cottage effect.

Hand weeding won't take long and will have to be done only about twice a year. A much bigger problem is cats. If you're plagued with them in the neighbourhood, they're likely to home in on your gravel as the easiest thing to scratch aside

If you use hard materials for the path, the edges tend to look rigid and formal, so plant low-growing subjects like this lavender to soften them.

before performing their ablutions. You can solve this problem completely by using larger gravel.

Stones about 13 mm (½ in) in diameter will generally deter them.

Finally, you'll find that the gravel sinks into the soil to some degree and also works its way into the borders as you tidy up any soil that may have fallen on to the path. You'll therefore have to put

1 The wooden edgings for a gravel path are held by pegs driven about 30 cm (1 ft) into the ground. Put them on the border side of the edging to hide them.

2 Put a sledge hammer behind the peg and nail the edging to it, checking with a spirit level at the same time. The nails should go right through and bend over.

3 To make the octagon where the paths cross, mark out a circle using a loop of string on a peg in the centre, fix the edging and cut off the excess.

down an extra barrowload of gravel about once a year or so, but the overall effect make it well worth the effort.

The Borders

The paths will look fine now, but the borders will be about 7.5 cm (3 in) below the level of the edging boards. That's good because it allows you to cultivate deeply and to work in some organic matter, which will raise the soil quite a bit more than the 7.5 cm (3 in). Remember Robinson's advice to 'look after the plot and make it fertile'.

If you can manage to double dig, then so much the better. It's hard work, but you'll have to do it only once and it's much the best thing for a new plot. But if you can't manage it, single digging will do.

To double dig, you take out a trench about 60 cm (2 ft) wide, putting the soil temporarily on to one of the adjacent beds. Break up the bottom of the trench with a fork and put in some manure, garden compost or one of the alternatives like composted straw or spent mushroom compost (but *not* peat), that you can buy in the garden centre. Then half-refill the trench with soil dug from the next one and thrown forward. Put in another layer of organic matter and completely refill, afterwards putting more organic matter on the top. The final trench is filled with the soil you dug out of the first one. Yes, it's hard work, but old William Robinson will be proud of you.

To single dig, you simply dig one spade deep, throwing the soil forward as you go to make a narrow, V-shaped trench. Put the organic matter in this trench and fill by digging out the next one and throwing the soil forward as before.

After all this exertion you'll find that not only will you feel *terrific*, but your soil will also have risen slightly above the edging boards and looks ready to welcome its first plants: exciting times.

Working with Wood

❀

The first Elizabethan cottage gardeners would not have had our resources. Garden centres were, to say the least, thin on the ground and even nurseries were very few and far between. Even in the Victorian era, cottage gardeners would have had very little money to spare for their gardens, though really keen plantsmen certainly spent quite large sums and travelled long distances to satisfy their irresistible urge for plants. We all know *that* feeling.

Artifacts and ornaments, however, would have largely been home-made. From necessity, most cottagers would have been quite handy with tools and there was always a certain amount of bartering of skills. The carpenter provided the bench for the blacksmith in return for a bit of

The initial digging is hard work, but you'll only have to do it once. Remember that the initial creation of fertility is the key to ultimate success. After that, the plants very nearly grow themselves.

decorative wrought iron and I can imagine the weaver exchanging a length of cloth with the farmer's load of manure for his precious auriculas.

In the main, though, cottage garden furniture was simple and home-made. These days most of us are immeasurably better off than our gardening predecessors and, perhaps after a little saving, we could no doubt buy most of our needs ready-made. If you do, believe me, you'll miss out on one of the most satisfying and creative aspects of the garden.

Even if you have no problem finding the ready cash for all your gardening needs, the pleasure

of making your own artifacts far outweighs the convenience of buying them. What's more, you can very often, with a little patience and ingenuity, design and build something far more suited to your special requirements and of far better quality than is available in the garden centre.

In the following pages I have suggested a few projects for the cottage garden. They were all made for the artisan's garden and none is difficult. They have all been designed for gardeners with minimum woodworking skills, and the only tools you'll need are a saw, a hammer, a drill, a spanner

If you can use a hammer and a saw, with a little ingenuity you could make a rustic bench like this. Probably the hardest part is finding suitable timber. Bear in mind that, without treatment, it'll be prone to rotting, so treat it annually with a colourless, matt-finish preservative.

to tighten coach screws and a screwdriver. Simply follow the drawings.

As a general rule, make sure that every bit of wood you use has been pressure-treated with preservative to ensure that it lasts.

Bench

One of the great pleasures in life is to sit in the sunshine on a summer's afternoon, listening to the buzz of the bees and the song of the birds and smelling the perfume of the plants while you shell the home-grown peas. So a bench is mantory.

Like everything else, it's made of pressure-treated softwood which has been planed all round and finished with a wood stain. I used a blue/grey finish but, of course, you'll want to choose the colour to suit your own taste.

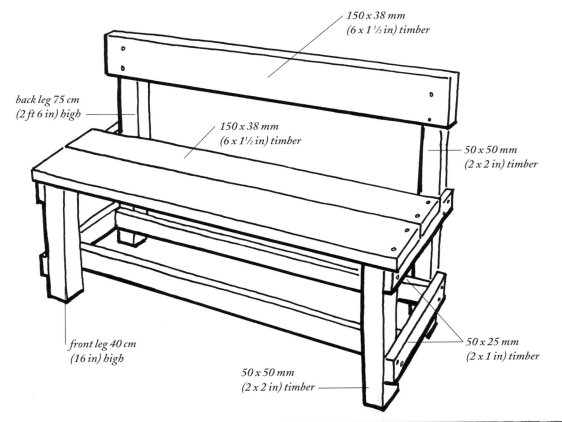

150 x 38 mm (6 x 1 ½ in) timber

back leg 75 cm (2 ft 6 in) high

150 x 38 mm (6 x 1 ½ in) timber

50 x 50 mm (2 x 2 in) timber

front leg 40 cm (16 in) high

50 x 25 mm (2 x 1 in) timber

50 x 50 mm (2 x 2 in) timber

All the timber measurements for the bench in the drawing above are 'nominal' – in other words, for rough timber before planing, so they finish slightly smaller.

Naturally the width is optional and should be made to fit your own garden. This one fitted exactly into the small sitting area in the artisan's garden and measures 1.2 m (4 ft) long. If you want to make a much longer bench, you may have to use thicker timber for the seat.

Facing south to catch the sun and surrounded by perfumed roses and with the small, aromatic herb border on one side, it makes a very pleasant place to sit.

Herb Table

The herb table was an idea I pinched from my friend the designer Dan Pearson. I've never seen it done before, but it's such a great idea for a cottage garden that I couldn't resist it. It's proof, if proof were needed, that the cottage garden style is, after at least four centuries, still evolving.

Don't skimp on the thickness of the timber: the table has to carry quite a lot of weight. Fill the central part of the table with a specially well-drained compost consisting of equal parts of good soil, coarse grit and either garden compost or fine bark. Then set a few slates or tiles into the compost. I found a few old thin stone roofing slates kicking around my garden and they're ideal. Try to find natural stone if you can. They should also be flat and set as level in the compost as you can make them, because it's here that you'll place your cup of tea or your plate when you're eating out.

Plant common thyme (*Thymus serpyllum*)

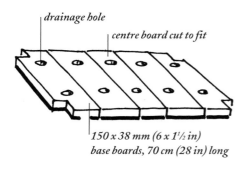

drainage hole

centre board cut to fit

*150 x 38 mm (6 x 1½ in)
base boards, 70 cm (28 in) long*

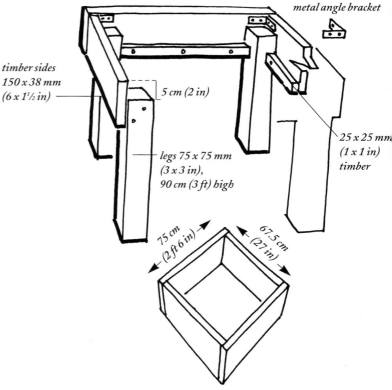

metal angle bracket

*timber sides
150 x 38 mm
(6 x 1½ in)*

5 cm (2 in)

*25 x 25 mm
(1 x 1 in)
timber*

*legs 75 x 75 mm
(3 x 3 in),
90 cm (3 ft) high*

*75 cm
(2 ft 6 in)*

*67.5 cm
(27 in)*

The herb table measurements are again nominal since it's best to make it in planed timber. It's also, of course, essential to have it pressure-treated with preservative because the wood will be constantly moist since the box is filled with compost. Again, the corners are held with metal angle brackets, but use ones at least 5 cm (2 in) long. If the wood twists, as it's likely to do, the brackets will be under considerable strain.

The finished table looks and smells wonderful. You'll have to water it from time to time in very hot weather, but don't overdo it; remember that these are Mediterranean plants and are quite happy in fairly dry conditions. The thymes can be clipped back after flowering to keep them compact and in check. They'll need little feeding but, if they look as if they're not growing well, give them a little organic fertilizer in the spring.

around the slates. Eventually this will spread out and merge together to form a complete, sweet-smelling mat which will release its delicious aroma every time you bruise a leaf or two. Romance? You can't go wrong.

Arbour and Love Seat

In the cottage garden the sun shines nearly all the time – at least, because of the bright borders, the strong fragrances and the constant bird song, it certainly *seems* to. So, as well as the bench and table in the sun, it's good to provide a quieter, shadier bower where you can relax in the late afternoon after a day's gardening, book in hand, cool drink at your side, and just dream.

I'm sure that the shady, perfumed arbour was an idea the cottagers copied from the gentry. Somehow it seems much more to suit the languid, pale-skinned maiden rather than the red-faced, buxom and probably slightly grubbly village lad and lass. Wherever it originated, it's become a traditional part of the cottage garden.

You can build an arbour from all kinds of materials. In older gardens the use of 'rustic' poles is quite common and they make attractive structures. But you'll need to be very careful about the wood you use. I learnt my lesson many years ago when I built one of pine poles which lasted no more than about three seasons before they rotted off. Oak, ash, hazel or chestnut seem to last longer but are pretty hard to come by. My recommendation would be to use sawn timber, again tanalized to prevent rotting.

Put the corner posts into metal sockets and concrete them in first, and then fit the timbers to them and hold them in place with coach screws. Naturally, you'll have to drill the wood beforehand, so you'll need a brace and bit or an electric drill for this job.

My last task was to nail to the front, one of the horseshoes I dug up when I was digging the garden. It was pretty rusty, but still perfect after its hundred years or so underground. Before putting it up I wire-brushed all the rust off and painted it with clear matt varnish to prevent further rusting and to stop it transferring brown rust marks on to the woodwork. But make sure that you put the horseshoe with the open end upwards because that's more or less guaranteed to bring you good fortune.

When the structure's finished, prepare the soil at either side with manure or compost and plant perfumed climbing roses and a clematis or two to add the final dimension.

To keep costs down, you can use all kinds of materials that would be considered junk by some. Here, two old tin baths have been painted and fitted with a seat. Bolt them to the wall and surround them with plants and you have an instant flowery bower for two.

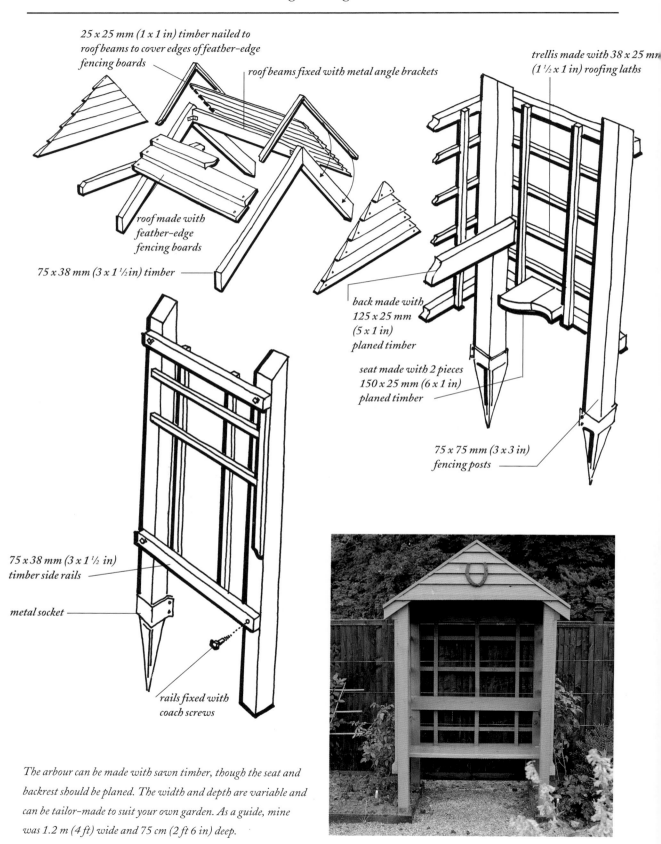

25 x 25 mm (1 x 1 in) timber nailed to roof beams to cover edges of feather-edge fencing boards

roof beams fixed with metal angle brackets

trellis made with 38 x 25 mm (1 ½ x 1 in) roofing laths

roof made with feather-edge fencing boards

75 x 38 mm (3 x 1 ½ in) timber

back made with 125 x 25 mm (5 x 1 in) planed timber

seat made with 2 pieces 150 x 25 mm (6 x 1 in) planed timber

75 x 75 mm (3 x 3 in) fencing posts

75 x 38 mm (3 x 1 ½ in) timber side rails

metal socket

rails fixed with coach screws

The arbour can be made with sawn timber, though the seat and backrest should be planed. The width and depth are variable and can be tailor-made to suit your own garden. As a guide, mine was 1.2 m (4 ft) wide and 75 cm (2 ft 6 in) deep.

Rustic poles are readily available at garden centres and can be used to make all kinds of garden furniture. It's important to choose wood that will last a while: some types will rot after only a few seasons. You need minimal carpentry skills for this kind of work – well-fitting joints are just not necessary. The poles are nailed or screwed together, but drill them first to prevent splitting. If you surround the seat with roses like this one, make sure that you have plenty of room to avoid getting scratched.

Obelisk

Opposite the arbour, at the far end of the path, I wanted a focal point to catch the eye and, in doing so, to make the path appear longer. It's a landscape trick that really does work. You can use anything eye-catching, like a statue, for example, or a bird bath. But both are really a bit too upmarket for this garden and in any case, in a space this small, I greatly begrudge the 'loss' of any land that could be used for plants.

My solution was again to grow climbers, but this time I fancied old-fashioned sweet peas – another group of plants capable of filling the whole garden with perfume and making a very good source of cut flowers for the house too.

The original cottagers would no doubt have simply banged a tall post into the ground and tied in the climbers to that, and it's a perfectly good way to grow them today. But the obelisk looks good even in winter when there are no plants on it, and it's very cheap to make.

It could quite easily be made from four lengths of 50 x 50 mm (2 x 2 in) timber for the uprights with thinner struts nailed across. I used 38 x 25 mm (1 ½ x 1 in) roofing lathes because you can buy them in bundles very cheaply from builders' merchants and they're already tanalized. I use them a lot around the garden and they also come in handy if you're making the trellis and love seat.

The ball on top of the obelisk is the plastic float from a modern lavatory cistern and you can buy those from builders' merchants too. Unfortunately the only one I could find was brilliant dayglo orange, so obviously it had to be painted.

Shortly after I'd made my obelisk I was very pleased to see an almost identical model in an up-market garden centre. It was priced at just under *ten times* the cost of my home-made effort.

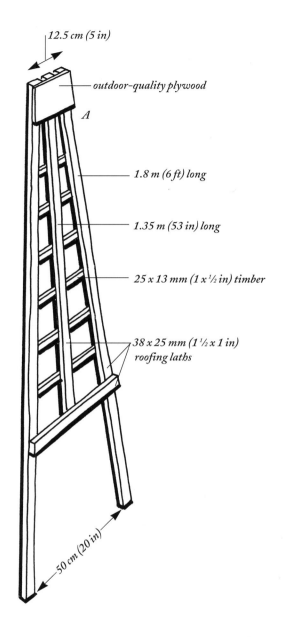

12.5 cm (5 in)

outdoor-quality plywood

A

1.8 m (6 ft) long

1.35 m (53 in) long

25 x 13 mm (1 x ½ in) timber

38 x 25 mm (1 ½ x 1 in) roofing laths

50 cm (20 in)

The obelisk is made with roofing laths with 25 x 13 mm (1 x ½ in) timber cross-pieces. It is, I confess, a bit of a fiddle to make and you'll need patience. The best way is to cut the roofing lath uprights to size, lay them on the floor and then fix the cross-pieces so that they overlap the uprights. When they're all fixed, cut off the excess later. It's also important to fix the thinner cross-pieces before you put the whole thing together.

It can be covered with sweet peas, clematis or climbing(but not the more vigorous rambler) roses.

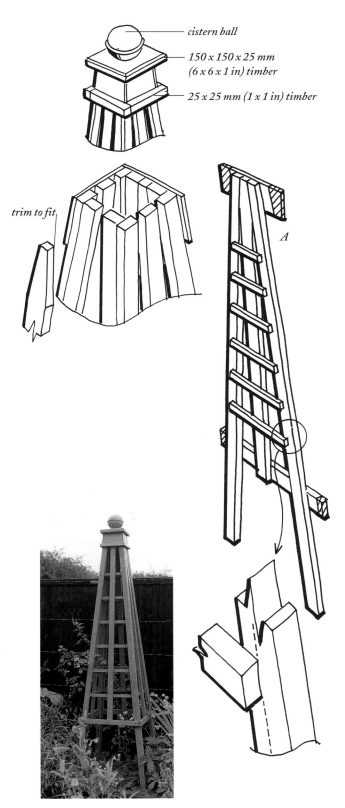

cistern ball

150 x 150 x 25 mm
(6 x 6 x 1 in) timber

25 x 25 mm (1 x 1 in) timber

trim to fit

A

Compost Containers

Cottage gardeners have always been thrifty. They've had to be. And even today, though we may not need to skimp and scrape like our less fortunate predecessors, it's pretty dumb to throw away resources and then have to buy them again.

Garden compost is an invaluable way to 'be good to your plot and make it fertile'. It avoids your having to buy expensive organic matter, or at least reduces the amount, and it gets waste out of sight quickly and conveniently. Returned to the soil, it does wonders.

It's possible to compost organic material by simply piling it into a heap and waiting. But if you can retain the heat generated by the working of bacteria, the rotting process will be speeded up considerably. Some form of container is therefore advisable.

Ideally, every garden should have at least two compost containers, so that the contents of one can rot down while the other is being filled up. If you have a small garden the containers don't need to be large, but even so, the problem is that they'll be constantly on view. You simply can't hide things away, and whatever you can see has to be easy on the eye – even compost containers. There are all kinds available at garden centres, but not one of them is good to look at, so you'll have to make your own. You can do it easily for half the cost of buying them.

My design is, of course, a copy of a traditional beehive, so it fits the cottage garden set-up very well. Note that there are no holes in the sides, because plenty of air will be able to get in between the boards, while high temperatures are still maintained. Here it's absolutely essential to use tanalized timber or, filled with rotting vegetation, the containers won't last five minutes. So that they fit in with the rest of the garden furniture, I've painted mine blue/grey, but you may prefer to

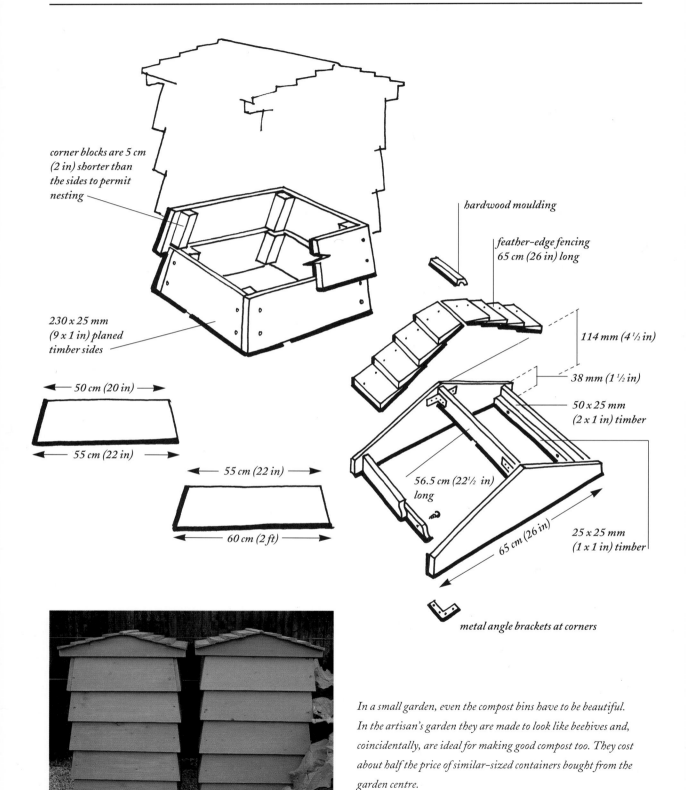

corner blocks are 5 cm
(2 in) shorter than
the sides to permit
nesting

hardwood moulding

*feather-edge fencing
65 cm (26 in) long*

230 x 25 mm
(9 x 1 in) planed
timber sides

114 mm (4 ½ in)

38 mm (1 ½ in)

50 x 25 mm
(2 x 1 in) timber

50 cm (20 in)

55 cm (22 in)

56.5 cm (22½ in)
long

55 cm (22 in)

25 x 25 mm
(1 x 1 in) timber

60 cm (2 ft)

65 cm (26 in)

metal angle brackets at corners

In a small garden, even the compost bins have to be beautiful.
In the artisan's garden they are made to look like beehives and,
coincidentally, are ideal for making good compost too. They cost
about half the price of similar-sized containers bought from the
garden centre.

You'll need to set the bevel square first and then it's best to
cut all the sides before assembling them.

make them more like proper beehives by painting them white. It's all a matter of personal preference, though I think that too bright a colour tends to detract from the plants, so I prefer to tone it down a bit.

ing them on a little earlier and greatly improving the quality.

Again, there are plenty of different designs available and a very few of them will fit in with this garden design – at a price. You can make your own for about a quarter of the cost of buying one

Coldframe

A coldframe is not an essential piece of equipment but will save you pounds at the end of the day and will greatly increase the interest of your gardening. You can use it to raise many ornamental plants and vegetables from seed and it's perfect for further increasing your stock of plants from cuttings. In the winter it comes in handy again to protect over-wintered vegetables, bring-

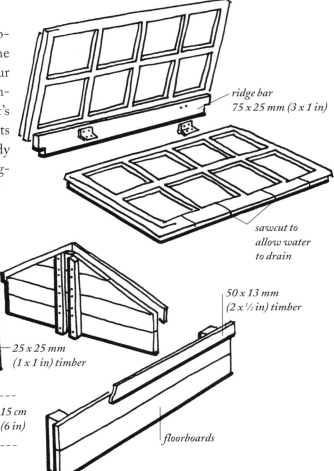

ridge bar
75 x 25 mm (3 x 1 in)

sawcut to allow water to drain

50 x 50 mm (2 x 2 in) timber

50 x 13 mm (2 x ½ in) timber

45 cm (18 in)

25 x 25 mm (1 x 1 in) timber

15 cm (6 in)

50 x 13 mm (2 x ½ in) timber

floorboards

The dimensions of the coldframe will depend on the window frames you use. As a guide, mine worked out to 90 cm (3 ft) wide and 107 cm (42 in) long. Note that the ridge bar is notched at the ends and drops between the two upright struts in the centre. Then screw it through both struts to hold it firm. In my prototype, rainwater collected in the window frames. I solved the problem with a sawcut through each frame to let the water drain away.

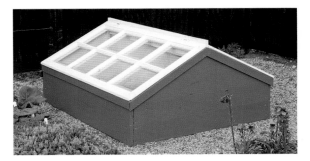

Enhanced by flowers in the borders and on the bare fence, even the working area can be made to look beautiful.

and it should be possible, with a little patience, to create a nice, old-fashioned look.

You need patience because I suggest that you make the glass top with two old window sashes, and you may have to wait a while before the ones you want turn up. Pay a visit to the local double-glazing or window-fitting firm. There is one in my local town from which I was able to get a couple of the wooden windows, removed when new aluminium jobs were being fitted. I wanted Georgian-style sashes with small, square panes, so I had to bide my time. Eventually they did appear and they cost me nothing.

Then, of course, you have to fit the body of the frame to the two sashes, so you may not be able to follow my measurements exactly. They refer only to my own two windows, but they give you the proportions at least, and the accurate measurements are easy to work out by measuring the sashes.

The body is made with floorboards, which

again I asked to be tanalized. Bear in mind, though, that if you buy your timber second-hand from a demolition contractor, you'll get it a lot cheaper, but you won't be able to have it preserved. So make sure that you give it a few coats of paint and that you keep the painted surface up to scratch to stop the timber rotting.

Tool Chest

If you have a shed or a garage, you won't need this. But many small gardens don't have storage space attached and I've even heard of gardeners with a garage who keep their car in it!

The chest is big enough to take all the tools you'll need, including even the mower if you decide to have a lawn too. Note that the top can be set level by engaging the flap along the front, so you can also use the top as a work-bench for potting and so on. I keep a sheet of outdoor-quality plywood in the chest to make a level surface.

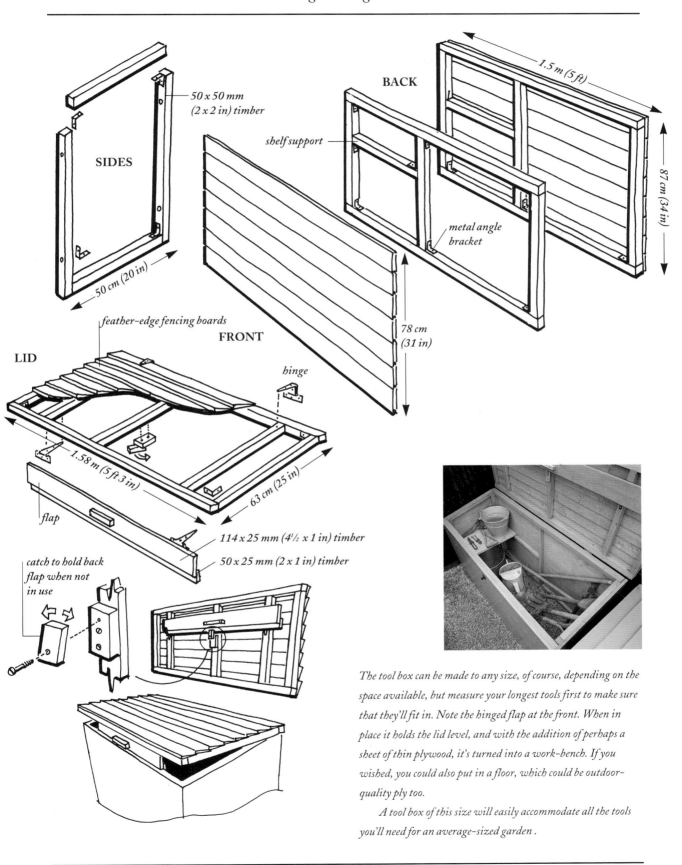

SIDES

50 x 50 mm
(2 x 2 in) timber

BACK

shelf support

1.5 m (5 ft)

87 cm (34 in)

metal angle
bracket

50 cm (20 in)

feather-edge fencing boards

FRONT

78 cm
(31 in)

LID

hinge

flap

1.58 m (5 ft 3 in)

63 cm (25 in)

catch to hold back
flap when not
in use

114 x 25 mm (4½ x 1 in) timber

50 x 25 mm (2 x 1 in) timber

The tool box can be made to any size, of course, depending on the space available, but measure your longest tools first to make sure that they'll fit in. Note the hinged flap at the front. When in place it holds the lid level, and with the addition of perhaps a sheet of thin plywood, it's turned into a work-bench. If you wished, you could also put in a floor, which could be outdoor-quality ply too.

A tool box of this size will easily accommodate all the tools you'll need for an average-sized garden.

Auricula Theatre

So obsessed were the old cottage 'florists' with their precious plants that they would build special 'theatres' in which to display them. These were often quite elaborate affairs with a proscenium, raked shelving and curtains and, as the gentry took up the challenge, they spent more and more on them and, in true Victorian fashion, produced some really rococo designs reminiscent of the Royal Opera House in London.

The 'theatres' were mostly used to display auriculas and, where there is in your own garden an area of wall or fence that perhaps has concrete or paving underneath, preventing you growing plants there, it might be a good idea to copy them. I wouldn't suggest that you go to quite the extremes that the Victorians did, and you won't want to restrict yourself to auriculas.

My 'theatre' is really no more than a set of shelves fixed to the fence, but it makes the perfect place to display windowsill plants like geraniums, calceolarias and fuchsias during the summer. The structure is simply fixed to the fence posts. There's also no reason why it shouldn't be fixed to the wall of the house by drilling the back supports and screwing them into pre-set wall plugs. Bear in mind that some water will always run through the pots so don't hang it over a border full of drought-loving plants.

SHELVES

15 cm (6 in) long

24 cm (9 ½ in) long

35 cm (14 in) long

88 cm (34 ½ in) long

90 cm (3 ft) long

The 'auricula theatre' is really just a set of shelves. The uprights are made from 38 x 25 mm (1 ½ x 1 in) roofing laths with shelves of 125 x 25 mm (5 x 1 in) timber. It can be any length you like, though it's easiest to make it 1.8 m (6 ft) long, so that it can be screwed to the fence posts. Mine was a little shorter; I therefore fixed some metal hooks on the top and simply hung it on a fence panel.

LEFT *When it's filled with flowering pot plants, the 'auricula theatre' makes a fine feature.*

Containers

The old cottage gardeners would have had a wonderful choice of plant containers for which we'd give our eye teeth today. Terracotta was, until around the 1950s, a common and cheap material used widely for all kinds of containers. The hand-made ones are still as beautiful but relatively expensive, though well worth saving for. More on those in the gentleman's cottage garden.

Artisan gardeners would also have had attractive containers made of wood, clay and other natural materials that were originally intended for something else. I managed, for example, to pick up a couple of potters' saggars – coarse clay pots that were used to protect china when it was put into the old bottle kilns.

Cottage gardeners would use just about any container for plants. Even this old washing-up bowl looks attractive. As ever, it's the plants that make it.

Potters were just as much cottage gardeners as weavers and spinners, even though they often lived in towns. They used old, damaged saggars as plant containers once they had been discarded. Cottage potters would sometimes even stack them one on top of the other to make walls between their back-to-back houses.

Modern saggars are still available, even though the bottle kilns are seen these days only in pottery museums. Now they're used in the production of colour pigments, but they're no longer hand-made, so they lack that attractive, craftsman finish. However, here and there you might find a modern reproduction as I did or, if you're ever in an area where pottery is made, you may even be lucky enough to find an original. They make marvellous plant pots with a good bit of history attached.

My own dissatisfaction with the modern saggars was really because of the colour – a very light biscuit brown. However, I found that a coat of ordinary matt paint completely transformed them. So again I used the blue/grey paint left over from the woodwork and the result was very acceptable.

A very appealing couple of pots can be made from an old copper water cylinder. You should be able to get one from your local plumber, though these days you'll have to pay for even an old, leaking cylinder, because the copper's worth quite a bit. But it should cost no more than a few pounds and you'll get two good containers from it. Of course, if you have your own water cylinder replaced, you'll already have the raw material – remember to ask the plumber to leave the old cylinder on site.

The first job is to remove the foam insulation which is sprayed on these days. It comes off easily with an old screwdriver. Before cutting the cylinder in half, mark a line all round by stretching a strap round, levelling it carefully and marking with a felt-tipped pen. Then you can cut through the thin copper with a hacksaw, a jigsaw with a metal-cutting blade or a small angle grinder. Remove the piping from inside, file down any rough edges and the job's done.

You'll need to support the domed part of the cylinder by putting it on perhaps a clay pot, while the tub made from the other, flat end is self-supporting.

Wooden containers are also quite easy to make in the style of the decidedly up-market Versailles tubs. Use tanalized timber throughout. The sides are made with tongued-and-grooved 'matching' and the decorative balls at the top are available at most good DIY stores.

Saggars were made of coarse clay and not really designed for use as plant pots. If you can find one, you'll need to drill drainage holes in the bottom, which is easily done with a masonry bit in an electric drill. If you don't like the colour, they can be painted with emulsion paint.

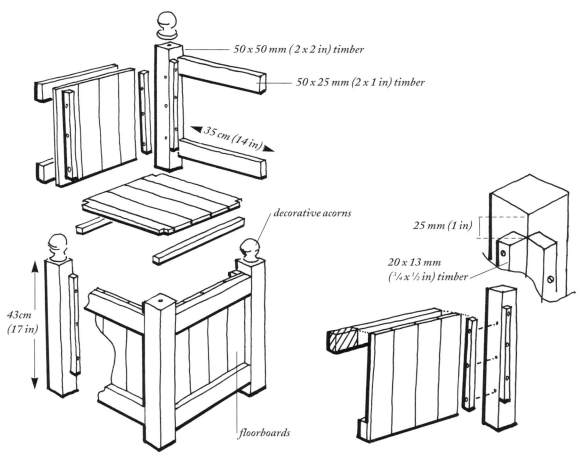

50 x 50 mm (2 x 2 in) timber

50 x 25 mm (2 x 1 in) timber

35 cm (14 in)

decorative acorns

25 mm (1 in)

20 x 13 mm (³/₄ x ¹/₂ in) timber

43cm (17 in)

floorboards

Basketwork Supports

The first Elizabethans grew all kinds of plants in pots, sometimes because they were tender and needed to be brought inside for frost-protection in winter and also when soil conditions in the borders were unsatisfactory. Of course, we do exactly the same thing today. Pinks and carnations were particularly prized in those days, but they do need good drainage, so where gardens were made on, for example, heavy clay these plants were grown in pots. They and many other similar plants have a lax habit of growth though, so some kind of support is always necessary. Naturally the supports themselves have to be decorative.

A wooden plant box is easy to make, requiring no complicated joints and costing a fraction of the shop price.

Four centuries ago all country people were adept at working with their hands and they had all the necessary materials for this sort of job growing on their doorstep. It was no problem to make plant supports much like the lobster pots and fishing traps, the baskets and containers that were a daily part of their lives.

We may have more difficulty finding the materials. You need flexible, straight, thin twigs, the ideal being willow. If you have a willow growing in your garden, you too will have to hand all the material you need. If not, you should be able to buy willow withies from a wattle fencing maker or perhaps cadge some from a friend at pruning time. If the worst comes to the worst, you can buy basket-making material from the craft shop.

Mine came from a golden willow (*Salix vitellina*) in my garden. It's pruned hard every year to keep it small and to encourage the new wood, which has much brighter bark. If you have room, it's a very worthwhile plant to brighten up the winter scene. There are other plants that could be used including the coloured-bark dogwoods which also need to be pruned hard in spring to encourage better colour.

Use the thinnest shoots, cut them to length and make them up in the pot you're going to use. If you fill it with garden soil first, the shoots are held firm while you tie and the job's much easier. Where the shoots cross, they're tied with florist's wire to make a really firm support.

'Lobster-pot' plant supports can be made from willow shoots or from the coloured-barked dogwoods. Use the thinner shoots and, if they're inflexible, soak them in water for a few days. Skilled basket-makers will experience no difficulties, but if you're a novice fix the withies where they cross with thin florist's wire.

Galvanized containers look very attractive filled with flowers, especially if you can find some with an unusual shape. I used an oval mop bucket and these florist's buckets normally used to hold cut flowers. They're still available.

The Gentleman's Garden

❁

Earlier in this book I railed against pretension. The cottage garden is very much an artisan's garden and should be 'hand-made' with love and patience. Yet my gentleman's garden is expensive and elaborate.

Well, I justify the building of it because I feel it's necessary to give all the options. I do firmly believe that there is far more enjoyment to be had from the garden if the plants are home-raised and if you make the artifacts yourself. It's not a matter of saving money (though that's not to be sniffed at!), but of sheer creative pleasure. However, today we can go out and buy beautiful things ready-made for the garden, and I suppose some

Above and below The design divides the short, wide plot into five distinct areas: a herb garden (A), a 'secret' garden (B), a vegetable plot (C), and a fruit and greenhouse area (D), plus, of course, the main central part which is the ornamental garden you'd see from the kitchen window (E).

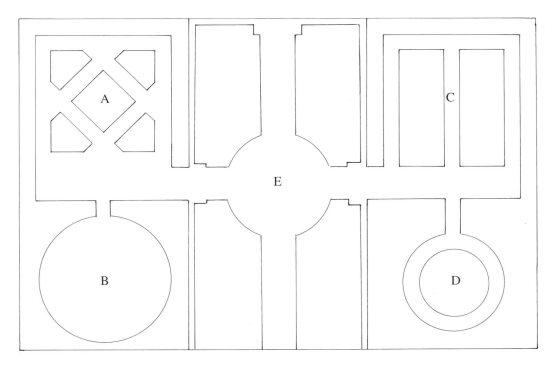

Opposite The gentleman's garden spares no expense. The paths, for example, are made with hand-made brick paviors which are far from cheap. I have tried to present something to aspire to and to suggest some more expensive ideas that could be used in either this or the artisan's garden depending on your budget. Hopefully you'll be able to take ideas from both gardens.

people may prefer to do that. What I hope is that you'll be able to pick some ideas from each garden to use in your own – to mix and match as appropriate for your individual situation. Naturally the plants I suggest in the next chapter will be suitable for both gardens.

The Design

As builders cram more and more houses together into smaller and smaller spaces, so the shapes and dimensions of the plots have to adjust. Not only are gardens shrinking, they're changing shape too. One result is the short, wide garden, which is difficult to plan and rarely catered for in design books.

I've therefore planned the gentleman's garden to suit that particular shape, but it's also done in modular fashion. With five separate gardens in one, you should be able to juggle around the component parts more or less to fit your own plot.

I confess that no expense has been spared. The bricks for the paving are hand-made and not cheap, the trelliswork and arches are built with expensive hardwood, the building was made by a well-paid craftsman and the whole plot is surrounded by slow-growing and therefore pricey yew hedging. Even the pots and containers are top-of-the-range.

No, I couldn't afford it all at once either! This is the kind of garden most of us will have to build slowly over several years, replacing, say, gravel with bricks later, upgrading the arbour from perhaps a rustic home-made job when the finances allow and even changing plants from cheap 'fillers' to more expensive specimens as we go along. Actually it's quite fun to make the dream come true gradually, and it's a very rewarding and creative exercise.

The principles of designing the garden are exactly the same as for the artisan's garden.

Decide first of all that the garden is there to be used and not just looked at, and then make a list of what you want to include.

Here there's space for a small vegetable plot and even a greenhouse, so the scope will be greater and the season of practical enjoyment longer. Again, there's a place to sit and enjoy the sunshine and there's space for a separate herb garden.

The 'secret' garden is simply a small area filled with attractive plants, perhaps in greens and pastel shades and certainly fragrant, where you can 'get away from it all' and simply sit.

I well remember, in my youth, my friend Harry, who was a real, genuine old cottage gardener. He must have been one of the last of the generation that worked on the farm with horses when he was a lad and he had his priorities right. Unnoticed, I watched him one summer's day for perhaps half an hour as he sat on his old bench outside his back door, gazing into space. When I asked him what he was doing, he replied, 'I were just cogitatin' my lawn, old 'un.' (He called everybody 'old 'un', though he was eighty-eight – I was nineteen at the time.) Somehow country folk know that's an important part of life and I look forward to doing it myself in my own secret garden.

Though planting schemes of the gentry's cottage gardens from the eighteenth century onwards were much more sophisticated, planned affairs, I have resisted the temptation to follow the Gertrude Jekyll example and make the planting 'blended and coordinated'. As I've already pointed out, that conflicts, in my view, so violently with the very idea of a cottage garden that it would turn it into something else. I've therefore used the same plants as in the artisan's garden. Some have been grown in cottage gardens for centuries and others are the improved versions of them that are available now.

One feature the artisan's garden would not have included is the small knot garden. Though later cottage gardeners did use clipped box to edge paths, there's no evidence I can find that they followed their wealthier neighbours by building knots and parterres. Still, well grown these do look wonderful, even on a very small scale, so there's no reason at all why you shouldn't include one, even if your garden's tiny.

Mind you, even a knot of this size uses plenty of plants which are by no means cheap. You may find that you have to buy only a few to start with and then to propagate your own from cuttings. Box is very easy to increase in this way and not nearly as slow as you might imagine.

Alternatively, you may wish to use other plants, which are cheaper and quicker to grow. Lavender, cotton lavender and rosemary all make superb dwarf hedges that can be clipped in the same way.

Building the Garden

❧

Boundaries

I surrounded my gentleman's garden with a yew hedge. If you have the room, I would recommend that you do the same, because there's no doubt that it's the finest boundary of all. It can be close-clipped to form a perfect green wall and it makes a much better windbreak than a solid barrier. Unfortunately yew is expensive and has a reputation for slow growth. It's certainly not as fast as other conifers like leylandii or Lawson's cypress, but if you prepare well (see page 48), it'll put on at least 20–25 cm (8–10 in) a year. It's well worth waiting for.

Plant about 1 m (3 ft) apart and, if the site is exposed to cold winds, erect some form of windbreak to protect the young plants until they get established. I used willow hurdles wired to strong posts. This puts the cost up, of course, but provides a temporary boundary (lasting about ten years) while the hedge is growing and it speeds up growth considerably. Alternatively plastic windbreak material is available, though it's not in the least attractive.

If you're in a desperate hurry, you can use either *Thuja plicata*, which makes a looser hedge but with fine, glossy, green foliage and grows about 60 cm (2 ft) a year, or *Cupressocyparis leylandii*

Yew, certainly the queen of hedging plants, will make a perfect green wall that can be clipped to form very straight, formal lines. It's evergreen, of course, and not as slow-growing as is generally believed. It has the extra advantage that it will grow out of old wood, so if it gets browned by freak cold winds, or if it becomes neglected and therefore scruffy, it can be cut hard back right to the main trunk and it'll regenerate in quite a short time.

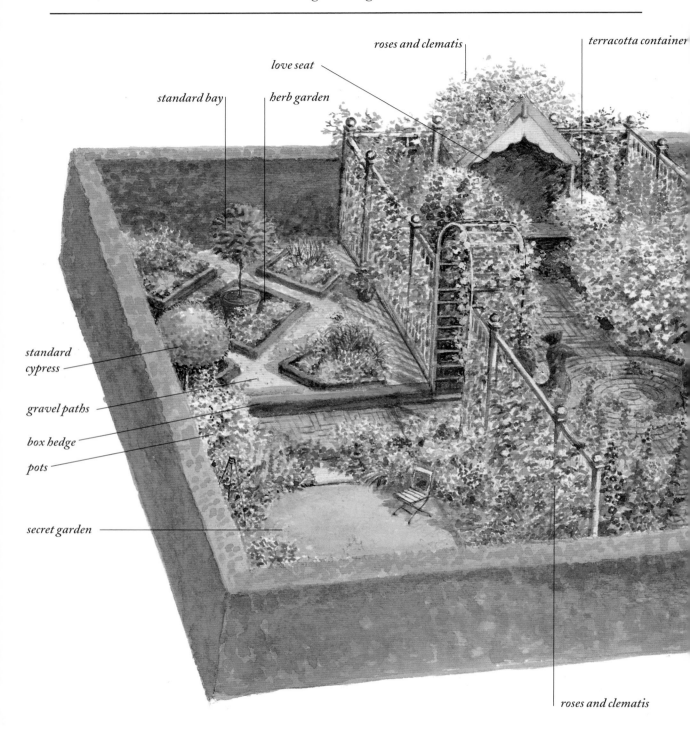

roses and clematis

terracotta container

love seat

standard bay

herb garden

standard cypress

gravel paths

box hedge

pots

secret garden

roses and clematis

which will easily win any growth race at the remarkable speed of 1 m (3 ft) a year.

Prepare and plant as recommended for other types of hedging (see page 48), setting the plants 1 m (3 ft) apart. Don't prune the tops until they've reached 30 cm (1 ft) above the required height and then cut them back to 15 cm (6 in) below the finished height. That allows for

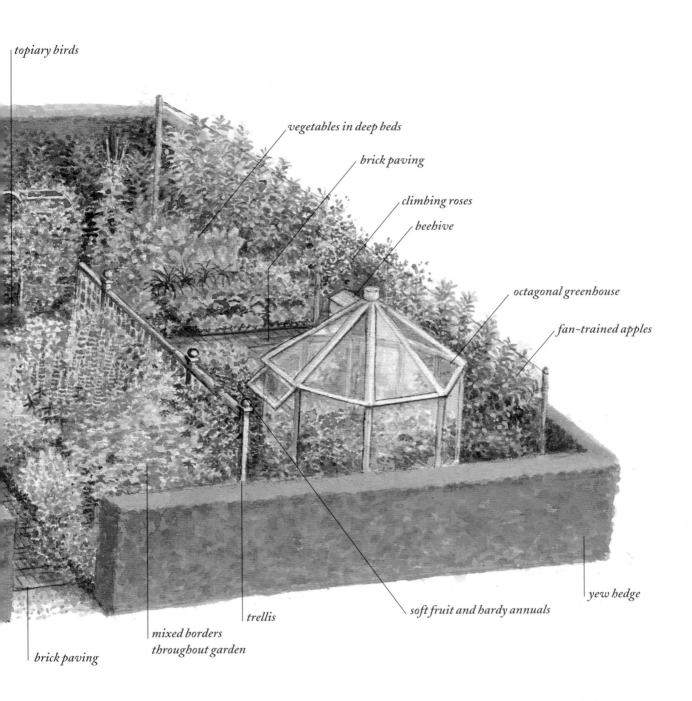

topiary birds

vegetables in deep beds

brick paving

climbing roses

beehive

octagonal greenhouse

fan-trained apples

yew hedge

soft fruit and hardy annuals

trellis

mixed borders
throughout garden

brick paving

re-growth to form a good, bushy top. The sides of the hedge should be trimmed as soon as they exceed the required width.

The one snag with coniferous hedges is that

When it's fully matured, the gentleman's garden should look like this. It'll be quite labour-saving, the main work being trimming and tying, though, because of the close planting, that's certainly a job you'll need to keep on top of.

they're not really suitable for growing climbers, except perhaps for the scarlet Scotch flame flower (*Tropaeolum speciosum*) – if you have acid soil – and a few of the less vigorous clematis.

Another good, close, formal hedge to consider planting is *Lonicera nitida*, but it can really be grown satisfactorily only up to about 1.5 m (5 ft) before it becomes floppy. It makes a perfect, low hedge, though, and is ideal for dividing the garden. Plant 30 cm (1 ft) apart and don't cut it back but clip it regularly when it reaches the required size.

Brick Paving

The brick paving in this garden is a real indulgence. It's possible to buy concrete brick paviors but they do tend to look a bit municipal and are not ideal in this situation. There's no doubt in my mind that hand-made bricks are the very best but, as you would expect, they're also the most expensive.

It's sometimes possible to buy second-hand bricks that are suitable, but it's essential to make sure that they're hard enough to withstand frost. Most bricks are intended for walling, where rain is quickly shed. If it stays on a horizontal brick, soaks in and then freezes, the surface will flake and look very messy indeed. It's best to buy special paviors intended for the job.

The edging bricks I used for the paths are moulded with an attractive Tudor rose design and are, alas, even more expensive. They're not absolutely necessary, of course.

The bricks are set on a sand base which has to be retained to stop it drifting out from underneath. You can set the edge rows of bricks on a mortar base and then lay the centre of the path, as I did when I used the special, decorated, edging bricks. Or you can take a cheaper route and make the edging with wood. I used 75 x 25 mm (3 x 1 in) pressure-preserved timber fixed with pegs exactly as recommended for the artisan's garden paths (see page 55).

Before fixing the bricks, lay them out on the ground in the pattern you're going to use, and

OPPOSITE *Sometimes you can find second-hand stock bricks that will do the job, but it's essential to ensure that they're hard enough to withstand freezing without flaking. Plants tumbling over the edges will soften hard lines and blend the path into the rest of the garden.*

1 To lay brick paving, put in the edging as recommended for the artisan's garden path (see page 55). Level it both sides, dig out and put in a layer of dry concrete.

2 Cover this with a layer of sand, consolidate it by treading it down hard and level it with a notched board to make a hard, level surface.

3 Lay out the bricks in the required pattern. Then brush in kiln-dried sand and consolidate the bricks by hand or, preferably, with a vibrator.

This larger area of brick paving has been softened by planting prostrate and low-growing herbs in a formal pattern to form a symbolic foot-maze.

measure the exact width. That'll save a lot of cutting later.

After setting the edging, dig out the soil between the boards and lay down a base of lean concrete. Use an 8:1 mix of ballast and cement mixed dry and just rake it out to make a 5 cm (2 in) bed. Tread it down, rake it again to level it roughly and cover with about 5 cm (2 in) of builder's sand.

Tread this layer down firmly and then make a notched board which will fit across the edging boards to level the sand accurately all over. Lay the bricks on the sand in the required pattern and brush fine sand all over it to fill in any spaces.

You can consolidate the bricks by putting a thick board across the path and bashing it down with a fence post. Alternatively you can hire a vibrating pad which does a much better job much more quickly.

The paved circle takes a lot more work because many of the bricks have to be cut. Hire an angle

grinder for the job and it'll not prove too arduous. In the centre of the circle all the bricks have to be cut to a wedge shape to fit. Later, as the diameter increases, a wedge-shaped brick is needed only now and then.

Make sure that you leave a few bricks out here and there in strategic places to provide planting pockets.

In the very centre of the circle I used an idea I borrowed from Gertrude Jekyll's working partner, Edwin Lutyens. The concentric circles are made by sinking a series of terracotta flower pots inside each other, adjusting the heights with sand. The small pot in the middle is inverted to complete the pattern.

When the brick paving is complete, you'll need to knock out the concrete at the bottom of the planting holes, fill with a gritty, soil-based compost and plant with low-growing, aromatic plants like thyme.

If I can refer back to the artisan's garden at this point, I should say that, if you started with gravel paths and have after a year or two decided to relay with bricks, the soil should be consolidated enough to do without the concrete base. Just rake a little cement powder into the top 5 cm (2 in) of the gravel and continue from there.

Slab Paving

I wanted to find space for a tiny greenhouse in this garden so, since there's not much room, I decided on an octagonal shape, 1.8 m (6 ft) across. This is erected on a paving base, using random-sized slabs.

After marking out the area, set a series of pegs over it, with their tops corresponding to the finished level of the paving. Level them carefully with a spirit level.

Then prepare a base exactly as recommended for brick paving but excluding the final layer of

Old, natural stone lifted from pavements is sometimes available. It makes a wonderful finish, but it's very expensive.

A small, octagonal greenhouse was erected on a paved base. Making a circle of rectangular paving presented some problems but, of course, a square base would do as well.

sand (see page 84). Lay the slabs on five points of mortar, one at each corner and one in the middle. Tap them down with the handle of a club hammer so that the top surface is exactly level with the pegs.

For my octagonal greenhouse I decided on a circular base, which does present some problems. I found that the best way round them was to lay the slabs out on the ground first and then to draw a circle on the slabs using a piece of string fixed to a cane at the centre. Then I cut the slabs where they were, again using the angle grinder. With the circle all laid out, it was a simple matter to transfer the cut slabs to their proper positions.

Naturally, to allow the concrete to harden, you shouldn't walk on the slabs for a couple of days after laying.

Trellis

The open nature of trelliswork allows you to divide the garden into separate 'rooms' without creating a claustrophobic effect. Because you can always see through the trellis in places, even when it's clothed with plants, you retain the feeling of the whole space of the garden and so get the best of both worlds.

This type of hardwood trellis is definitely not a do-it-yourself job. Each piece is jointed, a task that would take hours and quite a lot of skill to do

Trellis like this is really high-quality garden furniture and making it should not be attempted by the average do-it-yourselfer. When the weather tones it down to a light grey, it looks superb and it makes a light, airy division for the garden without giving a 'shut-in' feeling. As you would expect, it's expensive, but because it's made of hardwood it has a long life.

by hand, and the finish is superb. If you want something this stylish, I'm afraid you just have to pay for it.

Fortunately it's not difficult to erect. Because the posts are made of hardwood (naturally I checked that it came from sustainable plantations and is not contributing to the destruction of the rainforest), there's no problem of rotting in the soil, so they can be concreted straight in.

Check and measure very carefully to ensure that each post is at exactly the right height and, just as for panel fencing, put in a post, then a panel and then fit the second post to the panel. Never put in all the posts first. All the panels are pre-drilled when they arrive and brass screws are supplied.

The very attractive arches came as part of the trellis system and are also very easy to erect. In fact, because the arches are fixed by the position of the path underneath them, that's the place to start. If, when you fit the trellis, it finishes a few centimetres short of the yew hedging, it doesn't matter, but it certainly would if it didn't fit exactly over the path.

Grass

I've included a small area of grass as a restful foil to the borders in the 'secret' garden and as a place to lie and dream in the summer sun. Grass was a very common component of older cottage gardens, but it was there for a very different purpose. There would probably have been quite an area used to feed perhaps a cow, a sheep or a goat or two, and the hens and ducks would have scratched around on it too. Today it would be used for relaxation which is, of course, also a very important function.

However, I just can't see the bowling-green type of lawn in a rural cottage garden. In my view the grass should be kept quite a bit longer than that and the modern cottage gardener should

In larger gardens grass is the perfect foil for the borders, but in cottage gardens it's best not to treat it like a bowling green. Leave it to grow a bit longer.

not get worked up over the sight of a daisy or a dandelion. Indeed I think that, in moderation, they're to be positively encouraged.

The grass can be raised from seed or turf and the basic preparation is the same for both. Dig the soil over, incorporating coarse grit if it's very heavy. Rake it down roughly with the back of a fork and then, when the soil's dry enough not to stick to your boots, tread all over it with your weight on your heels to consolidate it thoroughly. Finally rake it level.

The difference between seed and turf is largely an economic one. Seed is much cheaper than the best turf but, of course, you'll have to wait longer to achieve results.

If you decide on seed, my recommendation would be for one of the new rye-grasses which make a tough, drought-resistant yet fine lawn. You'll need to sow at about 50 g per sq. m (1½ oz per sq. yd). On a small area it's not difficult to sow by hand. For a bigger lawn put two large plastic flower pots one inside the other and turn them so that the holes in the bottom don't coincide. Fill with seed and you'll find that you can shake it out very evenly. After sowing, rake it in with a wire lawn rake, aiming to cover about half the seed.

If you prefer turf, it pays hands down to choose a special, cultivated turf that has itself been raised from seed. There should be no weeds in it, it'll be evenly cut and will consist of good, fine grasses.

Lay out the edges first and then, working from the longest straight side, lay out the first row. When you get to the end of the row, lay the end of the last turf over the edging turf and cut off the excess with an old knife. Tap the turves in with the back of a rake.

Subsequent rows are laid in the same way working off wide boards laid on the turf to protect it from footmarks. When you've finished, make sure that the grass never goes short of water until it's rooted or the turves will shrink.

When you first mow either a seed or a turf lawn, raise the cutters as high as they'll go and lower them over the next two cuts until they're cutting the grass to a length of about 2.5 cm (1 in). That's plenty short enough for a cottage garden and will provide a good home for insects.

Wildflowers

In true cottage tradition you could turn your grass into a wildflower meadow. Even if it's quite a small area, it'll still attract millions of insects, birds and butterflies.

Instead of using straight grass seed, you could

A cottage lawn sown with wildflowers looks great and attracts many insects. But you should cut it only twice a year to allow the flowers to seed, and the grass must then be raked off to avoid overfeeding.

start off with a grass and wildflower mixture. If you do, never fertilize the soil either before or after sowing. Wildflowers are used to poor conditions and they wouldn't thank you. Alternatively, if you use turf or already have established grass, the easiest way is to raise the plants by sowing into modules just as for hardy annuals (see page 198). The plants can then be planted into the turf, where they should thrive.

Bear in mind that wildflower lawns should be cut only a couple of times a year, once after flowering and again, if necessary, in the early spring. It's essential to allow the plants to seed into the grass to maintain the population. And note that

this will change over the years as the species that are really happy thrive, while other species less content with their conditions will die out.

Knots and Parterres

Formal knot gardens and the French equivalent, parterres, were very popular with the gentry in their romanticized gardens and completely shunned by cottagers. They were often to be found in monasteries in medieval times, when they were sometimes fashioned into foot mazes representing man's journey through life. The idea was gradually adopted in grand gardens across Europe and reached a peak of popularity in the sixteenth century. Today knots and parterres are benefiting from a great revival of interest, perhaps because the formality of the design is ideally suited to small spaces.

You'll need to decide, first of all, whether you want a pure knot garden, which consists of dwarf hedging and nothing else, or if you want the hedges to retain flower borders. For borders, the scheme will need more room and have to be much more open and expansive in design.

Box is the favourite plant to use for the hedging, either the vigorous common box (*Buxus sempervirens*) or the dwarfer edging box (*Buxus suffruticosa*). You could also incorporate other plants like dwarf lavender (*Lavandula* 'Hidcote') or cotton lavender (*Santolina chamaecyparissus*). Both need clipping regularly to stop them sprawling. I've

This tiny knot in a small cottage garden measures only 1.5 m (5 ft) square, but it makes an attractive formal feature in what is an otherwise very informal garden. As a contrast to the dwarf box hedging, it's planted inside with a golden-foliage thuja and lavenders.

also used dwarf barberry (*Berberis thunbergii* 'Atropurpurea'), which adds a fine, red leaf colour to the scheme. Wall germander (*Teucrium chamaedrys*) is another traditional plant to provide a contrast of colour and texture, as is rosemary (*Rosmarinus officinalis* 'Miss Jessopp's Upright') or rue (*Ruta graveolens*).

Patterns can be quite complicated, though you should again bear in mind that, if you want to grow flowers or herbs inside the hedging, you'll need fairly wide areas to do so. Mark out the shape on the ground using sand poured from a wine bottle and plant about 15–23 cm (6–9 in) apart.

Always remember that it's essential to clip the hedges at least every autumn or spring, and some gardeners like to tidy them up in summer too.

The Vegetable Plot

Over my years of gardening I've come to the conclusion that the most effective way to grow vegetables in a small space is to put them into 1.2-m- (4-ft)-wide beds. The method of cultivation is covered fully later, but a word here about how they were made. It's essential, of course, for them to be decorative as well as productive.

The beds were edged with tiles of a Victorian design which are still available new, made with exactly the same materials and, indeed, in the very brickworks which produced many of those used by Victorian gardeners. They're set on a bed of mortar for extra rigidity, since constant cultivation is likely to move them if they're simply sunk into the soil. Set a tile at each end first and then

There's not much room for vegetables in the gentleman's garden, so they're grown in narrow beds with all the work being done from the paths. It's certainly the most productive way and it can be made very decorative too.

run a tight line along the top. This will mark both the lines and the level and make the rest of the laying quick and easy.

The paths were simply made with gravel on beaten soil like those in the artisan's garden (see page 55).

The Fruit Garden

The area housing the greenhouse was planted with fruit trees and bushes surrounded by flowering plants. Again, cultivation methods are covered in the next section, but this garden presents one problem. To maximize the small space available, I wanted to use fan-trained and espalier trees. But in the absence of a fence or wall, a post-and-wire structure had to be erected. The 2.4-m (8-ft) tanalized posts were set in concrete with 2 m (6 ft 6 in) above the ground. Three straining bolts were fixed at the end of each row to take wires at the top, 30 cm (1 ft) up from the bottom and one in the middle. To hide the posts, roses can be planted at the base and trained tightly to them.

The remainder of the garden round the greenhouse was planted with redcurrants and blackcurrants, raspberries in a column (see page 245), standard gooseberries and strawberries.

Fan-trained fruit trees look very attractive even in winter when the branches are bare. Contrary to popular opinion, they're extremely easy to prune and they certainly produce bumper crops. Train them on wires fixed to posts or to the wall or fence.

The Plants

COTTAGE GARDENERS, like any others, grew whatever plants they could get their hands on. We all know that, once enthusiasm takes a hold, there are no limits to your interest in trying something new. Even the old cottage gardeners would have felt the same way. So how do you define 'cottage garden plants'?

They started out, undoubtedly, as plants with a purpose. Primarily there would have been subsistence plants: the fruit trees and bushes and the vegetables to provide food for both the cottager's family and the livestock. Later, after the dissolution of the monasteries in the sixteenth century, there would have been medicinal herbs and some for the pot too. They've changed very little over the centuries and, of course, the modern cottage gardener will want to grow them as well. But what of the ornamental plants? They have been described as 'simple' or 'unpretentious' flowers, even as 'old-fashioned', but those descriptions don't really get to the nub of it.

I feel sure that cottage gardeners years ago would have given their eye teeth for some of the plants we grow today and would certainly not have turned up their noses because they were 'sophisticated', whatever that means. Yet look at any cottage garden and it's true that the charm does come from a simplicity in both the planting scheme and in the actual plants themselves. There's a decidedly *rural* feel about a real cottage garden, even if it's in the city.

Well, my own definition is perhaps more objective. I think that the old cottage gardeners would have grown whatever they could get their hands on. But they had to do so with very slim resources indeed. They would therefore have taken plants from the wild and later would have 'liberated' them from the gardens of the gentry where they worked. Then these would have been spread around other cottage gardens. So my own theory is that cottage garden plants are those that are essentially easy to grow and to propagate.

1 *Campanula persicifolia*

2 *Papaver rhoeas* 'Mother of Pearl'

3 *Paeonia lactiflora*

4 *Linaria purpurea* 'Canon Went'

5 *Rosa* 'Mischief'

6 *Rosa* 'Conrad Ferdinand Meyer'

7 *Linaria purpurea*

Typical cottage garden borders lack uniformity. There's a real charm in a glorious 'jumble' of colour like this.

Keys are provided to identify the main flowering plants in the photographs.

And that's exactly what modern gardeners want too. I don't think I could be accused of being patronizing when I say that most of us, certainly for the first several years of our gardening lives, find that the biggest restriction to developing our plots exactly as we want them is money. So we too will be looking for ways to reduce our expenditure on plants.

We'll want to grow them from seed, or from cuttings given to us by friends. We'll want to grow plants to swap too, just as our ancestors did in Thomas Hill's time, and we won't be able to spend a lot on the facilities to do it either: no expensive greenhouses with mist propagation and computerized heating and ventilation; no light-rooms and fogging machines; just the same simple equipment our predecessors have been using for centuries.

All the plants I've described here, then, the old favourites and a few newer ones too, can be grown with the simplest of equipment and, provided you can find a source of material, for a minimum of expense. Gardeners are generally delighted to swap plants and to give away cuttings and home-collected seed if you ask. So ask! The best bet is to join the local garden club or society, where you'll meet like-minded people, make a lot of friends and find that you can fill your garden for next to nothing. Even better, join a national society too, like the Cottage Garden Society, which distributes seeds to members each year and is generally eager to give away and exchange plants.

Of course, there's no sense in restricting ourselves to the old cottage plants for purely sentimental reasons. There are lots of excellent new ones that measure up to our criteria of simplicity of cultivation and propagation and would also fit our cottage scheme very well.

Indeed, there are examples of great improvements in the vigour and disease-resistance of some modern varieties. Roses, for example, are bred these days with an eye very much on disease resistance. Modern gardeners don't want to spend their lives spraying noxious chemicals, so if new varieties are prone to blackspot and mildew, they just don't get on the market. None are completely immune but many are now resistant.

Old-fashioned pinks have excellent flowers and superb perfume, but they only flower once. Many new varieties have been bred for the size of flower and repeat flowering, but in doing so have lost the delicacy of the old ones and much of their perfume too. Now a new race is being developed with the old-fashioned look plus the perfume and the long-flowering of modern varieties. That doesn't mean that we must abandon the old ones – heaven forbid! But we should certainly not turn up our noses at the new ones just because they are new. You can be sure that William Robinson wouldn't have done.

Planting

The old cottage gardeners would have done much by trial and error and would have learnt by observation. Being country people in the main and working with plants and animals every day, they couldn't have failed to glean much knowledge of the natural world. So if they dug a plant from, say, a shady woodland edge, they'd know to plant it in a similar position in the garden. Just like us, I daresay, they went wrong quite often too. But generally, if they did, they could go out and dig up another plant. These days, especially if we have to buy our plants, we won't be able to afford the luxury of getting it wrong too often. Even if you're raising your own plants from seed and cuttings, you'll lose heart if you fail more than is necessary.

It's important, therefore, to get to know your plants. Find out how tall they grow and how much they spread, when they flower and also their preferences as to soil and position. The list of plants here includes all those details.

However much you research, you'll nonetheless still go wrong from time to time. In my travels I have met several very experienced cottage gardeners who have been growing plants all their lives. They *all* admitted that they still made mistakes now and then. That's the bad news.

The good news is that, to a man (and woman), they all said the same thing. If you go wrong, don't worry. As soon as you realize that you've planted this plant too close to that one, or that you simply can't live with the colours of those two adjacent flowers, change them. All you need do is to pour a bucket of water over the plant to be moved, dig it up with as much soil as possible and plant it somewhere else. Then give it another good drink and it'll never know it's been disturbed. It's very comforting to know that, provided you move trees and shrubs within a season or two of their original planting, they'll be quite happy. And, of course, most herbaceous plants will love being shifted at any age.

As for positioning plants, remind yourself again that you're involved in an *artisan's* craft. I have to say that, in my own gardening, I have *never* been worried by clashing colours. That doesn't mean I've got it right every time – far from it. It's perhaps testament to my philistinism that the lovely jumble of colour I achieve more by luck than judgment looks spot-on to my eye. And in my garden that, of course, is what matters.

So, in the first instance at least, concentrate on finding the right soil and aspect for each plant and, as a general rule, putting the tallest at the back and the shortest at the front. Even that rule should not be hard and fast, because a change of height will add a lot more interest than a uniformly graded border.

In my view, one of the great interests of garden-ing lies in the critical appraisal of the borders you've planted and the re-arrangement of any-thing you feel could be improved. You might decide that two colours live uneasily with each other or that the addition of another one would add to the appeal of the grouping. You may feel that the delicate flowers of one plant would be better appreciated against a background of dull green, or it might be that one plant has grown more than you thought it would and so hides another. The fascination of gardening is that it never seems to stop. You'll *always* be adding, changing and improving.

Whatever you do, you *will* succeed. The fact is that nature's *really* in charge here and there's no more creative artist in this world or the next.

Many of the plants in this wonderful garden on the Isle of Wight were grown from seed from the Cottage Garden Society, while others were raised from cuttings given or more often exchanged through gardening friendships.

Trees

Trees were of much greater importance to the old cottage gardeners than they are to us today, because they were used for food, for fuel and to make most of what the cottager needed for his livelihood from buckets to hay forks, carts to thatching pegs. Thomas Tusser gives us an insight into the various uses of different timbers in the sixteenth century, in some more of his charming doggerel:

Save elme, ash and crabtree, for cart and for plough,
save step for stile, of the crotch of the bough.
Save hazel for forks, save sallow [willow] for rake,
save hulver [holly] and thorne,
thereof flaile for to make.

Naturally these were woodland trees, though some of them found their way into gardens for purely decorative reasons.

Trees are the only plants that don't fit the general specification I've laid down for cottage garden plants because, with a very few exceptions, they simply aren't subjects for home propa-gation. Some, like willows, alders and poplars, are pretty easy to raise from cuttings, but most of these are big, vigorous trees and not really suitable for our purpose. Others, like hawthorns, wild plums and cherries, can be raised from seed, but take so long that it's always best to buy them as young trees from a nursery. Many varieties are budded or grafted on to special rootstocks, so this really is a job for the grower.

It's likely that you'll want only one or at most two trees, so it's best to choose those that give you two or more displays through the year; perhaps flowers followed by berries or good autumn foliage colour, or even attractive winter bark.

All the trees listed below will grow in virtually any soil and position unless otherwise stated, but for the sake of the rest of the garden be careful with the siting. Trees will naturally cast shade and, though this can often produce another welcome type of habitat, in very small spaces it can shed so much gloom that you're stuck with growing shade-loving plants whether you like it or not.

When you buy a tree from the garden centre, you may find the suggested height misleading. To avoid putting customers off, they often state the

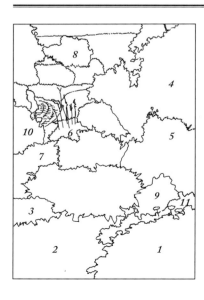

1 *Anthemis punctata cupaniana*

2 *Viola labradorica*

3 *Epimedium rubrum*

4 *Cotinus coggygria* 'Royal Purple'

5 *Geranium phaeum* 'Album'

6 *Thalictrum aquilegifolium*

7 *Pulmonaria officinalis* 'Sissinghurst White'

8 *Rosa* 'Canary Bird'

9 *Polemonium caeruleum*

10 *Osmanthus delavayi*

11 *Pelargonium* hybrid

Trees and shrubs form the basic bones of this border and act as a background to herbaceous plants.

height the tree will reach in ten years, but if you intend to stay in your garden for longer, expect a bigger tree. However, don't be alarmed at the eventual heights stated in the following list. Though a 10-m (33-ft) tree sounds huge, when you see it growing, it's really relatively small. What's more, the heights I've given are the eventual tallest expected. The trees would, in most cases, take many years to get there. I suppose, as a rule of thumb, that they would grow about a third of the stated height in ten years.

Planting

Bare-rooted trees should be planted in the dormant season between late autumn and early spring. Container-grown stock can go in at any time if you're prepared to water.

It's most important, first of all, to prepare a big area for a new tree. If you simply dig a hole in otherwise uncultivated soil, it'll drain all the surrounding water and become a sump.

Dig the hole and break up the bottom, checking that it's deep enough to allow you to plant at *exactly* the level the tree grew on the nursery. Before planting, bang in a short stake, which should come no more than a third of the way up the trunk. Next sprinkle fertilizer on the heap of soil you've dug out, using bonemeal in winter and a balanced organic feed in the growing season. Put the tree in the hole, refill with a little soil and shake the plant up and down a few times to settle the soil around the roots. Then completely refill, firming gently with your boot.

Fix the tree with a proper plastic tree tie which is held firmly to the stake with a nail. Then mulch round the plant with manure or compost to eliminate weed growth and retain moisture.

Most trees that fail do so because of lack of water, so check the soil for at least a year and water if necessary.

Make sure that trees and shrubs are planted at the depth they grew on the nursery. Even on heavy soil it's a mistake to use peat, which holds too much water. If any addition is necessary, use rotted manure or compost.

Choosing trees

If you have space for only a single tree, I'd have to say that I would go along with the old cottagers and state a preference for an apple. Here's a tree with stunning blossom in spring, followed by huge, attractive fruits in late summer that you can actually eat too. No other tree offers so much. But in small spaces, there are other ways to grow them that take up less room. All that's covered later.

Amelanchier lamarckii JUNEBERRY, SERVICEBERRY or SNOWY MESPILUS
Height: 12 m (40 ft). Spread: 9 m (30 ft).
The small, black berries produced by the Juneberry were once used as a substitute for

raisins, but the value of this tree is really in its three shows of colour. It has white flowers in spring, set off by lovely bronze young foliage. The leaves turn green through the year and then finally bright yellow if it's growing in shade or brilliant red in sunshine. It's not at all happy on very chalky soils, but I've found it fine on slightly alkaline land.

Arbutus unedo STRAWBERRY TREE
Height: 9 m (30 ft). Spread: 9 m (30 ft).
A native of Ireland, the strawberry tree makes a small, gnarled tree with reddish, shredding bark. It always looks good, summer and winter. It bears small, white flowers in drooping clusters in autumn, followed by red fruits. Often both are there at the same time. Its close relative *A. andrachnoides* is even lovelier, with cinnamon-red bark. These are slow-growing trees that won't take over, despite their eventual height. They do best on acid soil, but will tolerate some lime.

Betula spp. SILVER BIRCH
Height: 30 m (100 ft). Spread: 7.5 m (25 ft).
The native birch (*Betula pendula*) is a well-known woodland tree noted for its white bark, its delicate tracery of bare branches in winter and yellow catkins in spring. It would certainly have found a home in many old cottage gardens, but it's a bit large for most modern plots. The Himalayan birch (*Betula utilis* 'Jaquemontii') is a little smaller and has brilliant white, peeling bark.

Corylus spp. HAZEL
Height: 7 m (23 ft). Spread: 5 m (16 ft).
The native hazel (*Corylus avellana*) has always been valued for its timber, used for jobs like thatching pegs and in hedge laying, and for its crop of cob nuts.

Some varieties are valuable as ornamental trees and can be grown to produce a crop of nuts too,

The beautiful red fruits of the strawberry tree are often accompanied by white flowers in autumn, but it's well worth its place in the garden just for its fine reddish bark and gnarled shape.

provided you grow two varieties for pollination and can keep the squirrels at bay. They can also be used in a mixed hedge for a very traditional cottage effect. The varieties of *C. avellana* and *C. maxima* are the ones to grow.

'Kentish Cob', 'Butler' and 'Longue d'Espagne' are all good nut-producing varieties with excellent, long, yellow catkins in spring.

If you're determined to defeat the squirrels, you'll have to grow the trees with a stem at least 1.8 m (6 ft) high before the branches start. Plant them about 3.6 m (12 ft) from any other trees in the garden so that the squirrels can't jump from tree to tree and then, well before harvest time, wire a sheet of rigid plastic around each trunk.

The squirrels won't be able to get a grip on it and they'll be forced to leave the nuts for you.

The purple-leaf filbert (*C. maxima* 'Purpurea') makes an excellant large shrub or a small tree with superb, intense purple foliage, but it is not really a fruiting type.

Crataegus spp. FLOWERING THORN
Height: 10 m (33 ft). Spread: 10 m (33 ft).
A small tree, making a rounded head in the early years and eventually spreading. The common hawthorn (*Crataegus monogyna*) is the one the old cottagers would have grown. In spring this has large, fragrant clusters of white blossom known as 'May blossom', which is the subject of many old country sayings and superstitions. 'Ne'er cast a clout till May be out' is one of the more sensible. The blossom is followed by red berries in autumn. It's a fine tree and a really authentic cottage garden plant.

The 'Glastonbury thorn' (*C. m.* 'Biflora') was, according to legend, planted by Joseph of Arimathaea who brought it from the Holy Land. It can produce flushes of white flower during winter, but it's for sheltered gardens only.

There are various varieties of the Midland hawthorn (*C. laevigata*) available, like the double red 'Paul's Scarlet' and 'Masekii' which has double pink flowers. All bear red berries. These are perhaps the most suitable for small gardens. The species is a native, but the varieties are hybrids.

C. prunifolia has fine, shiny foliage and white flowers followed by large, red fruits, but its most notable feature is its superb autumn leaf colour. Its origin is unknown.

Euonymus europaeus SPINDLE
Height: 6 m (20 ft). Spread: 5 m (16 ft).
A native shrub or small tree, the spindle was often used in mixed hedgerows. It got its name

from the fact that the hard wood was used to make spindles. It bears small, greenish white flowers in spring followed by scarlet capsules which open to reveal orange seeds. The leaves also turn bright red in autumn. The variety 'Aucubifolius' has foliage which turns pinkish, mottled yellow and white in autumn.

Ilex aquifolium HOLLY
Height: 20 m (65 ft). Spread: 6 m (20 ft).
Another native, the holly is a plant with many religious and magical connections. Common holly (*Ilex aquifolium*) has been grown in gardens for centuries as a shrub or small tree, as hedging and as a subject for topiary. It has evergreen, glossy leaves and, if you have a male and a female plant or the self-fertile variety 'J. C. van Tol' or 'Pyramidalis', bright red berries too. The variety 'Bacciflava' bears handsome yellow berries.

All the hollies can be controlled by judicious pruning or by clipping to a formal shape.

Laburnum spp. GOLDEN RAIN
Height: 7 m (23 ft). Spread: 7 m (23 ft).
The laburnum has been grown in this country since about 1560. The variety originally grown would have been the common laburnum (*L. anagyroides*), but the best for modern gardens is certainly *L. watereri* 'Vossii', which carries long, pendulous racemes of yellow flowers in late spring to early summer. All parts of this plant are poisonous, but this variety sets very few seeds so it's an obvious choice where children live.

Malus spp. CRAB APPLES
Height: 6–8 m (20–26 ft). Height: 5–6 m (16–18 ft).
The native crab apple (*Malus sylvestris*) bears white flowers followed by yellow fruits flushed with red and was possibly taken from the woods and grown by cottage gardeners. However, the

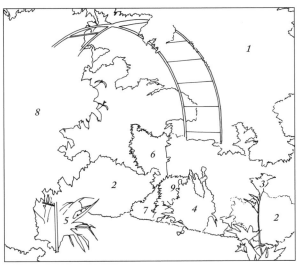

1 *Gleditsia triacanthos*
'Sunburst'

2 *Alchemilla mollis*

3 *Filipendula rubra*

4 *Sisyrinchium striatum*

5 *Phormium cookianum*
'Cream Delight'

6 *Daphne mezereum*

7 *Helichrysum petiolare*

8 *Cornus* 'Eddie's White
Wonder'

9 *Campanula persicifolia*

Even before the climbers have grown over this metal arch, the plants in the mixed borders have begun to take away its formality and blend it in with the rest of the garden.

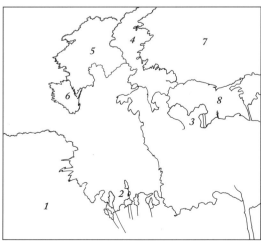

1 *Myosotis* 'Royal Blue'

2 *Tiarella cordifolia*

3 *Tulipa* 'Princess Margaret Rose'

4 *Prunus* 'Pink Perfection'

5 *Acer pseudoplatanus* 'Brilliantissimum'

6 *Cytisus praecox* 'Allgold'

7 *Camellia japonica*

8 *Hesperis matronalis*

This spring border is brightened by the young, pinkish foliage of an acer and the display of cherry flowers.

apple (*M. domestica*) has been here so long that it was more likely, because of its usefulness, that they grew some form of that in preference to the crab apple.

With the exception of the variety 'John Downie', which has long been used to make jam and jelly and is covered in the fruit section (see page 239), the newer hybrids are much more suitable for modern gardens if you're looking purely for ornament.

'Evereste' is one of the smaller ones and is covered with red buds opening to white flowers in spring followed by orange/yellow fruits.

'Golden Hornet' has pink buds which open to pinkish white followed by bright yellow berries. This is one of the best varieties for pollinating apples.

'Liset' has bronze/purple leaves and deep red flowers followed by small red fruits.

'Lemoinei' has the same colouring as 'Liset', but the flowers and fruits are larger.

There are many others with slightly different flowers and fruits, all worth growing.

Prunus spp. FLOWERING CHERRY
Height: 6–10 m (20–33 ft). Spread: 6–10 m (20–33 ft).
Many of the flowering cherries available today originated in Japan and can, by no stretch of the imagination, be called original cottage plants. But old cottage gardens certainly grew the sweet cherry and the 'gean' or 'mazzard' (*Prunus avium*).

These are big trees and, though superb if you have the space, are not appropriate for a small garden. The Japanese types will provide the same stunning spring blossom but on a smaller scale.

In my opinion the spring cherry (*Prunus subhirtella* 'Autumnalis') should be made obligatory in every garden. The white flowers appear on naked stems at intervals right through the winter

and then have a final, superb fling in early spring. Even better is the pink variety 'Autumnalis Rosea'. Both make small trees.

One of the earliest of the Japanese hybrids is 'Accolade', which forms a small, spreading tree and is unfailingly covered in deep pink blossom even on young plants. It's one of the earliest to flower in spring.

'Mount Fuji' is a real spring tonic. Again, it's a small, spreading tree but this time with fragrant flowers of snow white, set off by the freshest of spring-green foliage.

P. sargentii is a little gem. A small, round-headed tree, it has single, pale pink flowers in spring and is one of the first to colour fiery red in autumn.

The cherry plum (*Prunus cerasifera*) is not known in the wild, but was certainly cultivated in gardens in the sixteenth century. Its plentiful white flowers open before the leaves, which are very dark green. Better for modern gardens is the variety 'Nigra', which has deep red leaves and

The Japanese flowering cherries make superb substitutes for the much larger native species early cottage gardeners would have grown. This one, 'Accolade', is one of the first to flower and is totally reliable.

Robinia pseudoacacia 'Frisia' is a recent introduction but well worthwhile for a small cottage garden. It doesn't move well, so always buy it in a container.

pink flowers: a very striking tree indeed and easy to grow almost anywhere.

The one native that was pretty certainly grown in cottage gardens from earliest times, and which would fit even a small space, is the bird cherry (*P. padus*). The flowers, hanging in long, pendulous racemes of almond-scented white, are quite different from those of most other cherries. Look out too for the variety 'Colorata', which has coppery foliage and pink flowers.

If you wonder why I have not included the superb flowering peaches and almonds with the cherries, it's because of the debilitating disease peach-leaf curl to which they are prone. This fungus causes characteristic red blisters on the leaves and can be controlled only with constant spraying – which simply doesn't fit in with the cottage philosophy.

Rhus typhina STAG'S HORN SUMACH
Height: 6 m (20 ft). Spread: 5 m (16 ft).
Originally from North America, the stag's horn sumach was often grown in cottage gardens. It has superb, deeply cut foliage which turns fiery red in autumn. The fruits consist of large, brownish cones at the ends of the branches and the bark is an attractive, furry brown. It has the big disadvantage that it suckers badly, sending up shoots a good distance from the parent. You can easily control these by pulling them out, provided they don't appear in a lawn. The variety 'Dissecta' has very attractive, finely cut leaflets. Both trees will grow on quite dry soil in sun or shade.

Robinia pseudoacacia BLACK LOCUST
Height: 25 m (80 ft). Spread: 6 m (20 ft).
The black locust or common acacia was introduced to France from North America in 1601 and soon found its way to Britain, where it quickly became naturalized. It has attractive foliage and pendulous, white, pea-like flowers in mid to late summer. It's a bit big for most gardens, so the smaller variety 'Frisia' is to be preferred. This has bright golden foliage, which makes it an attractive tree, and though it dates from only 1935, you can bet that the old cottagers would have fought over it.

Sorbus aria WHITEBEAM
Height: 15 m (50 ft). Spread: 6 m (20 ft).
The native whitebeam (*Sorbus aria*) is a fine sight in spring. The new leaves are silvery grey, sparkling in the early sunshine. The tree has small, white flowers in spring, followed by red berries, but these are relatively insignificant.

The old cottagers would therefore have much preferred *Sorbus thibetica* 'John Mitchell', a Chinese species. It's much the same tree except that the silver-grey leaves are very much bigger and more dramatic.

Sorbus aucuparia ROWAN or MOUNTAIN ASH
Height: 8–15 m (26–50 ft). Spread: 6–8 m
(18–26 ft).
A native and therefore certain to have been
grown in original cottage gardens. The real
rowan (*Sorbus aucuparia*) makes quite a large,
conical tree with lots of white blossom in spring
followed by clusters of red berries in late summer.
Like most rowans it keeps its fruits until the birds
decide to have a go. Then they disappear rapidly.
So they're a very useful food source in early
winter.

The modern cottager would be well advised to
grow one of the varieties like 'Autumn Glow'
which has fiery red foliage in autumn, contrasting well with pinkish yellow fruits.

S. cashmiriana makes a small tree with large,
pink flowers in spring followed by pendulous
clusters of large, white berries, while the variety
'Joseph Rock' has bright yellow berries.

Sorbus domestica SERVICE TREE
Height: 20 m (65 ft). Spread: 6 m (20 ft).
The service tree has been cultivated in this country for centuries. It has typical rowan leaves and
slightly off-white flowers in spring, followed by
greenish yellow fruits which can be eaten when
bletted (partly rotted). Another genuine early
cottage garden tree.

Taxus baccata COMMON YEW
Height: 20 m (65 ft). Spread: 10 m (30 ft).
One of the only three native conifers, the yew is
part of the British heritage and has been grown
for centuries. It was an important tree since it was
used to make arrows; and, being poisonous to
livestock, it was often planted in churchyards
where it was presumed cattle wouldn't stray.

It's doubtful that a small cottage garden would
be able to afford the space for a fully mature yew
that has been allowed to grow unchecked. It can
be a dull plant unless it's clipped to a formal
shape: then it becomes a focal point and an
exciting sculpture (see page 203). It's also the best
possible hedging plant (see pages 81 and 132).

Climbers

Climbers add instant height to the garden and
should be used to cover the fences and walls more
or less completely. In a small garden the more leaf
cover you can get on the fences, the less claustrophobic they'll look. Of course, you should leave
space for productive plants like trained fruit trees,
but allow room to grow a climber of some sort

*Use all vertical structures in the garden – walls, fences, trellis
and so on – to add almost instant height by planting them
with climbers. This bare trellis in the gentleman's garden
will be transformed when it carries a mixture of climbing
roses and clematis.*

between them to add colour and interest.

Climbers can also be used to add height to the borders: simply grow them over free-standing supports. An obelisk is ideal (see page 66) or even just a post driven into the ground.

Where you're growing climbers over an arbour or round a seat, they should naturally be scented and, where they cover an arch, it's often better to avoid thorny roses to avoid scratching your unwary visitors.

Planting

By their nature climbers generally prefer a deep, rich, moisture-retentive soil, so take special care to prepare the planting holes well.

Remember that the soil at the base of the house wall is often the driest in the garden: it's therefore best to plant about 30 cm (1 ft) away from it and simply to point the climber where you want it to grow. It will eventually get there. You should also keep a special eye on it and water when it dries out – for at least the first season until it can fend for itself.

Most plants should be planted at the depth at which they grew on the nursery. Since you'll buy most in pots, that's easy to see. But there are   exceptions. It's best to put roses about 5 cm (2 in) below soil level to encourage growth right from the base of the plant. That goes for bush roses too.

Clematis should also be planted deeply, but for a different reason. They're subject to the fungus disease clematis wilt, which makes the plants wilt from the top and die. Since the fungus affects only parts above ground level, deep-planted plants will have plenty of buds left to regrow if the plant does succumb and has to be cut back.

After planting always give the plants a good handful of organic fertilizer, water them well, and mulch round them with compost.

Self-clinging plants can't be induced to stick to the wall or fence. It's only the new growth of ivy, Virginia creeper, climbing hydrangea and so on that will stick, so you have to leave it to them. Just point them at the wall. They'll be frustratingly slow until they do stick, but then they'll get away like a race-horse.

Some plants, like clematis and honeysuckle, climb by twining. They may need a little help to get started, but after that they'll roar away under their own steam. Others, like roses, will need to be tied in to wires and their shoots pulled horizontal to restrict sap flow and so encourage flowering.

Chaenomeles japonica Flowering quince
This wall shrub came to Britain from Japan in about 1869 and is quite different from the quince grown to eat, which was known in this country certainly in the seventeenth century, if not before (see page 240). The flowering quince is grown for its decorative value and was a popular Victorian cottage garden plant. It has bright orange flowers in spring, followed by large, yellow, pear-shaped fruits.

Chaenomeles speciosa arrived in Britain at about the same time and there are several more modern seedlings in a range of colours, but with the authentic cottage feel. 'Apple Blossom' is white, tinged pink; 'Brilliant' is scarlet; 'Rosea Plena' is a double with pink flowers; and 'Nivalis' is pure white.

Quinces are very hardy and will grow on a fence or wall, where they will need tying in and training. Propagate by softwood cuttings in June in the coldframe (see page 200).

Clematis spp.
Old man's beard or traveller's joy was grown in gardens of old, but it's much too rampant for modern gardens. Its small, white flowers and

Two varieties of Clematis viticella *climb happily through shrubs in late summer, providing another season of flower. After flowering they can be cut back hard to give the shrubs light and air and both will give a repeat performance the next season.*

hairy seed heads are not that exciting in any case. Some other species and varieties have also been grown for centuries and no cottage garden should be without these attractive twining plants. The new cottager has a wealth of wonderful clematis to choose from.

The main point to bear in mind is that the small-flowered species are generally much more vigorous than the large-flowered hybrids, so choose carefully. While a species like *C. montana* can be used to cover a building or a large pergola, it's not suitable for an obelisk and certainly not for growing through another plant as some of the less vigorous types are.

Pruning sometimes baffles gardeners, so remember the simple rule of thumb. If it flowers before the end of June, prune it after flowering by cutting side shoots back to within a bud or two of the main branches. If it blooms later, cut it hard back to within 15 cm (6 in) of the ground in February. Propagate by cuttings in June (see page 200).

Clematis alpina, introduced in 1792, is not too vigorous for small gardens. It has smallish, blue flowers with a white central tuft and flowers in April and May. Its varieties 'Frances Rivis' with larger blue flowers, 'Ruby' with red flowers and 'White Moth' are also worth growing.

The hybrid 'Bill Mackenzie' is a vigorous variety with thick petals of bright yellow. It flowers from July to October and the flowers are followed by fluffy white seed heads.

C. flammula was certainly grown in the sixteenth century. It's quite vigorous and covered in tiny, white, sweetly scented flowers from August to October, followed by silky seed heads.

C. macropetala is a lovely early-flowering species, producing violet-blue flowers paling towards the centre and again followed by attractive seed heads. 'Lagoon', with blue flowers, 'Markham's Pink' and 'White Swan' are also good.

C. montana is vigorous to rampant and bears small, white flowers in profusion in May. Its varieties, the pink 'Elizabeth' and 'Tetrarose', have much the same habit.

C. viticella has been cultivated in cottage gardens since the sixteenth century and is useful for growing through other plants to give a late show. After flowering it should be cut right down and the old growth removed to give its host plant a free run. The flowers are red/violet or blue. Much later varieties offer the modern gardener a wider range. Look for the wine-red 'Madame Julia Correvon', the deep pink 'Margot Koster' and the violet 'Etoile Violette' especially.

The large-flowered hybrids date from the late nineteenth century onwards, but are wonderful cottage plants. There's a huge choice, so visit a nursery before buying. Popular varieties include:

'Comtesse de Bouchaud' – pink flowers with yellow stamens from June to August.

'Ernest Markham' – petunia-red flowers from June to September.

'General Sikorski' – blue flowers, red at the base, in June and July.

'Gravetye Beauty' – bell-shaped, cherry-red flowers from July to September.

'Hagley Hybrid' – shell pink flowers with brown anthers from June to September.

'Jackmanii Superba' – violet-purple flowers from July to September.

'Lasurstern' – deep lavender-blue flowers with golden stamens in May and June and again in autumn.

'Mrs Cholmondeley' – pale blue flowers from May to August.

The large-flowered clematis hybrid 'Hagley Hybrid' is a very free-flowering variety introduced in 1956. Prune it hard in early spring.

'Perle d'Azur' is a vigorous variety introduced in 1885. Try growing it through dark foliage plants like yew which will display the pale-coloured flowers to their best advantage.

'Nelly Moser' – mauve/pink flowers with a central carmine bar on each petal in May and June and again in late summer.

'Niobe' – deep red flowers with yellow anthers from July to October.

'Perle d'Azur' – light blue flowers from June to August.

'The President' – purple-blue flowers with a silver reverse from June to September.

'Ville de Lyon' – carmine-red flowers with golden stamens from June to October.

'Vyvyan Pennell' – double, blue/purple flowers with a carmine centre from May to July.

Hedera spp. IVY

The common ivy (*Hedera helix*) is a native and was certainly grown in cottage gardens since the Middle Ages and before. It has numerous folk-lore connections and has been used since before early Christian times at Christmas.

Ivy is particularly useful for growing on north-facing walls and in soils where nothing else will do. It will cling to both walls and fences and can also be used as a scrambling plant to cover difficult areas of soil. The flowers are insignificant, but the evergreen leaves are most attractive. It's an excellent wildlife attractor, providing a home for many insects and a favourite nesting site for several species of birds.

In 1577 Thomas Hill suggested that garlands of ivy be tied around trees to attract ants, where they could then be killed.

There are several new varieties of ivy which you may like to grow, but for a genuine cottage garden avoid the more contrived forms like the bright yellow 'Buttercup' and the green-and-yellow 'Goldheart'. 'Green Ripple' is an interesting variation, bearing leaves with wavy edges, while the other native, the Irish ivy (*H. hibernica*), is noted for larger leaves than the English form. Well worth growing. Propagate by layering.

Humulus lupulus HOP

Hops have been grown by cottagers for centuries and were used to make ale which was consumed in much greater quantities than today. Indeed, even quite small children were weaned on the stuff!

These days, gardeners rarely have the space to grow hops for brewing, but they make decorative (if very rampant) plants. The young shoots can also be eaten like asparagus.

For the small garden it's advisable to stick to the slightly less vigorous golden hop, the variety 'Aureus'. It has soft yellow leaves and is best grown up a free-standing post or an obelisk, where it will twine happily. But make sure that you control the running roots by digging them out where they're not wanted.

If you want to grow hops really well and you have access to pigeon manure, take Thomas Tusser's sixteenth-century advice: 'For hop ground cold,/Dove doong woorth gold.' Otherwise farmyard manure is the next best thing. Propagate by division.

Jasminum spp. JASMINE or JESSAMINE

The common white or poet's jasmine has been seen in cottage gardens since 1548. This twining plant is still a great favourite and it's not hard to see why. It produces numerous small, white and very fragrant flowers and, if you grow it on your own cottage wall, it'll perfume your days all summer. In colder districts it needs a south wall and some shelter. Thomas Hill recommends growing it over a willow arbour, where it 'not only defendeth the heat of the sun but yieldeth a delectable smel much refreshing the sitters under it'.

The winter jasmine (*Jasminum nudiflorum*) can be grown as a wall shrub. It bears bright yellow flowers from November to February and soon covers a wall, though it needs tying in initially.

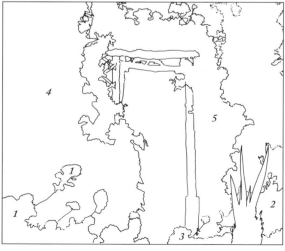

1 *Centranthus ruber*
2 *Campanula persicifolia*
3 *Alchemilla mollis*
4 *Hedera canariensis* 'Gloire de Marengo'
5 *Rosa* 'Albertine'

The large, evergreen leaves of ivy make it an excellent climber, especially where the soil or conditions are not ideal. It's a plant that will grow almost anywhere.

J. stephanense is much more modern, but worth growing for its variegated creamy yellow, young leaves and fragrant, pink flowers in summer.

Propagate jasmines by layering or hardwood cuttings in autumn.

Lathyrus odoratus Sweet pea

The sweet pea is a twining, summer-flowering annual which first came to Britain from Sicily in 1697. By 1754 there were three colours, but in 1870 Henry Eckford began a very successful breeding programme and by 1900 there were 264 varieties. The flowers were smaller than modern varieties and mostly had frilled edges, but the perfume was always mentioned as sweet and strong. They were great favourites with cottage gardeners.

Modern varieties were bred for size and began to lose their frilled edges and their fragrance. Now perfume has largely been bred back in, using varieties found in old cottage gardens where seed had been collected for generations. When selecting new varieties always ensure that perfume is mentioned in the description. There's no point in growing sweet peas that don't smell.

They come in a vast range of pastel colours and are very easy to raise each year from seed sown in February in special sweet-pea tubes (or rolled-up newspapers or even old toilet-roll centres) in a coldframe. Grow them in full sun.

Lathyrus latifolius Perennial sweet pea

This perennial sweet pea is a European native, first mentioned in 1596, and was enthusiastically grown by the earliest cottagers. The species has rose-pink flowers, but there are good white, pink and red forms too. Propagate by seed sown in spring, and once the plants are established, don't move them. Grow in full sun. They look especially good when they are allowed to scramble through a shrub.

Lathyrus nervosus Lord Anson's blue pea

Brought from Patagonia in 1744, this perennial has clear blue, perfumed flowers. It's very rare, but if you can find it, grow it.

Lonicera periclymenum Honeysuckle or woodbine

A British native and an absolute must. I say that not purely sentimentally, but because the common honeysuckle is, in my opinion, still the very best. In summer it has gloriously scented, creamy white flowers which are purple or yellow on the outside. The flowers darken with age in a most attractive way and they're followed by bright red berries.

Honeysuckle is a twining plant that will grow in sunshine or shade, flowering slightly better in sun, but less prone to attack from greenfly in shade. Propagate by layering.

Other good varieties include the early Dutch honeysuckle, called 'Belgica', with red/purple

The perennial sweet pea is an old cottage plant and invaluable for growing through shrubs and over herbaceous plants to give another season of flower.

flowers fading to yellow; its similar, later cousin 'Serotina'; and the wonderful *L. tellmanniana* with large, red buds opening to coppery yellow flowers.

Parthenocissus quinquefolia VIRGINIA CREEPER

A very popular, rampant, self-clinging climber introduced to Britain in 1629. The leaves are glossy and attractively shaped and turn brilliant red in autumn.

The later introduction *P. henryana* has leaves beautifully veined with white. It's especially good on a shaded north wall. It grows in any fertile soil and can be propagated by layering or hardwood cuttings.

Passiflora caerulea PASSION FLOWER

Perhaps surprisingly the passion flower has been a favourite cottage garden climber in warmer counties since 1609. Given a south-facing wall, it makes a very vigorous twining plant and should produce many flowers during the summer. They're undoubtedly one of the most complex, interesting and beautiful of all flowers and folklore has it that they represent the instruments of Christ's Passion – the nails, the crown of thorns, the wounds and the halo. Plants may get cut down by frost during the winter but, if the base is protected, they generally re-appear the following spring. Propagate by cuttings in late summer in the coldframe.

Ribes speciosum FUCHSIA-FLOWERED GOOSEBERRY

Grown in Britain since 1828, this spiny wall shrub bears superb, pendulous, red flowers in late spring. The foliage is glossy and semi-evergreen. In colder districts it needs a south-facing wall (where it requires tying in), but will thrive in any reasonably fertile soil. Propagate by hardwood cuttings in autumn.

Rosa spp. and varieties

Climbing and rambling roses are obviously such a traditional part of the cottage garden that there's simply no question of excluding them. Older varieties have such superb shape and perfume that they're irresistible, even though some of them flower for only a short period.

Many of the newer climbers in particular flower repeatedly and lots of them produce the most exquisite perfume. There's absolutely no point and no need either to buy roses that have had the perfume bred out.

The big difference between ramblers and climbers is this. Ramblers are more vigorous and will give a superb show of flower but generally only in one fine flush. The flowers are smaller and borne in large clusters. Climbers are less vigorous but flower continually, on and off, during the summer or have one good flush and another later but with fewer flowers, which are generally larger but sparser. Prune ramblers after flowering by

'Bobbie James' is a vigorous rambler rose ideal for growing through quite large trees.

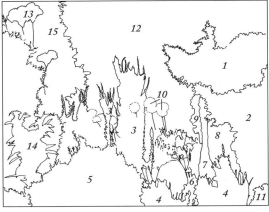

1 *Rosa glauca*

2 *Cotinus coggygria* 'Royal Purple'

3 *Linaria purpurea*

4 *Eschscholzia californica* 'Alba'

5 *Cistus hybridus*

6 *Lychnis coronaria*

7 *Atriplex hortensis rubra*

8 *Astrantia major* 'Rubra'

9 *Campanula persicifolia*

10 *Allium aflatunense*

11 *Lotus hirsutus*

12 *Rosa* 'New Dawn'

13 *Rosa* 'Pink Peace'

14 *Lilium* 'Corsage'

15 *Buddleia davidii*

The climbing rose 'New Dawn' dominates this border with its large, white flowers which are touched with a soft pink flush.

removing old wood and shortening side shoots. Climbers are pruned in early spring in much the same way.

Climbers and ramblers can be grown against a wall or fence or they can be trained up pergolas, arches, obelisks and arbours. Both need tying in. When training, always try to pull branches downwards to restrict growth and encourage flowering. The majority prefer a south- or west-facing wall, but there are one or two that are successful facing north or east. Propagate by hardwood cuttings in autumn.

As with clematis, there are hundreds of varieties to choose from and it's impossible to describe them all here. This list includes many that were grown in old cottage gardens and those which have, in my view, an old cottage garden appeal. Still, you'd be well advised to visit a specialist nursery or to get hold of a catalogue. If you do visit, do so when you want your roses to flower, see them blooming and order for later delivery or, if they're pot-grown, take them away with you.

That roses were appreciated for their ornamental quality in the sixteenth century is confirmed by Thomas Tusser, who recommends that they should be grown as decoration in the fruit plot:

The Gooseberry, Respis [raspberry],
and Roses, al three,
with strawberies under them trimly agree.

Most of the 'old-fashioned' climbers we associate with cottage gardens were raised in France from the nineteenth century, but long before that a few varieties were dug up from the wild and were certainly grown by cottagers.

The dog rose (*Rosa canina*) entwined itself through their hedges to provide flowers in summer and could still be used in the same way today. Its simple, single, pink, perfumed flowers are a real delight and they're followed by bright red hips in autumn. The hips are used to make rose-hip syrup as they have been by generations of country folk.

If you've ever allowed one of your budded modern roses to be overcome by suckers, you could well have discovered some beautiful pink blooms and prolific hips. That's because the rootstock on which it has been budded is a close relation of the old dog rose.

This is an imaginative planting of roses, using relatively modern varieties. 'American Pillar' was introduced from the USA in 1909 and 'Eye Paint' came from New Zealand in 1975.

1 *Penstemon* 'John Nash'
2 *Rosa* 'Eye Paint'
3 *Rosa* 'American Pillar'
4 *Anemone magellanica*

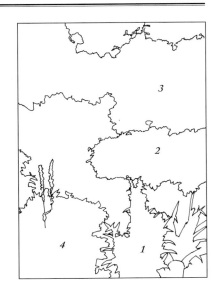

Climbing or rambler roses are the ideal plants to clothe a garden arch. In a small garden it's probably best to choose varieties that flower on and off all summer, but the once-flowering old-fashioned varieties are very hard to resist.

The sweet briar or eglantine rose (*R. eglanteria*) is another native that's been grown for centuries in gardens. It should certainly grace some part of your cottage garden and is also at its best growing through a hedge. It has soft pink, single flowers followed by good, red hips. But its real charm lies in the fragrance of apples given off by the leaves, especially after rain. Trim the plants back each year to encourage fresh, young growth, because the tips give off the strongest perfume.

All old-fashioned roses are susceptible to disease, so may need spraying.

Old Climbers

'Aimée Vibert'. A Noisette rose bearing clusters of small, double, pure white flowers with yellow stamens and a fine perfume. Good, glossy foliage. Repeat flowers. Introduced in 1828.

'Blairii No. 2'. This Bourbon rose has pale pink outer petals, deeper pink inside and with a superb perfume. It flowers once and is recommended for a north wall. Raised in 1845.

'Blush Noisette'. Small, semi-double flowers, pink fading to white throughout the summer. Good perfume. Raised in 1816.

'Gloire de Dijon'. A Bourbon rose with pendulous flowers of buff-yellow tinted with pink and superbly perfumed. Flowers continuously and is good on a north wall. Raised in 1853.

'Guinée'. A Hybrid, the deepest crimson of them all. The flowers are large and very well scented. Flowers once with a few blooms later. Raised in 1938.

'Lady Hillingdon'. A Tea rose whose warm apricot-yellow flowers look marvellous against its bronze foliage and whose perfume is magnificent. Flowers through the summer. Raised in 1917. Not to be missed

'Madame Alfred Carrière'. This Noisette rose bears large blooms of white with a tinge of pink and a lovely perfume. Flowers all summer and is ideal for a north wall. Introduced in 1879.

Rosa banksiae normalis. A vigorous Banksian rose with perfumed, single, white flowers and thornless stems. Introduced in 1877.

Rosa banksiae alba plena. As above but with double flowers. Introduced in 1807.

Rosa banksiae lutea. The yellow Banksian rose. Produces large trusses of small, double, yellow flowers in late spring. Slightly scented. Introduced in 1825.

'Zéphirine Drouhin'. A Bourbon rose bearing semi-double, deep pink flowers with a strong perfume which are produced all summer. Thornless and good on a north-facing wall. Introduced in 1868.

Ramblers

'Albéric Barbier'. A Wichuriana rose whose yellow buds open to large, creamy yellow flowers with an excellent perfume. A very reliable flowerer with one large flush followed by a few flowers later. Recommended for a north-facing wall. Introduced in 1900.

'Albertine'. This Wichuriana is one of the most popular. It has large, copper-pink flowers and an excellent perfume. Introduced in 1921. Flowers once.

'Félicité et Perpétue'. A much-branched Sempervirens variety with creamy white flowers and a delicate fragrance. Flowers once in late summer. Introduced in 1827.

'Léontine Gervaise'. A Wichuriana with fragrant double flowers of clear pink tinged with orange. Shiny foliage. Once-flowering. Introduced in 1903.

'May Queen'. A Wichuriana bearing large, deep pink, scented flowers in a single, magnificent flush. Introduced in 1898.

'Rambling Rector'. This Moschata hybrid is worth growing just for the name! Large clusters

The very old variety 'Rambling Rector', which produces large trusses of white flowers with yellow stamens, is ideal for growing through trees.

of small, creamy white, semi-double flowers with a fine perfume. Probably introduced in Tudor times.

'Veilchenblau'. A Multiflora bearing large clusters of flowers of magenta fading to blue, purple and then lavender with a fine fragrance. Introduced in 1909.

Newer Climbers

'Anne Dakin'. An attractive variety with flowers of the 'old-fashioned' shape. Coral pink fading to creamy pink in summer. Introduced in 1974.

'Breath of Life'. Apricot-pink, Hybrid Tea flowers with a pleasant fragrance. Repeat flowering and not too vigorous. Introduced in 1981.

'Compassion'. Salmon-pink, Hybrid Tea flowers suffused with orange and a superb fragrance. Its repeat flowering and fine, glossy foliage make it one of the best. Introduced in 1973.

'Climbing Crimson Glory'. A sport of the favourite bush rose, it produces masses of deep crimson blooms in early summer and a few later too. Excellent perfume. Introduced in 1935.

'Dreamgirl'. Delicate coral-pink flowers with the 'old-fashioned' shape and an excellent fragrance. Introduced in 1944.

'Climbing Ena Harkness'. 'Ena Harkness' is a favourite bush rose with crimson/scarlet flowers with a fine perfume. The heads tend to droop, so it's better as a climber. One flush in summer and a few flowers later. Introduced in 1954.

'Golden Showers'. Masses of golden-yellow, semi-double flowers throughout the summer. Excellent fragrance and good for a north wall. Introduced in 1956.

'Highfield'. A fine yellow sport of 'Compassion' and just as good. Introduced in 1980.

'Kathleen Harrop'. A sport of 'Zéphirine Drouhin' but with soft pink, very fragrant flowers which repeat. Introduced in 1919.

'Lady Sylvia'. A lovely deep pink suffused with apricot, and with a wonderful fragrance. Repeat flowers. Introduced in 1933.

'Lawrence Johnston'. A strong grower with large, double yellow flowers with a strong

Old cottage gardeners grew wild roses through their hedges and there's no better way to brighten up an otherwise dull boundary. Even better, grow roses and clematis together, like this rose 'New Dawn' with the clematis 'Perle d'Azur'.

fragrance. Once-flowering. Introduced in 1923.

'Madame Grégoire Staechelin'. Huge, deep pink flowers in clusters and with an exquisite fragrance. Once-flowering. Introduced in 1927.

'Maigold'. Bronze/yellow, semi-double flowers with golden stamens and a strong perfume. Flowers once with a few blooms later. Introduced in 1953.

'Mrs Herbert Stevens'. A Tea rose with white flowers tinged with green and a delicate yet strong perfume. Flowers once. Introduced in 1922.

'New Dawn'. Large clusters of silvery pink flowers with a fruity fragrance and glossy foliage. Introduced in 1930.

'Paul Lede'. A Tea rose which has a lovely old-fashioned look. Buff-yellow flowers with a superb perfume and very free, repeat flowering. Introduced in 1913.

'Pink Perpétue'. Large clusters of deep pink, almost red flowers throughout the summer. An excellent rose, but only a slight fragrance. Good on a north wall. Introduced in 1965.

'Souvenir de Claudius Denoyel'. Strongly perfumed, bright crimson flowers in June and again later. Vigorous. Introduced in 1920.

Tropaeolum majus NASTURTIUM

A rampant hardy annual introduced to Britain from Peru in 1684, this easy-to-grow, twining plant has been a favourite cottage plant ever since. In Elizabethan times it was called 'yellow larkes heels'. It has highly attractive, shield-shaped leaves and masses of lovely trumpet flowers in bright yellow, red, orange, crimson and pink. It's available with single, semi-double and double flowers too. The seeds can be pickled to use as a substitute for capers. It will flower from early summer to the first frosts and does best in poor soil. Sow it in spring where it's to flower and stand back!

There's surely no easier climber to grow than the nasturtium. It can be sown direct in the soil without any preparation whatever and it will often resow itself the following year. It's an ideal first plant for children to sow too.

Canary creeper (*Tropaeolum peregrinum*) came to Britain in 1810 and this has small, yellow flowers. It's best sown inside and grown on in the frame. Otherwise grow it in the same way as nasturtium.

Look out too for the tuberous-rooted perennial *T. tuberosum* 'Ken Aslet', with typical nasturtium flowers in yellow and scarlet. In colder areas it's worth covering the tubers with a thick mulch in winter. Propagate by division.

Vitis vinifera GRAPE VINE

Grapes were grown widely in England in the monasteries and, after the dissolution, they were to be found in cottage gardens. Their cultivation for wine is covered on page 246.

For purely decorative purposes, choose varieties with large leaves turning red and purple in autumn. They'll also produce fruit, of course, but if they're allowed to ramble freely, it'll be small.

The variety 'Brandt' is a vigorous variety often used for wine. The leaves turn purple in autumn and the fruits are numerous and deep red.

The most spectacular of all vines is *V. coignetiae* which has huge leaves turning crimson-scarlet in autumn, but it needs a lot of space.

Generally vines, which are twining plants, like a sunny position. The best autumn leaf colours come from plants growing in poor soil. Propagate by layering or hardwood cuttings in the cold-frame in autumn.

Border Plants

Of course, there are hundreds of plants that will fit well into a cottage garden. I've restricted myself mainly to those that are old or derived from 'old-fashioned' plants that were grown in the earlier cottage gardens. In a new garden there's no reason at all to stick to the list, but if you want to keep the genuine 'feel' of a country cottage, you'll need to choose carefully.

I think it's vital, especially if your budget's tight, to make sure that your plants can be grown and propagated easily in the way they have been for centuries by gardeners with limited facilities. You'll note that even when you choose older plants, better, newer varieties of them are often available.

I've classified the plants in the following lists according to height. Obviously you'll want to place the tallest plants at the back and the shortest at the front of the border – usually. A little variation of this rule adds interest and avoids the 'serried ranks' look.

In fact I have included some slightly taller plants among those suggested for the front of the border, but they're ones that will flop slightly to break up the hard line of the path edging.

Cottage gardens have always relied mainly on herbaceous plants, but you'll need at least a framework of shrubs and especially evergreens that will give you something to look at in winter.

Bulbs should not be forgotten: they really take up no space at all and many will provide a welcome show of colour when there's little else about.

All types of plant will be grown in the same mixed borders of course, so my lists include every one you'll be likely to grow – shrubs, herbaceous plants, roses and bulbs – simply classified by size. Only the food plants (which start on page 211) have been deliberately excluded. But don't discount the possibility of raising vegetables and fruit in the borders too. They can look very attractive grown that way and you'll be carrying on a tradition that began when our ancestors started gardening. Earlier gardeners did not categorize their plants as we do today, so it was quite common to find patches of vegetables and herbs growing amonst the flowers

Planting

Bare-rooted shrubs should be planted from autumn to spring exactly as for trees (see page 100), except that no stake is necessary.

Herbaceous perennials can go in during spring or autumn unless they're pot-grown, in which case any time will do. They're generally planted in prepared soil, using a trowel and firming with your fingers (see below). A dressing of organic fertilizer and a good watering in afterwards are essential.

Bulbs that flower in spring are planted in late summer and autumn, summer flowerers in spring and autumn flowerers in summer. There are exceptions, but normally it's best to plant in groups either with a trowel or, if in heavy soil, by taking out a hole, putting in a layer of grit and covering. The grit simply protects the vulnerable base-plate.

Before planting it's always a good idea to spend a bit of time improving the soil with garden compost, manure or one of the alternatives. For plants requiring free drainage, include an equal quantity of coarse grit.

Scatter a little organic fertilizer and then plant with a trowel, making sure that the plant is at the level it grew in the nursery. Firm down well with your fingers and always water in well afterwards.

Plants for the Back of the Border

Plants that are suitable for the back of the border will be mostly shrubs and herbaceous plants. There are, of course, some bulbs that are tall enough, but my own view is that they're much better used among lower-growing plants to rise above them and add another level of interest.

In island beds like those in the artisan's garden, these taller plants will go in the middle rather than at the back.

Shrubs

Berberis vulgaris BARBERRY
Height: 1.8–2.7 m (6–9 ft). Spread: 1.5–1.8 m (5–6 ft). Flowers: Late spring to early summer.
Grown since the sixteenth century, the berries of the barberry were pickled, or candied and used to decorate meat. The native species is no longer grown because it harbours wheat rust. There are better decorative varieties, many of which also make superb, impenetrable hedges. They grow well in shade and in poor soils. Propagate deciduous species by half-ripe cuttings in late summer and evergreens by hardwood cutting in autumn.

B. julianae. A dense evergreen, especially good for hedging. Flowers are yellow followed by shiny, black fruits.

B. lologensis. Evergreen with an upright habit and bright orange flowers.

B. ottawensis 'Superba'. A fine variety with purple leaves.

B. stenophylla. A superb, graceful shrub with arching branches swathed with yellow flowers in spring. There are also some orange varieties.

B. thunbergii. A useful shrub with green leaves and excellent for its superb autumn colour and bright red berries. The variety 'Atropurpurea' has red/purple leaves. Dwarf varieties are suitable for the middle of the border (see page 142).

Buddleia davidii BUTTERFLY BUSH
Height: 2.4 m (8 ft). Spread: 1.5 m (5 ft).
Flowers: Late summer.
Not introduced until 1890, but well known to cottagers from the late Victorian era onwards, buddleia is especially prized as an attractor of butterflies in their hundreds. It produces long, cylindrical clusters of florets in several colours from white, through pink and blue to deepest purple. Grow in sunshine in any soil. Prune last year's growth back hard in early spring. Propagate by hardwood cuttings in autumn.

Chaenomeles speciosa FLOWERING QUINCE
Height: 1.2 m (4 ft). Spread: 1.5–1.8 m (5–6 ft).
Flowers: Late winter to mid-spring.
Can be grown as a free-standing shrub. See under 'Climbers', on page 108, for a full description.

Cytisus scoparius COMMON BROOM
Height: 1.5 m (5 ft). Spread: 1.2 m (4 ft).
Flowers: Late spring.
A native British shrub, well-known to the gardeners of the Middle Ages, common broom bears butter-yellow flowers in profusion, rather like gorse but without the spines. It grows well in full sun and will flower best in poor soil. Prune carefully after flowering, avoiding cutting into old wood. Propagate by half-ripe cuttings in summer. There are several named varieties, the best being:

'Andreanus' – yellow marked brown and crimson.

'Cornish Cream' – creamy white.

'Firefly' – deep yellow and crimson.

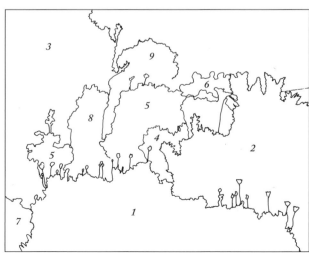

1 *Osteospermum* 'Lady
Leitrim'
2 *Lonicera nitida*
'Baggesen's Gold'
3 *Rosa* 'Canary Bird'
4 *Lavandula stoechas
pedunculata*
5 *Lunaria annua*
6 *Tulipa* 'Black Swan'
7 *Alchemilla mollis*
8 *Aquilegia* 'Hensol
Harebell'
9 *Cytisus praecox* 'Allgold'

*Shrubs provide both flower
and foliage colour in this
spring border.*

'Fulgens' – orange and crimson.

The Warminster broom (*Cytisus praecox*), which is slightly more compact, and has masses of cream flowers, arose in 1867. There are a few good varieties:

'Albus' – white.

'Allgold' – yellow.

'Gold Spear' – deep yellow.

Deutzia hybrida

Height: 1.5–2.4 m (5–8 ft). Spread: 1.2–1.5 m (4–5 ft). Flowers: Early summer.

Deutzias have been grown in cottage gardens since the nineteenth century, with many new hybrids becoming available from France in the early twentieth century. Look for 'Magicien', with purple buds opening to reveal pink, white-edged flowers. 'Mont Rose' is smaller with pink flowers and yellow stamens, while 'Pink Pompom' is larger with arching branches hung with double pink flowers fading to white.

D. scabra is an older species and more vigorous, growing to 1.8 m (6 ft). 'Pride of Rochester' is double-flowered with white inside and pink outside, while 'Candidissima' is double white.

Deutzias are easy to grow in any well-drained soil in sun or part-shade. Propagate by hardwood cuttings in autumn or softwood cuttings in summer.

Forsythia spectabilis

Height: 1.8 m (6 ft). Spread: 1.5 m (5 ft). Flowers: Spring.

One of the best-known shrubs of all and deservedly popular. Its arching branches are massed with yellow flowers and it's very easy to grow. There are now several named varieties, but this older one remains one of the best.

Look out too for 'Lynwood', 'Beatrix Farrand' and 'Karl Sax', which tend to have larger flowers. Forsythia can be grown successfully in any reasonable soil in either full sun or part-shade. Propagate by hardwood cuttings in autumn.

Garrya elliptica SILK TASSEL BUSH

Height: 4 m (13 ft). Spread: 3 m (10 ft). Flowers: Early winter to late winter.

Introduced in 1828, this elegant evergreen became a cottage favourite. It produces long, silvery tassels when there's little else in flower. Look for the variety 'James Roof', which has the longest tassels of all. It's especially good on a north-facing wall, thriving on most soils, but dislikes cold winds. Propagate by hardwood cuttings in autumn.

Garrya elliptica *'James Roof' is a vigorous male variety with catkins that can be as long as 20 cm (8 in). It's not an old variety, having been raised in California in about 1950, but old cottage gardeners would have gladly grown it.*

The shrub in the front of this border, Berberis thunbergii
*'Rose Glow', is a modern introduction and probably got its
variegation from a virus.*

Kerria japonica 'Pleniflora' JEW'S MALLOW
Height: 1.8–2.4 m (6–8 ft). Spread: 1.8 m (6 ft).
Flowers: Spring.
A vigorous, suckering shrub that needs regular
pruning to keep it in control. It may also need to
be restrained with a spade at the roots from time
to time to stop it spreading, so it's not for the tiny
garden. Well-grown, the green, cane-like shoots
hung with yellow balls are most attractive. It'll
grow in almost any soil but prefers a little shade
to prevent the flowers fading. Propagate by
detaching a shoot or two with a piece of root.

Leycesteria formosa HIMALAYAN HONEYSUCKLE or
NUTMEG TREE
Height: 1.8–2.4 m (6–8 ft). Spread: 1.5 m (5 ft).
Flowers: Late summer/autumn.
This is a vigorous shrub introduced in 1824. It
produces a clump of tall, hollow, green stems,
topped by white flowers with conspicuous red
bracts, followed by purple fruits in warmer areas.
It needs a retentive soil in sun or part-shade.

Prune it hard to the ground every few years, or even every year, to keep it in check and growing tidily. Propagate by seed or hardwood cuttings in spring. The fruits are very attractive to pheasants so they were planted as cover on estates and the berries were much sought after by poachers!

Myrtus communis MYRTLE

Height: 3 m (10 ft). Spread: 2 m (6 ft 6 in).
Flowers: Late summer.

The aromatic, evergreen common myrtle has been grown in England since the sixteenth century, when it was valued for its aromatic properties and recommended for planting round arbours. Its white flowers are followed by purple/black berries. Unfortunately it's not reliably hardy; it needs full sun and preferably a south-facing wall. Myrtle grows on any soil and is especially recommended for seaside areas. Propagate by half-ripe cuttings in late autumn.

Philadelphus spp. MOCK ORANGE

Height: 1–2.4 m (3–8 ft). Spread: 1–1.8 m (3–6 ft). Flowers: Early to mid-summer.

A relatively recent introduction at the end of the nineteenth century. Many hybrids have been raised since, a number of which have the true cottage garden qualities. Most produce white flowers, some with attractive markings and excellent perfume. They thrive in almost any soil in sunshine and flower in summer. Propagate by hardwood cuttings in autumn.

'Belle Etoile' is one of the best, with single, creamy white flowers splashed purple at the base and an excellent perfume.

'Manteau d'Hermine' is much more compact and could do for the middle of the border too. It has superb, creamy white, double flowers and is also very fragrant.

'Beauclerk' has large, single, creamy white flowers with a band of cerise towards the centre.

Ribes sanguineum FLOWERING CURRANT

Height: 1.8 m (6 ft). Spread: 1.5 m (5 ft).
Flowers: Spring.

A popular and easy-flowering shrub introduced from the USA in 1826. The flowers are deep pink with white petals and hang down from leafless branches at first, but are soon complemented by fresh, green, young leaves. The whole bush has a pungent smell of blackcurrants.

There are several varieties: 'Tydeman's White' has white flowers, 'King Edward VII' is deep crimson, while 'Pulborough Scarlet' has red flowers. Look out too for the strongly clove-scented *Ribes odoratum*, which bears attractive yellow flowers. They'll grow in any soil in sun or light shade. Prune annually, removing old wood to the base. Propagate by hardwood cuttings in autumn.

Rosa spp. and varieties

There are, of course, hundreds of rose varieties to choose from, so I've listed only those I think most suited to the cottage garden. This, you'll notice,

The pure white flowers of the mock orange produce the sweetest perfume that pervades the whole garden. It's one of the easiest shrubs of all to grow and definitely not to be missed.

doesn't include many modern Hybrid Teas or floribundas. Somehow they don't seem quite to match the rather looser, informal nature of growth of older varieties, and the more stylized shape of the blooms and the vivid colours tend to jar. You may agree. Obviously what you need before you buy is a specialist's catalogue or, better still, to visit a nursery at flowering time and make a choice based on first-hand knowledge.

However, my list would not exclude modern roses entirely. There are some excellent modern shrub roses, and the range of 'English' roses has great advantages. The latter combine the old-fashioned cabbage shape with the modern rose's ability to repeat flower, so they're a great improvement for the new cottage garden.

A few words of warning: the breeders of some of the newer roses have concentrated on other factors and ignored the plant's ability to resist disease. So a few are prone to attack from rust, blackspot and mildew. If you don't want to spray regularly, they're to be avoided. However, disease resistance is a top priority with breeders, so in the main modern varieties tend to be more disease resistant than older ones.

Since I would rarely contemplate a rose without perfume, all my selection can be considered to be scented unless otherwise stated.

'Abraham Darby'. Height: 1.5 m (5 ft). Spread: 1.5 m (5 ft). An English rose bearing deeply cupped blooms of apricot-yellow from early summer to autumn.

'Ballerina'. Height: 1.2 m (4 ft). Spread: 1.2 m (4 ft). A modern shrub rose with large, hydrangea-like heads of small, single, pink flowers. One of the most continuous and free-flowering of all, but with only a slight scent.

'Baroness Rothschild'. Height: 1.8 m (6 ft). Spread: 1.2 m (4 ft). A very large-flowered, pink Hybrid Perpetual rose, freely flowering in summer and again in the autumn.

'Belle Amour'. Height: 1.5 m (5 ft). Spread: 1.8 m (6 ft). A strong-growing moss rose with dusky purple flowers and a good perfume. Flowers once in the summer.

'Belle de Crécy'. Height: 1.2 m (4 ft). Spread: 1 m (3 ft). A Gallica rose, which is the parent and forerunner of all the cottage roses. It opens rich pink and fades to purple. Flowers once in the summer.

'Blanc Double de Coubert'. Height: 1.5 m (5 ft). Spread: 1.8 m (6 ft). A Rugosa rose with semi-double, ivory-white blooms throughout the summer.

'Boule de Neige'. Height: 1.5 m (5 ft). Spread:

That I suggest growing a rose with only a little perfume is a recommendation for its other qualities. 'Ballerina' is not to be missed because it flowers reliably right through the summer, looking superb when the flowers are young and even when they begin to fade.

1 m (3 ft). Small, white, ball-shaped flowers with a fine perfume.

'Buff Beauty'. Height: 1.5 m (5 ft). Spread: 1.2 m (4 ft). A fine modern shrub rose with buds opening deep apricot and maturing to buff-yellow throughout the summer.

'Cardinal de Richelieu'. Height: 1.2 m (4 ft). Spread: 1 m (3 ft). A rich, dark purple Gallica. Flowers once in summer.

'Centifolia'. Height: 1.8 m (6 ft). Spread: 1.5 m (5 ft). Grown in the sixteenth century, a superb pink and very heavily perfumed.

'Comte de Chambord'. Height: 1 m (3ft). Spread: 60 cm (2 ft). A superb Damask rose which repeat flowers through the summer. The flowers are strong pink with lovely, ruffled petals and a fine fragrance.

'Fru Dagmar Hastrup'. Height: 1.5 m (5 ft). Spread: 1.5 m (5 ft). A fine Rugosa with very attractive, single, pink flowers throughout the summer and a stunning display of large, orange hips in autumn.

'Frühlingsgold'. Height: 2.1 m (7 ft). Spread: 2.1 m (7 ft). A large, arching, modern shrub rose with richly fragrant, creamy yellow flowers in early summer.

'Général Kléber'. Height: 1.2 m (4 ft). Spread: 1 m (3 ft). One of the best Moss roses. Soft pink with a superb perfume. Flowers once in summer.

'Gertrude Jekyll'. Height: 1.2 m (4 ft). Spread: 1 m (3 ft). A deep, rich pink English rose with large, rosette-shaped flowers. The scent was selected for making real rose perfume for the first time in 250 years. Flowers all summer.

'Golden Wings'. Height: 1.2 m (4 ft). Spread: 1.2 m (4 ft). A modern shrub rose with large, single, yellow flowers all summer.

'Graham Thomas'. Height: 1.2 m (4 ft).

'Graham Thomas' is a fine English rose with a long flowering habit and the typical 'cabbage' blooms of the older roses. In my garden the glossy foliage has proved to be fairly resistant to disease.

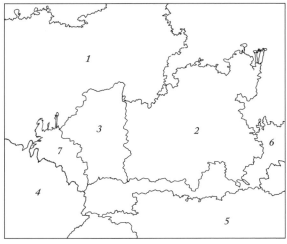

1 *Rosa* 'Canary Bird'

2 *Lunaria annua*

3 *Aquilegia* 'Hensol Harebell'

4 *Lotus hirsutus*

5 *Sedum* 'Ruby Glow'

6 *Myosotis scorpioides*

7 *Lavandula stoechas pedunculata*

Here a standard rose provides height in the border above a colourful display of herbaceous perennials and biennials.

Spread: 1.2 m (4 ft). An English rose with cup-shaped flowers in rich yellow all summer.

'Heritage'. Height: 1.2 m (4 ft). Spread: 1.2 m (4 ft). An English rose with very fine, cup-shaped, pink flowers all summer.

'La Reine Victoria'. Height: 1.5 m (5 ft). Spread: 1.2 m (4 ft). Bourbon rose with delicate pink, cup-shaped flowers all summer.

'Nevada'. Height: 2.1 m (7 ft). Spread: 2.4 m (8 ft). One of the most striking modern shrubs with large, semi-double, creamy white flowers in early summer. Not scented.

'Queen of Denmark'. Height: 1.5 m (5 ft). Spread: 1.2 m (4 ft). One of the best Albas with strong pink flowers, paler on the margins. Flowers once in summer.

Rosa gallica officinalis. Height: 1.2 m (4 ft). Spread: 1.2 m (4 ft). The 'apothecary's rose' with bright crimson flowers and golden stamens.

Rosa moyesii 'Geranium'. Height 2.4 m (8 ft). Spread: 2.1 m (7 ft). A large shrub rose with great arching branches with single, bright red flowers followed by lovely, orange, flagon-shaped hips. Flowers once in summer.

Rosa mundi. Height: 1.2 m (4 ft). Spread: 1.2 m (4 ft). The oldest striped rose from the sixteenth century. Pink with pink/purple stripes. Flowers once in summer.

Rosa mutabilis. Height: 1.8 m (6 ft). Spread: 1.2 m (4 ft). A China rose with copper-coloured buds opening to yellow and fading to pink. Flowers once in summer.

Rosa xanthina 'Canary Bird'. Height: 2.4 m (8 ft). Spread: 1.8 m (6 ft). Masses of single yellow flowers borne on ferny foliage in early spring. Unfortunately it has no scent. One of the earliest roses to flower and often grown as a standard.

'William Lobb'. Height: 1.8 m (6 ft). Spread: 1.5 m (5 ft). Dusky purple and prolific. Flowers once in summer.

Sambucus nigra ELDER
Height: 3 m (10 ft). Spread: 2.4 m (8 ft).
Flowers: Summer.
A native shrub or small tree, long cultivated and still well known for its aromatic white flowers and black berries used for cordial and wine-making. Elder is ideal as a hedge plant, but in the small garden and for purely decorative purposes it's best to grow one of the varieties with decorative leaves.

'Laciniata' has deeply cut, green leaves, but the brightest is 'Aurea' with golden leaves. Cut back to two buds each spring to keep the plant to size and to generate the brightest colouring. It grows absolutely anywhere. Propagate by hardwood cuttings in autumn.

Syringa vulgaris LILAC
Height: 2.4–3 m (8–10 ft). Spread: 1.5–1.8 m (5–6 ft). Flowers: Mid-summer.
Introduced to England in the sixteenth century, lilac has naturalized itself in many parts of the

The wonderful, large flowers of lilacs will perfume the whole garden. They come in many colours and this one, 'Congo', is among the best lilac reds. Look for micropropagated plants to avoid suckering.

country. The common variety has lilac flowers, of course, with a superb perfume and is still one of the best. It does, however, have a nasty habit of suckering, but modern propagation methods have solved the problem. It's now possible to buy plants that have been raised by micropropagation and these don't sucker. They'll grow in any soil and are especially useful in lime. They'll flower best in a sunny spot. Propagate by layering. Look out also for some of the many varieties – there are over 500, but here are a few:

'Congo' – lilac/red.

'Hugo Koster' – purple/crimson.

'Madame Charles Souchet' – soft lilac/blue.

'Mont Blanc' – green in bud, opening white.

'Souvenir de Louis Späth' – wine-red.

'Belle de Nancy' – red in bud, opening lilac/pink; double.

'Charles Joly' – dark purple-red; double.

'Katherine Havemeyer' – purple/lavender.

'Madame Lemoine' – pure white; double.

'Président Grévy' – lilac; very large, double flowers.

For small gardens it's also worth searching out *Syringa meyeri* 'Palibin', which has violet-purple flowers on a small-to-medium-sized shrub.

Viburnum opulus GUELDER ROSE

Height: 1.5–1.8 m (5–6 ft). Spread: 1.2–1.5 m (4–5 ft). Flowers: Early to mid-summer.

A large, vigorous native, grown in gardens since the sixteenth century, the guelder rose bears showy white flowers like those of lacecap hydrangeas, followed by glistening red berries and superb autumn foliage colour. It thrives in wet conditions.

An excellent and popular variety is the snowball tree (*Viburnum opulus* 'Roseum' or 'Sterile'). This produces white globes of flowers but no berries. Propagate by hardwood cuttings in autumn or half-ripe cuttings in late summer.

Viburnum tinus LAURUSTINUS

Height: 1.2–1.5 m (4–5 ft). Spread: 1.2–1.5 m (4–5 ft). Flowers: Winter to mid-spring.

A popular evergreen grown since the sixteenth century. The bushy habit and dark, glossy leaves make a superb background and the white, pink-budded flowers, which appear from autumn to early spring, are especially welcome. Propagate by softwood cuttings in summer or half-ripe cuttings in late summer.

The old favourite laurustinus is one of the best winter-flowering evergreens of all and deservedly popular. It will spread to form quite a large bush, but can be kept in control easily by judicious pruning. Especially recommended is the variety 'Eve Price', which is more compact with pink-tinged flowers.

Taxus baccata COMMON YEW

Height: 20 m (65 ft). Spread: 10 m (30 ft).

Obviously yew is far too big to grow unfettered as a tree (see page 107), but it was and still is widely used to make probably the best hedge of all and for topiary. Trimmed regularly, it makes a splendid specimen. It's not at all fussy as to soil, will tolerate quite heavy shade and can be cut hard back, even if quite old, when it will always re-grow. Propagate by seed sown in a coldframe in autumn or by stem cuttings also in a coldframe at the same time.

The Irish yew (*Taxus baccata* 'Fastigiata') was found in Ireland in 1780. It forms a green column and retains its shape well. There's also an attractive golden form, 'Fastigiata Aureomarginata'.

Herbaceous Plants

Acanthus mollis BEAR'S BREECHES
Height: 1.5 m (5 ft). Spread: 1 m (3 ft). Flowers: Late summer.
Grown since medieval times when it was known to herbalists as 'brank-ursine'. It has long, shiny, green leaves and produces tall spikes of foxglove-like mauve/pink flowers. It grows well in sun or shade. Propagate by seed sown in late spring or division in late winter.

Acanthus spinosus. Similar but with more divided, spiny leaves and it flowers more freely.

Achillea filipendulina YARROW
Height: 1.2 m (4 ft). Spread: 45 cm (1½ ft).
Flowers: Late summer.
A well-known plant introduced in 1803. It has attractive, feathery leaves and plates of golden flowers. 'Gold Plate' is the best-known variety. It requires good drainage and a sunny spot. Propagate by seed, division or basal cuttings, all in spring.

Aconitum carmichaelii MONKSHOOD or
WOLF'S BANE
Height: 1.2 m (4 ft). Spread: 30 cm (1 ft).
Flowers: Autumn.
Introduced in 1886, though the original native

monkshood was mentioned in the tenth century. This one is far better than the native species, having rich green foliage and Wedgwood-blue flowers, hooded on top. Note that all parts of the plant are poisonous. In medieval times the poison extracted from the plants was used to kill wolves when it was put on to arrow tips and on meat used as bait.

Monkshood likes full sun or part-shade and a retentive soil. Propagate by division in autumn.

Aconitum napellus is a native but has been cultivated in gardens since the sixteenth century. The flowers are indigo-blue and there are white and pink forms.

Alstroemeria PERUVIAN LILY
Height: 1–1.2 m (3–4 ft). Spread: 45 cm (1½ ft).
Flowers: Early summer.
Introduced to Britain in the nineteenth century, the original species have been superseded by modern hybrids. Called 'princess lilies', they have small, lily-like flowers, beautifully marked and in various colours from yellow through orange and

The 'princess lilies' are modern hybrids of the traditional cottage alstroemeria and are particularly valuable for their long flowering period from early summer to the autumn.

pink to deep red. Give them full sun and good drainage. On heavy soils dig in some grit and compost and plant the roots deeply. Propagate by division.

Althaea spp. HOLLYHOCK
Height: 2.7 m (9 ft). Spread: 1 m (3 ft). Flowers: Summer/autumn.

Hollyhocks are synonymous with cottage gardens, where they've been grown since the sixteenth century. They're quite short-lived perennials, so need to be replaced frequently. They're easily raised from seed sown in spring, then should be potted up and over-wintered in a frame, and planted out the following spring. The plants must be staked. They're excellent bee plants.

Althaea rosea. Height: 2.4 m (8 ft). Spread: 1 m (3 ft). Flowers: Summer. The cup-shaped flowers are borne up the tall stem and can be white, yellow, cream, pink, red or deep crimson. Look out for the double-flowered 'Chater's Double'.

A. ficifolia. The 'Antwerp hollyhock' is another popular form, with yellow or orange flowers.

Anemone hybrida JAPANESE ANEMONE
Height: 1.5 m (5 ft). Spread: 60 cm (2 ft). Flowers: Autumn.

Introduced in 1848, this wonderful autumn flowerer produces heads of striking, rounded, pink blooms with golden stamens. There's also a stunning white, 'Honorine Jobert'. They'll grow in almost any soil in sun or part-shade and can become mildly invasive, though never a problem. Propagate by division or root cuttings in autumn.

Campanula spp. BELLFLOWER
All the tall bellflowers prefer sun and must be staked. They can be propagated by seed sown outside in late spring, by division in autumn or spring and by basal cuttings in early spring.

Campanula lactiflora. Height: 1.8 m (6 ft). Spread: 60 cm (2 ft). Flowers: All summer. A fine perennial, grown in cottage gardens since the early nineteenth century. It produces tall spikes topped by branching heads of lilac bellflowers.

C. latifolia. Height: 1.2 m (4 ft). Spread: 60 cm (2 ft). Flowers: Summer. This native of Britain makes a fine spire of violet, blue or white flowers. It seeds itself freely, so it may be necessary to cut down the spikes after flowering.

C. pyramidalis. Height: 1.5 m (5 ft). Spread: 60 cm (2 ft). Flowers: Summer. The 'chimney bellflower' has been grown since 1596 and is still one of the most attractive. It's a short-lived plant best treated as a biennial, but worth the extra trouble for its huge spikes of cup-shaped flowers in pale blue or white. Propagate by seed sown in late spring.

Delphinium spp.
Height: 1.2–2.4 m (4–8 ft). Spread: 1 m (3 ft). Flowers: Summer.

Among the classic cottage garden plants, the delphinium hybrids produce tall flower spires in all shades of blue, white and pink. Hybrids have been produced since 1875 and specialists are still breeding named varieties. They also produce selected seed, which is excellent value, but only if you're prepared to coddle the plants a little. Otherwise grow Pacific hybrids or Belladonna hybrids.

To produce the best spikes, they need a rich, well-fed soil, sun and shelter. It's essential to stake the tall flowering spikes as they grow. They can be raised from seed sown in May outside, but will not come true, so if you get a good one, propagate it by root cuttings in late winter.

Echinacea purpurea CONEFLOWER
Height: 1.2 m (4 ft). Spread: 45 cm (1½ ft). Flowers: Mid- to late summer.

The tall spires of delphiniums are an absolute 'must' for any cottage garden. They're easy to grow provided you can keep them free from the attentions of slugs. They're most vulnerable in the early spring when the soft, young shoots are just coming through.

Wonderful, large heads of daisy flowers in shades of purplish pink, rose-pink or white with a striking central boss of deep brown. It likes a sunny spot and well-drained, retentive soil.

The species came to England from the USA in 1699 and was widely grown in cottage gardens as it can be raised from seed. It has more or less disappeared now, to be replaced by even better hybrids like the rich mauve/crimson 'Robert Bloom' and a new variety, 'Magnus', with huge, rose-pink flowers. The hybids can be propagated by division but with some difficulty because in my experience they don't transplant well, so take root cuttings in late winter or collect and sow seed as soon as it's ripe.

Echinops ritro GLOBE THISTLE
Height: 1.2 m (4 ft). Spread: 60 cm (2 ft).
Flowers: Late summer.
Grown in gardens since 1570, this striking plant has jagged, thistle-like foliage and steely blue balls of flower on strong spikes. However, a much better plant is *Echinops ruthenicus*, which has more attractive foliage of shining green with a silvery sheen beneath and flowers of strong, bright blue. It will grow in most soils in full sun. Propagate by division or, for *E. ritro*, by seed.

Eremurus stenophyllus FOXTAIL LILY
Height: 1.5 m (5 ft). Spread: 60 cm (2 ft).
Flowers: Summer.
A majestic plant grown since 1885. It produces slender spikes of clear yellow flowers, fading to orange so that the two colours are on the plant together making a very attractive sight.

The delicate pink flowers of gypsophila in the front spill over the path and make a fine contrast to the bolder blooms of the ornamental onion. This excellent cottage plant is easy to grow and to raise from seed.

Perhaps even better is *Eremurus robustus*, introduced in 1874. It's a towering plant with 1.2-m (4-ft) flower spikes laden with pink flowers with a brown basal blotch and a green keel: very striking. It needs good drainage and full sun. New crowns should be planted just below the soil's surface and care must be taken not to damage them. Protect them with straw, compost or leaf litter in the first winter. New crowns tend to work upwards and these should be lifted and split off for re-planting after the leaves have died down in late summer. They're well worth the extra trouble.

Euphorbia characias SPURGE
Height: 1.2 m (4 ft). Spread: 1 m (3 ft). Flowers: Early spring.
A striking evergreen plant producing great towering spikes of green. Look out for the variety *Euphorbia characias wulfenii* with wider spikes forming large cylinders of greenish yellow. The varieties 'Lambrook Gold' and 'John Tomlinson' have improved yellow flowers.
They'll grow in most well-drained soils and in sun or shade. Propagate by seed or basal cuttings in spring, but avoid getting the irritant sap on your hands and particularly in your eyes.

Gypsophila paniculata BABY'S BREATH or CHALK PLANT
Height: 1–1.2 m (3–4 ft). Spread: 1.2 m (4 ft).
Flowers: Summer.
Introduced in 1759, this plant produces a great cloud of white stars on a mass of delicate foliage. Grow 'Bristol Fairy' which is double white, and 'Flamingo' which is double pink. It's particularly valuable to contrast with bolder foliage plants like hostas and is much sought after by flower arrangers. It likes full sun and poor, dry soil. Propagate by seed (though the resulting plants can be variable) or cuttings in July.

1 *Eschscholzia californica*
'Alba'
2 *Lychnis coronaria*
3 *Campanula persicifolia*
4 *Nigella damascena*
5 *Atriplex hortensis rubra*
6 *Santolina pinnata*
neopolitana 'Sulphurea'
7 *Allium aflatunense*
8 *Linaria purpurea*
9 *Rosa* 'New Dawn'

Even with a whole range of different colours, there's perfect harmony in this border.

Helenium autumnale SNEEZEWEED
Height: 1.5 m (5 ft). Spread: 45 cm (1½ ft).
Flowers: Early autumn.
Brought to Britain in 1729, this bears vivid yellow, sunflower-like flowers. But there are better hybrids now, like 'Bressingham Gold'; 'Bruno', which has crimson/brown blooms; and 'Coppelia', whose flowers are coppery orange.

They like a retentive soil in full sun. Lift and divide every couple of years to prevent deterioration. Propagate by division.

Helianthus decapetalus SUNFLOWER
Height: 1.5 m (5 ft). Spread: 60 cm (2 ft).
Flowers: Summer.
The sunflower has been with us since 1596 and is a great favourite with record-breakers. It's a somewhat coarse flower, but fun to grow. The best hybrid is 'Loddon Gold', which grows tall and has huge, bright yellow, double, daisy-like blooms which don't need supporting.

The sunflower likes sun and heavy soil. Propagate by division. The annual sunflower, of course, is raised by direct-sown seed.

Hemerocallis fulva DAY LILY
Height: 1.2 m (4 ft). Spread: 1 m (3 ft). Flowers: Summer.
The old day lily dates from 1576. It has bright orange flowers with a brown marking on the throat and an apricot line on the petals. It likes a sunny spot and a retentive soil. Propagate by division in autumn. The variety 'Maculata' is particularly choice, with copper flowers with a darker centre. Other varieties are shorter (see page 154).

Hesperis matronalis SWEET ROCKET or
DAME'S VIOLET
Height: 1.2 m (4 ft). Spread: 60 cm (2 ft).
Flowers: Summer.

A cottage garden favourite since the fourteenth century, this is a 'must'. It produces tall, branching stems decked with white or lilac flowers rather like those of a stock in appearance and with a superb perfume.

It'll grow in any soil in sun or part-shade, but it's a short-lived plant. However, if you stick to the single-flowered varieties (much better in any case), they'll seed themselves freely. Either collect the seedlings or the seed and raise it yourself or, better still, allow it to find its own home.

Kniphofia spp. and hybrids RED HOT POKER
The red hot pokers, which make a brilliant show of spiky blooms in the border, have been grown since the eighteenth century. Unfortunately they have untidy foliage that looks a bit messy for a small garden. However, with judicious planting around them to hide the leaves, they're a valuable addition to the mixed border.

Kniphofia uvaria. Height: 1.5 m (5 ft). Spread: 60 cm (2 ft). Flowers: Autumn. Grown since 1707, this striking plant produces pokers of coral pink, changing to red, orange and then greeny yellow. It's not entirely hardy.

'Royal Standard', one of the best of the tall hybrids, is just a little shorter than the above. It has scarlet buds which open to reveal yellow flowers.

'Wrexham Buttercup' is clear yellow. There are several other good hybrids, but watch out if you live in a cold area because not all will survive. Give them a sunny spot and propagate by division in spring.

Lavatera olbia TREE MALLOW
Height: 1.8 m (6 ft). Spread: 1.2 m (4 ft).
Flowers: Summer to autumn.
This large, vigorous, shrubby mallow has been grown since 1570 in cottage gardens, where its masses of pink flowers make a brilliant display.

The hybrid lavateras are showy and easy to grow but it must be borne in mind that they're short-lived plants. Just in case, take cuttings in summer.

The variety 'Rosea' is generally grown. However, it is a plant that needs quite a lot of space, so for smaller gardens it's probably best to stick to the varieties of *Lavatera thuringiaca*, which is slightly shorter and more open. The variety 'Barnsley', which has light pink flowers, is very popular, as is the crimson-flowered 'Burgundy Wine' . They need a sunny spot and will grow in most reasonable soil. Prune them back quite hard in early spring when they start to shoot. Propagate by cuttings in late summer.

Lythrum salicaria PURPLE LOOSESTRIFE
Height: 1.2 m (4 ft). Spread: 45 cm (1½ ft).
Flowers: Summer.
This British native must have been grown in the earliest cottage gardens. It produces slender flower spikes of pink or red. The variety 'Robert' has clear pink flowers, while 'Firecandle' and 'The Beacon' are deep red. They prefer wet, even boggy soil but are very adaptable, also flowering well in dry conditions. Either way, they like sunshine. Propagate by division.

Malva alcea MALLOW
Height: 1.2 m (4 ft). Spread: 60 cm (2 ft).
Flowers: Summer.
Introduced in 1797, mallow produces large, cup-shaped, mauve/pink flowers. It'll do well in poor soil in sun and is a very reliable flowerer. Propagate by seed.

Polygonum amplexicaule KNOTWEED
Height: 1.2 m (4 ft). Spread: 1.2 m (4 ft).
Flowers: Summer/autumn.
Makes big clumps which slowly increase and produce large spikes of crimson flowers. There's also a bright red, 'Firetail', and a white with a pink tinge. They like a moist, retentive soil and sun or part-shade. Propagate by division.

Cottage garden planting doesn't have to be entirely random. In this border mainly purples have been grouped together to give a very pleasing effect with purple hebe in front, lupins and the bright, round blooms of ornamental onions behind and, right at the back, the blue spires of camassias.

Rudbeckia maxima CONEFLOWER
Height: 1.2 m (4 ft). Spread: 60 cm (2 ft).
Flowers: Summer.
Introduced in 1818, this is the big brother of the

more common *Rudbeckia fulgida* (see page 162). It has large yellow daisy flowers with drooping petals and a central boss of deep brown. Give it a sunny spot in ordinary soil and it should do well. Propagate by division.

Sidalcea malviflora WILD HOLLYHOCK
Height: 1–1.2 m (3–4 ft). Spread: 45 cm (1½ ft).
Flowers: Summer.
Introduced in 1838 and popular in cottage

gardens ever since. It produces branching spikes of small, silky, hollyhock-like flowers in various shades of pink. Look for 'Sussex Beauty' and 'The Reverend Page Roberts'. Slightly shorter are 'Loveliness', 'Oberon' and 'Puck'.

They grow well in sun or part-shade in any reasonable soil. Propagate by seed, root cuttings or division and bear in mind that seed-raised plants don't come true to type and are rarely as good as the named varieties. Still, if you have the space they're worth growing because some of the seedlings could produce even better flowers. This, after all, was the way that existing named varieties arose.

Solidago canadensis GOLDEN ROD
Height: 1.2 m (4 ft). Spread: 60 cm (2 ft).
Flowers: Late summer/autumn.
This is a rather rank plant now replaced by the variety 'Mimosa', which is definitely an improvement. It produces tall stems topped by spikes of bright yellow flowers. It's easy to grow in sun or part-shade in any soil. Propagate by division. There are also shorter varieties (see page 181).

Thalictrum delavayi MEADOW RUE
Height: 1.5 m (5 ft). Spread: 60 cm (2 ft).
Flowers: Summer.
A tall, stately plant with delicate, divided foliage and great, airy sprays of flowers. Look closely at the individual flowers for the creamy white stamens hanging from the crown of lilac petals. It likes a rich, retentive soil in part-shade, though it will thrive in sun if the soil doesn't dry out. Propagate by seed.

Verbascum spp. and hybrids MULLEIN
Height: 1–1.2 m (3–4 ft). Spread: 45 cm (1½ ft).
Flowers: Summer.
Some of the mulleins are biennials, but there are several perennials you should never be without.

They form tall spires with delicate pastel flowers all the way up. One of the most commonly grown is *Verbascum chaixii*, which has small, yellow flowers with a purple centre, and there's a good white form too.

Never be without the purple mullein (*V. phoeniceum*), which flowers in several fine pastel shades. It's a short-lived plant, often lasting only one season, but it has the happy knack of seeding itself around, so my own borders have never been without it. Of course, they seed where *they* want to be, but in a cottage garden, that's just as it should be. This was one of the most prolific seeders in the gravel paths in my artisan's garden. Any seedlings growing where they were not wanted were easy to transplant.

There are several good hybrids too, like the light brown 'Helen Johnson', the apricot-yellow 'Royal Highland', the superb 'Cotswold Queen' (buff-orange with a touch of purple) and the white 'Mont Blanc'.

All like well-drained soil and full sun. Species can be propagated by seed, but the hybrids must be done by root cuttings.

Bulbs

Allium spp. ORNAMENTAL ONION
The onions have been grown for centuries in gardens and there are two that are especially good for the back of the border. Both require full sun and may need staking.

Allium aflatunense. Height: 1.2 m (4 ft). Spread: 30 cm (1 ft). Flowers: Late spring. This produces large, round heads of tiny, lilac flowers, and there is a white variety 'Album'. Plant the bulbs in early autumn 12.5 cm (5 in) deep. Propagate by division in autumn or by seed.

Allium giganteum. Much the same as the above but with larger heads in summer.

Plants for the Middle of the Border

Shrubs

Artemisia 'Powis Castle' LAD'S LOVE or
SOUTHERNWOOD
Height: 75 cm (2½ ft). Spread: 75 cm (2½ ft).
One of the best of all the artemisias, this
produces a mound of silver, finely cut foliage and
is a great improvement on the larger *Artemisia
abrotanum*, grown since at least the tenth century.
Look out also for wormwood (*A. absinthium*),
which is much the same. The variety 'Lambrook
Silver' is the best. They absolutely *must* have a
well-drained soil, so work in plenty of coarse grit
before planting and give them a sunny spot.
Propagate by softwood cuttings in summer.

Berberis thunbergii 'Atropurpurea Nana'
BARBERRY
Height: 60 cm (2 ft). Spread: 60 cm (2 ft).
Flowers: Spring.
A small, rounded bush with fine, red foliage
turning orange in autumn. Also recommended is
the variety 'Aurea' with golden foliage. Propagate
by half-ripe cuttings in autumn.

Cistus purpureus ROCK ROSE or SUN ROSE
Height: 1.2 m (4 ft). Spread: 1 m (3 ft).
Flowers: Summer.
Grown since 1790, this sun-lover has crimson
flowers with chocolate-brown centres, rather like
a single rose, and is very free-flowering. If it's a
bit too large for the centre of your border, grow
one of the smaller named varieties. 'Grayswood
Pink' grows to about 1 m (3 ft) and 'Warley Rose'

to about 60 cm (2 ft). Give them a dry soil and
a sunny spot and propagate by half-ripe cuttings
in autumn. They're not long-lived plants, so
propagate every three or four years.

Cytisus purpureus BROOM
Height: 45 cm (1½ ft). Spread: 60 cm (2 ft).
Flowers: Early summer.
A low-growing plant with arching branches
covered in lilac flowers. There's also a white
variety, 'Albus'. 'Atropurpueus' has deeper-purple
flowers. Give them a sunny spot and well-
drained soil and propagate by half-ripe cuttings
in summer.

Daphne mezereum MEZEREON
Height: 1 m (3 ft). Spread: 60 cm (2 ft).
Flowers: Late winter/early spring.
Introduced in 1561, it was doubtless not long
before a few cuttings of this little gem reached
cottage gardens. It bears pink/lilac flowers all
the way up naked stems and fills the garden
with sweet perfume. The variety 'Alba' has white
flowers; 'Rubra' has deep red ones. It can be
subject to virus attack and is not generally a
long-lived shrub, but well worthwhile none
the less. Grow it in well-drained soil in sun or
part-shade. It thrives in chalky soils.

The British native spurge laurel (*D. laureola*) is
about the same size but it's evergreen, with good,
shiny foliage. It bears slightly scented, yellow
flowers in early spring. It prefers a retentive soil
in full or partial shade. Propagate by seed.

Deutzia 'Nikko'
Height: 60 cm (2 ft). Spread: 1 m (3 ft).
Flowers: Early summer.
A fairly recent introduction, this delightful shrub
forms a compact mound of fresh green foliage
covered with small, white flowers. It grows in any
well-drained soil and prefers full sun. Propagate

by hardwood cuttings in early autumn or softwood throughout the summer.

Fuchsia hybrids
Height: 30 cm–1.2 m (1–4 ft). Spread: 30 cm–1.2 m (1–4 ft). Flowers: All summer/autumn.
Invaluable plants for the middle of the border. Some do grow a bit tall, but can be pruned hard in winter so that they don't become an embarrassment. They're quite hardy and produce lovely, skirted flowers, often in two colours. Look for 'Mrs Popple', a taller one with deep red and violet blooms; 'Tom Thumb', one of the smallest with flowers of the same colour; and 'Eva Boerg' with two-tone pink flowers. They like a sunny spot and a well-drained soil is essential. In colder areas cut back the shoots in winter and cover the root with leaf litter or straw; otherwise prune hard in spring before the new shoots start to grow. Propagate by softwood cuttings in summer.

The hardy fuchsias, like 'Mrs Popple' here, never fail to fill with bloom in late summer.

Genista tinctoria DYER'S GREENWEED
Height: 45 cm (1½ ft). Spread: 1 m (3 ft).
Flowers: Late spring/early summer.
Grown since 1570, the species is not really worthwhile as an ornamental plant, having not very conspicuous, yellow flowers. But two more recent varieties cover themselves in bright yellow, double blooms. Look for 'Golden Plate' and 'Plena'. 'Royal Gold' is more upright, growing to about 1 m (3 ft).

Hydrangea macrophylla
Height: 1–1.5 m (3–5 ft). Spread: 1–1.5 m (3–5ft). Flowers: Summer.
Most cottage gardens would have a hydrangea or two. The mophead varieties, or 'hortensias', bear large, round heads of pink or blue florets, though even blue varieties will show their true blue colours only on acid soils. Otherwise they stay pink unless treated with 'blueing agent', available at garden centres. There are many named varieties, like the deep rose-pink 'Altona'; 'Blue Prince'; the large-flowered pink or deep blue 'Goliath'; the dwarfer, deep red 'Souvenir du Président Paul Doumer'; and more.

Then there are the lacecaps, which bear large, flat flowers, surrounded by a ring of florets. They have a more delicate, airy look and are ideal for the cottage effect. 'Blue Wave' has blue flowers surrounded by pink florets; 'Lanarth White' is blue or pink surrounded by white; and 'Tricolor', has flowers varying from pink to white and leaves variegated green, grey and yellow.

All prefer to be in a semi-shaded place and a free-draining but retentive soil. Prune shoots that have flowered in the following spring and propagate by softwood cuttings in late summer.

Hypericum androsaemum TUTSAN
Height: 1 m (3 ft). Spread: 1 m (3 ft).
Flowers: Summer.

Grown since 1370, the hypericums, with their bright yellow flowers and long flowering period, became popular cottage garden subjects. The fresh green leaves are almost hidden by masses of yellow, saucer-shaped flowers most of the summer and these are followed by attractive, shining, red fruits which later turn black. Unfortunately the plants are somewhat prone to rust disease these days, but it won't strike every year. When it does, I cut the stems right down to ground level and burn them: the plants re-grow happily the following season.

Also popular is the variety 'Hidcote', with similar flowers but without the fruits. It doesn't seem nearly so prone to rust. Grow hypericums in a sunny spot in reasonable soil and propagate by dividing the roots or by softwood cuttings.

The lacecap hydrangeas bear large blooms with a central boss of flowers surrounded by a ring of florets, sometimes of matching colours, sometimes different, depending on variety.

Potentilla hybrids Cinquefoil
Height: 1.2 m (4 ft). Spread: 1.2 m (4 ft).
Flowers: All summer.
A very adaptable and tough shrub, popular because of its long flowering period and range of flower colours. They include the superb, pure white 'Abbotswood'; the peachy cream 'Daydawn'; the canary yellow 'Elizabeth'; the rich gold, dwarfer 'Goldfinger'; the vermilion 'Red Ace'; and the orange 'Hopley's Orange', a good, recent introduction.

They prefer full sun, but some of the newer hybrids tend to fade, so a little shade is probably better. They'll grow in almost any well-drained soil. Prune them after flowering by clipping with shears and propagate by softwood cuttings in summer.

Rosa varieties
'Brother Cadfael'. Height: 1 m (3 ft). Spread: 1 m (3 ft). An English rose with very large, peony-like, soft pink flowers.
'Cottage Rose'. Height: 1 m (3 ft). Spread: 75 cm (2½ ft). An English rose producing cupped flowers of real old-fashioned shape in warm pink. Repeat flowers well.

'Duchesse de Buccleugh'. Height: 1 m (3 ft). Spread: 1 m (3 ft). A Gallica rose with large, quartered flowers of lilac-pink.

'Evelyn'. Height: 1 m (3 ft). Spread: 1 m (3 ft). A delightful English rose with shallow, cup-shaped blooms of apricot and yellow.

'Félicité Parmentier'. Height: 1 m (3 ft). Spread: 1 m (3 ft). A lovely Alba rose with delicate, pale pink flowers, deeper-coloured in the centre and turning to pale pink as the flower opens.

'Glamis Castle'. Height: 1 m (3 ft). Spread: 75 cm (2½ ft). A pure white English rose with cupped flowers and a fragrance of myrrh.

'Gloire de France'. Height: 1 m (3 ft). Spread:

1 m (3 ft). A Gallica rose with cupped flowers of pink with a deeper pink centre.

'Hermosa'. Height: 1 m (3 ft). Spread: 1 m (3 ft). A lovely China rose with cupped flowers of mid-pink. It hangs its head slightly to give a delicate appearance and flowers all summer.

'Jayne Austin'. Height: 1 m (3 ft). Spread: 75 cm (2½ ft). An English rose with rosette blooms of soft yellow with a hint of apricot.

'Pompon de Bourgogne'. Height: 1 m (3 ft). Spread: 60 cm (2 ft). Introduced in 1664, this bears the smallest flowers of all the old roses. It has tiny, dark green leaves and small, deep red flowers. Often used to make hedges in parterres.

'Rose de Rescht'. Height: 1 m (3 ft). Spread: 75 cm (2½ ft). A compact Portland rose with crimson flowers. Flowers throughout summer.

'Sharifa Asma'. An English rose with flowers of blush pink fading to white on the outer petals.

'Soupert et Notting'. Height: 1 m (3 ft). Spread: 75 cm (2½ ft). Full flowers of strong lilac-pink.

'Souvenir de la Malmaison'. Height: 1 m (3 ft). Spread: 75 cm (2½ ft). A lovely Bourbon rose with large, pink flowers touched with light brown which repeat throughout the summer.

'The Countryman'. Height: 1 m (3 ft). Spread: 1 m (3 ft). An English rose forming flat, many-petalled rosettes of clear pink. Two flowerings a year with some in between.

'The Dark Lady'. Height: 1 m (3 ft). Spread: 1 m (3 ft). A deep red English rose producing large blooms like those of a tree peony.

Rosmarinus officinalis ROSEMARY
A fine decorative shrub for the middle or front of the border, covered under 'Herbs' on page 231.

Senecio 'Sunshine'
Height: 1 m (3 ft). Spread: 1.8 m (6 ft).
Flowers: Summer

A lax, spreading shrub which forms a mat of felty grey leaves topped by yellow daisies. It needs a well-drained soil and sun. Prune lightly after flowering and cut old, straggly plants back hard to the ground every so often to rejuvenate them. Propagate by softwood cuttings in summer.

Herbaceous Plants

Achillea hybrids
Height: 60 cm (2 ft). Spread: 38 cm (15 in).
Flowers: Throughout summer.
The native British yarrow was no doubt dug up and planted in early cottage gardens, but is certainly not worth growing now, having been replaced by much better species and hybrids. They all like a retentive, well-drained soil in full sun and can be propagated by division, seed or basal cuttings, all in spring.

'Moonshine' is an excellent modern hybrid with sulphur-yellow flowers. From Germany come several others certainly worth a place: 'Cerise Queen' has cherry red flowers; 'Apple Blossom' is lilac-pink; 'Great Expectations' is buff-primrose; and 'Salmon Beauty' is salmon-pink.

Alchemilla mollis LADY'S MANTLE
Height: 45 cm (1½ ft). Spread: 60 cm (2 ft).
Flowers: Early summer.
Introduced in 1874, this is a plant that will grow almost anywhere, in sun or deep shade, though it looks best in shade. Its delightful, rounded, fresh green leaves catch droplets of rain which sparkle in the sun and they're topped by yellow flowers on delicate stems. It will seed itself readily, so it may be best to remove the flower heads when they fade. Propagate by seed or division.

Anthemis tinctoria 'Grallach Gold'
Height: 1 m (3 ft). Spread: 1 m (3 ft).
Flowers: Summer.

A striking plant producing masses of stunning, acid-yellow daisies over a long period. Propagate by basal cuttings or division. (See also page 172.)

Anthemis sancti-johannis. Height: 60 cm (2 ft). Spread: 60 cm (2 ft). Flowers: Summer. Like the above but with bright orange flowers and somewhat shorter petals. A short-lived plant but easily raised from seed or cuttings.

Aquilegia spp. and hybrids COLUMBINE
These are real cottage garden plants dating from about the thirteenth century. They've been grown in cottage gardens since the earliest times. I've included them in the middle of the border, but some should certainly drift towards the front where their delicate flowers and foliage can be best seen.

Aquilegia canadensis. Height: 60 cm (2 ft). Spread: 30 cm (1 ft). Flowers: Early summer. This graceful plant has delightful red-and-yellow flowers and typical dark green divided foliage. It prefers well-drained soil and sun. Propagate by seed.

Long-spurred hybrids. Height: 60–90 cm (2–3 ft). Spread: 45 cm (1½ ft). Flowers: Early summer. These are the really well-known 'granny's bonnets' that are as much part of cottage gardens as hollyhocks. They have beautifully shaped blooms with a long spur on the back, in various shades of yellow, pink, red, purple and mauve: not to be missed. They also like good drainage and a sunny spot. Propagate by seed sown in pots in the coldframe in late summer. Some will also seed themselves.

A mass of lady's mantle at the front of this border lights up an otherwise shady spot with a foam of yellow flowers. After rain, the drops will be caught in the cupped leaves and will sparkle like jewels.

Arum maculatum LORDS-AND-LADIES or
JACK-BY-THE-HEDGE

A British native that must have been dug up in
early times by cottagers to grow in their gardens.
That's illegal now, of course, but there's a much
better garden variety anyway.

Arum italicum 'Pictum'. Height: 45 cm (1½ ft).
Spread: 30 cm (1 ft). Flowers: Spring. This variety has large, sword-shaped leaves of glossy green
marbled with cream and grey, making a fine show
in winter. The flowers are greenish white spathes
with purple staining at the base and a creamy
central spadix. Give it a moisture-retentive soil
and a sunny position, though it will take some
shade. Propagate by division in spring.

Astrantia major MASTERWORT
Height: 60 cm (2 ft). Spread: 45 cm (1½ ft).
Flowers: Summer/autumn.

Introduced in 1597, this fine old cottage
favourite forms branched heads of interesting
flowers with their central florets surrounded by a
ruff of bracts. The flowers are greenish white
with a pale green collar. Look for the variety
'Shaggy', which is particularly good. 'Rubra'
has beautiful red flowers and a new variety,
'Sunningdale Variegated', has leaves striped with
yellow. They like a well-drained soil in sun or
partial shade and can be propagated by division
or seed.

Catananche caerulea BLUE CUPIDONE
Height: 60 cm (2 ft). Spread: 30 cm (1 ft).
Flowers: Summer.

Introduced in 1596, this was one of the plants
grown by the herbalist John Gerard (1545-1612)
in his own garden. It makes a clump of grassy
leaves and numerous wiry flower stems with
small, deep blue flowers surrounded by a papery
'everlasting flower' calyx: most attractive. There
are some good named varieties like 'Perry's

White', the lavender-blue 'Major', and 'Bicolor'
which is white with a dark blue centre. Give them
a sunny but sheltered position and propagate by
seed or, in the case of the named varieties, by root
cuttings in early spring.

Centaurea montana MOUNTAIN KNAPWEED
Height: 45 cm (1½ ft). Spread: 60 cm (2 ft).
Flowers: Early summer.

Gerard called this the 'Great Blew-Bottle or
Corne-Floure' and it has been grown in cottage
gardens since 1596. It produces large, cornflower
blooms of deep blue with a red centre. There are
also white and pink varieties. It grows in almost
any soil and is most at home in sun. Propagate by
division in autumn or spring.

Centranthus ruber VALERIAN
Height: 60–90 cm (2–3 ft). Spread: 45 cm
(1½ ft). Flowers: Summer.

A popular cottage plant often to be found growing on walls. It loves chalky soil and a sunny spot
and, given the right conditions, it'll seed itself
freely. The seedlings should be controlled where
they're not wanted. It has large, elongated heads
of small pink flowers. Best of all are the white
form 'Albus' and the deep red 'Atrococcineus'.
Propagate by seed sown outside in early summer.

Chrysanthemum maximum or correctly
Leucanthemum superbum SHASTA DAISY
Height: 1 m (3 ft). Spread: 45 cm (1½ ft).
Flowers: Summer.

A wonderful, easy, strong grower that has been in
cottage gardens since 1816. It produces masses of
white daisies over a long period. There are also
some selected forms, like the well-known 'Esther
Read', that are very worthwhile. It'll grow almost
anywhere in any soil but prefers sun or part-shade
and a retentive soil. Propagate by division in
autumn. It does best when divided regularly.

The shasta daisy is the easiest of plants to grow, simple to propagate and one of the most reliable flowerers: a perfect cottage garden plant.

Dendranthema hybrids
HYBRID CHRYSANTHEMUMS
Height: 45 cm–1 m (1½–3 ft). Spread: 30 cm (1 ft). Flowers: Late summer.
There are hundreds of florist's chrysanthemums that are too tender for our purposes, but also several hardy varieties. Get hold of a specialist catalogue, but don't miss 'Anastasia', which has small pink 'buttons', and 'Emperor of China', known as the 'old cottage pink', with pink flowers with a crimson centre right through to the first frosts. 'Innocence' is a single pink well worth growing. They like a sunny position and may be propagated by cuttings in spring.

Coreopsis verticillata TICK SEED
Height: 60 cm (2 ft). Spread: 45 cm (1½ ft). Flowers: Summer/autumn.
Brought to Britain from the USA in 1759, this must have been readily accepted by cottage gardeners. It has bright green, narrow foliage and brilliant yellow, daisy-like blooms over a long period. Look for the variety 'Grandiflora', sometimes called 'Golden Shower', which has a richer yellow colour, and 'Moonbeam' which is primrose-yellow. It'll grow in any soil in sunshine. It's a short-lived plant, but can easily be raised from seed sown in spring outside.

Dianthus hybrids CLOVE CARNATION
Height: 45 cm (1½ ft). Spread: 30 cm (1 ft). Flowers: Summer.
Carnations or 'gillyflowers', like the old crimson clove, have been grown since the sixteenth century. It's dark red and has a very strong perfume. 'Lord Chatham' bears bright pink, perfumed flowers. Grow plants in full sun and well-drained soil and stake them early to prevent the flowers flopping. Propagate by cuttings in early summer.

Diascia rigescens
Height: 45 cm (1½ ft). Spread: 45 cm (1½ ft). Flowers: Summer.

Not exactly a traditional cottage garden plant, but one I'm quite sure the old cottage gardeners would have loved. It has masses of deep pink flowers that cover the stems over a long period. It could be tender in colder areas and must have full sun and excellent drainage everywhere. Prop-agate by cuttings in mid-summer.

Dicentra spectabilis BLEEDING HEART or DUTCHMAN'S BREECHES
Height: 60 cm (2 ft). Spread: 45 cm (1½ ft).
Flowers: Late spring.
Introduced in 1810, this plant has the distinction of more common names than any other, I'm sure. It produces beautiful, white-tipped, red, pendulous, locket-shaped flowers which dangle from arching stems. And it's worth growing just for its attractive much-divided foliage. It needs a shady spot and retentive soil. Propagate by division.

Dicentra formosa was introduced from the USA in 1796. It also makes tussocks of lovely, ferny foliage and has pendulous flowers. They're red/purple and there are a few varieties like the dark pink 'Luxuriant' and the soft pink 'Boothman's Variety' that are worth hunting out. Grow them like *D. spectabilis*.

Doronicum plantagineum LEOPARD'S BANE
Height: 75 cm (2½ ft). Spread: 30 cm (1 ft).
Flowers: Early spring.
An easily grown plant introduced about 1570 that forms large clumps of attractive, fresh green foliage from which arise masses of bright yellow daisies. It likes retentive soil and some shade, though it will put up with sun if the soil is moist. Propagate by division in autumn.

Erigeron hybrids FLEABANE
Height: 45–60 cm (1½–2 ft). Spread: 45 cm (1½ ft). Flowers: Summer.
Grown in cottage gardens since the nineteenth century, but the older species have now been replaced by better hybrids. They produce masses of daisy flowers rather like Michaelmas daisies, only on shorter plants. Look out for the single, pink 'Amity' and 'Charity'; the violet-blue 'Dignity'; and the red 'Rotes Meer'. All like a sunny site and well-drained soil. Propagate by division.

Eryngium maritimum SEA HOLLY
Height: 30 cm (1 ft). Spread: 30 cm (1 ft).
Flowers: Summer.
The British native sea holly must have been grown in coastal cottage gardens by the earliest gardeners, but is now quite rare. Like all the sea hollies, it has attractive, thistle-like foliage and very blue flowers. Two other sea hollies are worth considering:

Eryngium alpinum. Height: 75 cm (2½ ft). Spread: 45 cm (1½ ft). Flowers: Summer. Introduced in 1597, this striking plant has the largest, blue, conical flowers of all. Look out for the improved variety 'Donard'.

E. bourgatii. Height: 60 cm (2 ft). Spread: 30 cm (1 ft). Flowers: Summer. Striking, deeply cut foliage with white veins is one of the features of this species. The flowers are green.

All need a very well-drained, dry soil in full sun. Propagate by carefully lifting self-sown seedlings or by root cuttings in autumn.

Erysimum hybrids PERENNIAL WALLFLOWER
Height: 30–60 cm (1–2 ft). Spread: 30 cm (1 ft).
Flowers: Spring/summer.
Wallflowers were great favourites in cottage gardens and still should be. However, they're biennials, so they take a lot of room to grow each year. The perennial wallflowers are therefore especially useful where space to grow the biennials is not available. There are several good varieties, but they're all fairly short-lived, so it's

advisable to take cuttings every couple or three years as an insurance. They all like a sunny spot or part-shade and retentive but well-drained soil. Look out for the yellow 'Harpur Crewe'; the purple 'Bowles' Mauve'; 'Chelsea Jacket', which is orange and pale mauve; and the shorter 'Jacob's Jacket', whose flowers change from bronze to orange and then to lilac.

Euphorbia spp. SPURGE or MILKWEED
Some of the spurges are native to Britain and, even though treated as weeds in many gardens, are actually quite attractive, so they will have been nurtured in early cottage gardens. There are several great improvements to be found in the plants available today.

Euphorbia palustris. Height: 1 m (3 ft). Spread: 1 m (3 ft). Flowers: Late spring. Grown in the sixteenth century, this species makes a spectacular splash of yellow in spring followed by green plumes all summer which turn orange and yellow in autumn.

E. polychroma. Height: 45 cm (1½ ft). Spread: 45 cm (1½ ft). Flowers: Late spring. This type of spurge forms well-rounded clumps of fresh green with masses of yellow flowers over a long period.

Euphorbia polychroma *produces a rounded bush covered in spring flowers of bright greenish yellow. Be careful of the irritant, milky-white sap.*

It's best to plant them alone or you lose the beauty of their rounded shape.

Euphorbias will grow in sun or partial shade. Propagate by softwood cuttings in summer – and wear gloves as protection against the sap, which can be irritant.

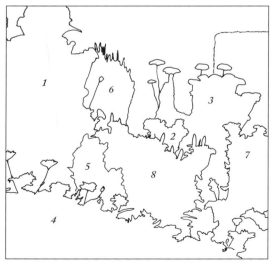

1 *Helianthus* 'Loddon Gold'
2 *Erigeron* 'Serenity'
3 *Achillea filipendulina* 'Gold Plate'
4 *Argyranthemum* 'Jamaica Primrose'
5 *Phlox paniculata* 'Brigadier'
6 *Linaria purpurea*
7 *Astrantia major*
8 *Lilium* hybrid

A summer border full of bright yellow really catches the eye and lifts the spirits.

Gaillardia grandiflora BLANKET FLOWER
Height: 60 cm–1 m (2–3 ft). Spread: 45 cm
(1½ ft). Flowers: Summer.
An easily grown, striking plant existing in various
forms in cottage gardens since the eighteenth
century. The clumps of foliage produce spikes of
daisy-like flowers in yellow to deep maroon with
a brown centre. They'll grow almost anywhere
and are easily raised from seed.

Geranium pratense CRANESBILL
Height: 60 cm (2 ft). Spread: 60 cm (2 ft).
Flowers: Summer.
This British native was grown by the very earliest
cottagers and is still a superb plant, making
mounds of violet flowers. However, it tends to
seed rather too freely so, unless you have a wild
garden, it's perhaps best to stick to the double
forms like 'Mrs Kendall Clarke' with greyish pink
flowers and 'Plenum Violaceum' which produces
tight rosettes of deep blue. There are dozens
more species and varieties, so it's worthwhile

*Geranium oxonianum 'Claridge Druce' is a vigorous grower
producing masses of flowers over a long period in summer.
It will need to be controlled.*

getting hold of a specialist's catalogue, especially
as some will thrive in the difficult area of dry
shade. I list only a few.

Geranium endressii. Height: 45 cm (1½ ft).
Spread: 60 cm (2 ft). Flowers: Summer to
autumn. Introduced in 1812, this low-growing
spreader has chalky pink flowers.

G. 'Johnson's Blue'. Height: 30 cm (1 ft).
Spread: 60 cm (2 ft). Flowers: Early summer.
Good, divided leaves and blue flowers with dark
blue veins.

G. macrorrhizum. Height: 30 cm (1 ft). Spread:
60 cm (2 ft). Flowers: Late spring. A vigorous
grower, even in dry shade. It produces pink
flowers in profusion and the leaves turn bronze in
autumn and generally stay on the plant all winter.

G. maculatum. Height: 60 cm (2 ft). Spread:
45 cm (1½ ft). Flowers: Spring. Introduced from
the USA in 1732, this is a superb plant with
excellent, soft-looking foliage topped by masses
of lilac-pink flowers. Not to be missed.

G. riversleaianum 'Russell Prichard'. Height:
23 cm (9 in). Spread: 1 m (3 ft). Flowers:
Summer to autumn. A fine plant that seems to
produce its chalky pink flowers right through the
summer. It should also be considered for the front
of the border for edging a path.

G. sanguineum. Height: 30 cm (1 ft). Spread:
45 cm (1½ ft). Flowers: Early summer. Known as
the bloody cranesbill, this has deep magenta
flowers, while its better form, *G. s. lancastriense*,
bears light pink flowers with deep crimson veins.

Geraniums will grow in almost any soil except
bog and will thrive in sun or shade. Propagate by
seed or division.

Helleborus corsicus HELLEBORE
Height: 60 cm (2 ft). Spread: 1 m (3 ft). Flowers:
Winter to spring.
A spreading, bushy plant with fine, leathery,
green foliage. The thick stems produce clusters of

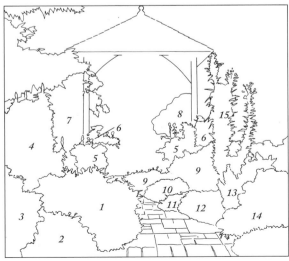

1 *Hebe* 'Primley Gem'

2 *Geranium sanguineum* 'Shepherd's Warning'

3 *Ruta graveolens*

4 *Agastache foeniculum*

5 *Petunia* hybrids

6 *Rosa* 'Margaret Merril'

7 *Rosa* 'Bantry Bay'

8 *Rosa* 'Pink Perpétue'

9 *Geranium riversleaianum* 'Russell Prichard'

10 *Artemisia schmidtiana*

11 *Phlox douglasii*

12 *Aubrieta gloriosa*

13 *Nepeta faassenii*

14 *Rosa* 'The Countryman'

15 *Lilium* 'Connecticut King'

A brick and paving path is softened with plants sprawling over the edges. Maintenance is needed from time to time to keep everything in check.

green bells that hang down from the ends of the branches. It grows in shade or sun on almost any soil, but does need support if it's not to flop. Cut off old, flowered stems after flowering when the new leaves start to show. Propagate by division.

Helleborus orientalis. Height: 45 cm (1½ ft). Spread: 60 cm (2 ft). Flowers: Early spring. Known as the Lenten rose, this wonderful plant is one of the great joys of spring. It has cup-shaped flowers varying from pure white to deep maroon, many with intricate spotting. It's a promiscuous plant, so it'll cross with its fellows, producing lots of seedlings around the plants in spring. They're worth searching out and transplanting to a nursery bed to grow on. All of them will be worth keeping. The Lenten rose likes a retentive soil and will revel in shade, but will grow in sun too. Cut off the old leaves in spring to display the flowers better: a new crop will soon grow. It resents disturbance, so try to leave clumps alone.

Hemerocallis hybrids DAY LILY
Height: 38 cm–1 m (15 in–3 ft). Spread: 60 cm (2 ft). Flowers: Summer.
There are numerous new hybrids that are a great improvement on most of the older ones. 'Anzac' has red flowers; 'Canary Glow' is yellow; 'Hyperion' is scented yellow; 'Stella D'Oro' is gold; 'Pink Damask' and 'Varsity' are pink. They all like sun or partial shade in most soils and are propagated by division.

Iris spp.
The irises have been grown in cottage gardens since earliest times. They're all easy to cultivate and will increase quite fast.
Iris florentina. Height: 60 cm (2 ft). Spread: 30 cm (1 ft). Flowers: Early summer. The ground, dried rhizomes of this plant, which was known as orris, were used in ancient times to make toiletries and pot-pourri. The leaves are typical, sword-shaped iris leaves and the flowers are greyish white and sweetly scented.

I. foetidissima. Height: 45 cm (1½ ft). Spread: 60 cm (2 ft). Flowers: Early summer. A British native grown in the earliest cottage gardens, the gladdon or stinking gladwyn, as it is known, produces a fine sheaf of leaves which are supposed to smell of roast beef when crushed. The greenish flowers are not striking, but in autumn the pods burst to show bright orange seeds. It's well worth growing and seems to survive almost anywhere.

I. sibirica. Height: 1 m (3 ft). Spread: 25 cm (10 in). Flowers: Summer. Grown since the sixteenth century, this clump-forming plant produces grassy leaves and masses of flower spikes. There are several good named varieties of which I grow 'White Swirl', the violet 'Tycoon' and light blue 'Papillon'. They grow almost anywhere, but prefer a moist soil in sun and are ideal bog plants.

Hemerocallis *'Stella D'Oro' produces a succession of gold flowers over a long period in summer. Ideally day lilies should be grown in sun where they'll clump up quickly. Divide them every three or four years.*

The bearded irises like this one, 'Helga', are easy to grow and to propagate. Give them a sunny spot and make sure that the fleshy rhizomes are planted at soil level.

I. germanica. Height: 60 cm–1 m (2–3 ft). Spread: 45 cm (1½ ft). Flowers: Early summer. Known as the bearded iris, this is the most common cottage iris, still seen in many gardens. The flowers are purple with darker 'falls'. There are hundreds of varieties available in many colours, so get hold of a specialist catalogue. I like the brown-and-white 'Kent Pride'; 'Shampoo', which is brown and green; and the yellow 'Berkeley Gold'.

All the irises do best in full sun and the rhizomatous kinds should be planted with the rhizomes exposed. Divide them every three or four years by splitting off young rhizomes with a fan of leaves. Cut the leaves back by half before replanting.

Clump-forming types are propagated by simple division and can be raised from seed.

Kniphofia dwarf hybrids RED HOT POKER
Height: 1 m (3 ft). Spread: 45 cm (1½ ft).
Flowers: Summer.
Ideal for making a strong contrast in mixed borders, there are several good colours. 'Canary Bird' is dark yellow; 'Little Maid' is the palest ivory; and 'Firefly' is orange-red. There are many others. They like full sun and a retentive soil. Propagate by division in spring.

Linum narbonense FLAX
Height: 60 cm (2 ft). Spread: 45 cm (1½ ft).
Flowers: Summer.
Introduced in 1759, flax is used to make linen and now to produce oil for the linoleum industry. It produces many silky, open flowers of the loveliest azure-blue. Look out for the variety 'Six Hills' and the white 'Saphyr'. It likes full sun and a well-drained soil. Propagate by cuttings.

Lupinus polyphyllus LUPIN
Height: 1.2 m (4 ft). Spread: 60 cm (2 ft).
Flowers: Early summer.
Introduced from North America in 1826, this bright flower is a great cottage garden favourite. From a clump of attractive, divided foliage come tall spikes of blooms, and there are many colours.

The most famous hybrids, the Russell lupins, were bred and selected by nurseryman George Russell in the 1930s and were widely grown. However, in recent years they deteriorated, mainly as a result of virus diseases. They have, however, been re-selected to form the 'New Generation' hybrids, which are even better than the originals.

Lupins like a sunny spot and a retentive soil and can be raised from seed to produce mixed colours. After flowering, cut them back and they should flower again later.

To propagate a particularly good colour, increase by basal cuttings in early spring.

No cottage garden would be complete without lupins, seen here in the artisan's garden at Barnsdale. They're very easy to grow and can be raised cheaply from seed, though it's worth seeking out the re-selected hybrids. After flowering, be sure to remove the flower spikes or the plant will be short-lived: this may also encourage the bonus of another, sparser flowering later in the year.

Lychnis chalcedonica MALTESE CROSS or JERUSALEM CROSS
Height: 1 m (3 ft). Spread: 30 cm (1 ft).
Flowers: Summer.
Supposedly brought to Britain by the Crusaders, this plant has been grown since 1593. It produces brilliant red flowers over a long period. There's also a rare, double-flowered variety and a white. Give it a sunny but sheltered spot and propagate by seed or division.

Lychnis coronaria ROSE CAMPION or DUSTY MILLER
Height: 1 m (3ft). Spread: 45 cm (1¹/₂ ft).
Flowers: Summer.
From clumps of grey, felted leaves arise magenta flower heads. Some gardeners feel that the colour is impossible to use in gardens, since it's so bright, but in a cottage garden it fits perfectly. The plant

likes full sun and a well-drained soil and can be propagated by seed or division.

Malva moschata MUSK MALLOW
Height: 1 m (3 ft). Spread: 60 cm (2 ft).
Flowers: Summer.
This British native has attractive, finely cut foliage and large, cup-shaped flowers of pink or white. It flowers over a very long period. Grow it in any soil in sunshine and propagate by seed.

Monarda didyma BEE BALM or BERGAMOT
Height: 1 m (3 ft). Spread: 45 cm (1¹/₂ ft).
Flowers: Summer.
Introduced from the USA in 1744, this plant quickly found favour in cottage gardens because it was used to make a soothing tea and it's also a very good bee plant. The flowers are hooded and rather like those of sage. The best varieties to

grow are *Monarda* 'Adam', which is rich red, and the pale pink 'Beauty of Cobham'. It needs sun and a moist, retentive soil. Propagate by division.

Monarda fistulosa is much the same plant but about 30 cm (1 ft) taller. Look for the varieties 'Croftway Pink'; 'Cambridge Scarlet'; and the dark purple 'Prairie Night'. This species will grow happily in dry soil and is also propagated by division.

Nepeta gigantea GIANT CATMINT
Height: 1 m (3 ft). Spread: 1 m (3 ft).
Flowers: Summer.
A tall version of catmint, this has spikes of lavender flowers over greyish foliage. It tends to be hardier than catmint and is, of course, twice as big. Give it a sunny spot and well-drained soil and propagate by division.

Paeonia spp. PEONY
Peonies have been grown in British cottage gardens since the tenth century and they're highly valued for foliage and flowers. The early leaves are often deep red or pinkish and deeply cut, and the flowers, though not long-lasting as a rule, are one of the garden's most sumptuous.

Paeonia officinalis. Height: 60 cm (2 ft). Spread: 60 cm (2 ft). Flowers: Late spring to early summer depending on variety. Attractive green foliage sets off sometimes single flowers, sometimes doubles. Look out particularly for 'Anemoniflora Rosea', a deep pink with a tufted centre of stamens that are crimson edged with yellow. 'China Rose' bears an excellent salmon-pink, single flower with orange stamens. Also recommended are the double crimson 'Rubra Plena', the pink 'Rosea Superba Plena' and the white 'Alba Plena'.

P. lactiflora. Height: 1 m (3 ft). Spread: 60 cm (2 ft). Flowers: Early summer. A superb, large, single, white flower with yellow stamens and red foliage. Much appreciated also as the likely beginning of a race of Chinese hybrids that have really taken over now. There are dozens of them in all colours and most, if not all, are worth growing. These are the ones normally offered in garden centres.

P. mlokosewitschii. Height: 60 cm (2 ft). Spread: 60 cm (2 ft). Flowers: Spring. Nicknamed 'Molly-the-Witch' for obvious reasons, this most attractive of spring flowerers has soft, grey/green foliage with large, primrose-yellow blooms and golden anthers.

Peonies like full sunshine and a retentive soil and they hate being moved. They do often take a year or two to settle down before flowering, but don't be tempted to dig up the crown and move it or you'll be back where you started. Enjoy the foliage for a while instead. They're propagated by division, but it's best to delay that for as long as possible because it means doing without flowers for a couple of years again. When planting the crowns, don't plant them too deeply: covering with 2.5 cm (1 in) of soil is enough.

Papaver orientale ORIENTAL POPPY
Height: 60 cm–1.2 m (2–4 ft). Spread: 60 cm (2 ft). Flowers: Early summer.
Introduced to Britain in 1714, this is one of the most striking plants in the garden. It has its snags, in that it tends to flop, especially after rain, so it needs support and, after flowering, it must be cut back to induce new foliage, thus leaving a space in the border. But it's so striking that it's worthwhile growing a pot or two of something else to fill the space while the leaves are growing.

'Beauty of Livermere' is a strong, single red; 'Harvest Moon' is orange and semi-double; 'Cedric Morris' is greyish pink with deep red, almost black blotches; 'Turkish Delight' is clear pink; and 'Perry's White', you will not be surprised to hear, is white.

Penstemon spp. BEARD TONGUE

Often slightly tender plants, the first of which came to Britain from the Americas in the eighteenth century, these are not suitable for cold gardens, though one or two have proved quite hardy in my own, far-from-Mediterranean plot.

To give penstemons the best chance of survival, make sure that you grow them in a sunny, sheltered position and improve the soil drainage with coarse grit.

Penstemon barbatus. Height: 1 m (3 ft). Spread: 30 cm (1 ft). Flowers: Summer. From a tuft of leaves grow branching stems with rose-red, tubular flowers touched with pink in the hairy throat.

P. venustus. Height: 45 cm (1½ ft). Spread: 60 cm (2 ft). Flowers: Summer. Mauve flowers in profusion over a long period. This one is perfectly hardy in my own garden.

Hybrids. Height: 45–60 cm (1½–2 ft). Spread: 60 cm (2 ft). Flowers: Early summer to autumn. There is a wide variety of hybrids in a full range of colours. 'Blackbird' is purple; 'Charles Rudd' has pink flowers with a white throat; 'Cherry Ripe' is red; 'Drinkstone' is deep pink; 'King George' is crimson with a white throat; 'Osprey'

Penstemon *'Alice Hindley' flowers over a very long period in summer and is easy to propagate.*

is creamy white and pink. There are many others to choose from, all worth growing.

Don't be put off by the fact that they may not be hardy, because all are very easy to propagate by soft cuttings in August. They'll over-winter happily in the coldframe provided you cover up on very cold nights.

1 *Monarda* 'Vintage Wine'

2 *Tanacetum parthenium*

3 *Helichrysum angustifolium*

4 *Artemisia abrotanum*

5 *Dianthus plumarius*

6 *Filipendula ulmaria*

7 *Nepeta melissifolia*

8 *Agastache foeniculum*

A bright cottage border that might have existed centuries ago since all the plants have ancient uses.

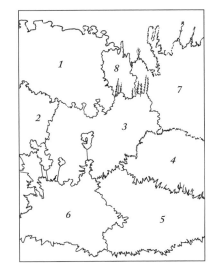

Phlox maculata *has been overshadowed by its showier cousin* P. paniculata, *but is an excellent cottage plant none the less. It may need staking, but it's much less prone to eelworm attack.*

Phlox spp.

Phlox maculata

Height: 1 m (3 ft). Spread: 45 cm (1½ ft). Flowers: Summer.

An elegant plant introduced in 1740 and not so flamboyant as its cousin, *Phlox paniculata*. It produces cylinders of small flowers on strong stems that don't need staking. The species is lavender-pink and fragrant, while 'Omega' is white with a red eye and 'Alpha' is pink. They like a light soil and a sunny or partially shaded spot. They're much less prone to eelworm attack than *P. paniculata*, but should still be propagated by root cuttings.

P. paniculata. Height: 1.2 m (4 ft). Spread: 60 cm (2 ft). Flowers: Late summer. Introduced to Britain in 1730, this is a showy perennial that grows well on light soil with a little shade. It's very subject to eelworm attack, which causes twisting and swelling of the stems, so buy plants propagated by root cuttings from clean soil.

Look out for the varieties 'Eva Callum' (pink); 'Blue Ice' (white with a blue tint); 'Red Indian' (deep red); 'Mary Fox' (salmon pink with a red eye); and 'Marlborough' (violet-purple).

Remove weak shoots in spring, to concentrate the plant's energies on the remaining flowers. Some shoots can be shortened before flowering to produce branching shoots which will flower later than the main batch. It's best to stake plants, though in dry areas with little wind it's not always necessary. I grow mine through a 'lobster-pot' support made with prunings from my coloured-bark dogwoods.

Physalis franchetii Chinese lantern

Height: 60 cm (2 ft). Spread: 1 m (3 ft). Flowers: Summer/autumn.

The Jacob's ladder is an ancient cottage garden plant, well worth growing for its superb flowers which vary in shade from white to deepest blue. It'll hybridize freely, so it's worth saving seedlings.

A better plant than the ancient bladder cherry (*Physalis alkekengi*), grown since 1549 for its red lanterns and edible fruit. This one has larger lanterns in autumn and more flowers in summer. It has running roots, so needs control and will grow almost anywhere. Propagate by division.

Physostegia virginiana OBEDIENT PLANT
Height: 1 m (3 ft). Spread: 60 cm (2 ft).
Flowers: Late summer.
The running roots of this plant, introduced in 1683, produce a dense clump of shoots with small flowers of pink, white or mauve. If moved from one side to another, the flowers stay where they're put – hence the name. It grows in any reasonable soil and prefers shade. Propagate by division.

Polemonium caeruleum JACOB'S LADDER
Height: 60 cm (2 ft). Spread: 60 cm (2 ft).
Flowers: Early summer.
This ancient plant was grown by the Romans and has been present in cottage gardens ever since. It has attractive, green foliage topped by clear blue bells with orange stamens.

There are several forms to look out for, among them the pinkish white 'Dawn Flight' and the rich blue 'Richardsonii'. They grow in any soil in sun or partial shade and will seed themselves readily, sometimes producing varying colours. Propagate by seed.

Polygonatum hybridum SOLOMON'S SEAL
Height: 1 m (3 ft). Spread: 30 cm (1 ft).
Flowers: Late spring.
An ancient plant, introduced into Britain in 1265. It produces arching stems hung with greenish white bells. There's also a double form, 'Flore Pleno'.

Polygonatum grows well in retentive soils in shade and can be propagated by division of the fleshy rhizomes when the leaves die down.

Ranunculus aconitifolius
BACHELOR'S BUTTONS, FAIR MAIDS OF FRANCE
or FAIR MAIDS OF KENT
Height: 1 m (3 ft). Spread: 1 m (3 ft).
Flowers: Spring.
Introduced in 1579, this is a strong, vigorous plant and was a great favourite with cottage gardeners of old. It bears single, white buttercups on branching stems. The variety 'Flore Pleno' is supposed to be connected with Huguenot refugees, hence the name 'fair maids of France'. It has double, white flowers. Another variety, 'Grandiflorus', bears larger, white flowers.

Ranunculus likes to be planted in a moist soil and in sun or part-shade. They can be propagated by seed or division.

Rudbeckia fulgida CONEFLOWER
Height: 60 cm (2 ft). Spread: 30 cm (1 ft).
Flowers: Summer/autumn.
Introduced in 1760, this easy plant produces masses of vivid yellow daisies with drooping, yellow petals round a striking, dark brown centre. Look out for the variety 'Goldsturm'. It grows happily in almost any soil in full sun. Propagate by division.

Rudbeckia fulgida *'Goldsturm' is one of the best of the coneflowers. It increases freely, forming large clumps quite quickly, so it's easy to propagate by division.*

Saponaria officinalis SOAPWORT
Height: 1 m (3 ft). Spread: 1 m (3 ft).
Flowers: Summer.
A native of Europe and naturalized in Britain, this was once used to make soap and is still used for cleaning very fine materials like old tapestries.

It's a coarse, untidy plant for the larger garden and has campion-like single or double flowers of white, pink or crimson. It grows in almost any soil and prefers full sun. Propagate by division or seed.

Scabiosa caucasica SCABIOUS
Height: 60 cm (2 ft). Spread: 60 cm (2 ft).
Flowers: All summer.
Lovely, long-stemmed pincushion flowers surrounded by a ring of petals in white, blue or lavender. Look for 'Clive Greaves' (lavender), 'Moerheim Blue' and 'Loddon White'.

There are also two good new varieties, 'Butterfly Blue' and 'Butterfly Pink', which are more compact. Give them a sunny position and divide the plants every two years and re-plant.

Stachys byzantina LAMB'S EARS
Height: 45 cm (1½ ft). Spread: 30 cm (1 ft).
Flowers: Summer.
This well-known plant was introduced in 1782 and makes a fine, grey carpet of woolly leaves. It produces magenta-coloured flowers on woolly stems, but after flowering looks rather unkempt. So a few non-flowering varieties have been selected and these are generally to be preferred. The variety 'Silver Carpet' is the best and looks wonderful under roses. It needs a free-draining soil in sunshine and should be propagated by division.

Thalictrum aquilegifolium MEADOW RUE
Height: 1 m (3 ft). Spread: 60 cm (2 ft). Flowers: Early summer.
Introduced in the early eighteenth century, this stately plant is noted for its delicate foliage (hence the Latin name, which indicates that it has leaves like those of a columbine). It produces mauve/purple flowers and there's also a good white. It likes retentive soil and a sunny spot.

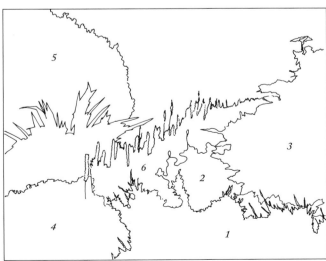

1 *Fabiana imbricata*

2 *Meconopsis cambrica*

3 *Anemone hybrida*

4 *Geranium himalayense*

5 *Clematis* 'Alba Luxurians'

6 *Salvia nemorosa*

In mid-summer the mixed planting in this border looks wonderful: lots of colours but not a jarring note.

Propagate by seed or division. There are taller kinds too (see page 141).

Veronica gentianoides SPEEDWELL
Height: 45 cm (1½ ft). Spread: 45 cm (1½ ft).
Flowers: Early summer.
Introduced in 1784, this is a mat-forming plant which produces spikes of pale blue flowers.

Veronica spicata grows to about the same size, but forms clumps. There are several named varieties worth growing, like 'Heidekind' with rosy red flowers; 'Icicle' (white); 'Romiley' (dark violet); and 'Pink Damask' (dusky pink).

All are easy to grow in well-drained soil in sun. Propagate by division.

Bulbs

Allium spp. ORNAMENTAL ONION
The onions have been grown in cottage gardens since earliest times. Even edible onions produce grey, spiky foliage that looks good among flowers. Try planting a few leeks in the flower border after you've finished digging the crop for the table. The following summer they'll produce fine, large, rounded heads of blue/grey flowers.

However, it's the cultivated ornamentals that really steal the show. Some are quite tall, but they belong in the middle of the border where they'll rise above other plants.

Allium cernuum. Height: 45 cm (1½ ft). Spread: 23 cm (9 in). Flowers: Summer. A smaller, clump-forming plant, valued for its pretty onion foliage and lilac flowers which hang down on small stalks.

A. christophii. Height: 60 cm (2 ft). Spread: 45 cm (1½ft). Flowers: Summer. This produces fine, rounded heads about 25 cm (10 in) across in a rich violet colour.

A. schubertii. Height: 60 cm (2 ft). Spread: 45cm (1½ ft). Flowers: Summer. Carries large, loose globes of lilac-pink flowers at varying heights. Later, the seed heads are most attractive.

A. tuberosum, known as garlic chives, has starry white flowers and leaves that have a mild taste of garlic. It is also often grown in the herb garden and used in the kitchen.

All the alliums like full sun and a well-drained soil. Propagate by seed or division.

Fritillaria imperialis CROWN IMPERIAL
Height: 1 m (3 ft). Spread: 45 cm (1½ ft).
Flowers: Spring.
One of the good old cottage garden standbys this has been grown since before 1590. It produces large heads of big, bell-shaped flowers at the top of stout stems, topped by a tuft of green leaves. Most are yellow, but the orange variety 'Aurora' makes a fine contrast. There are two with variegated leaves, 'Aureo-marginata' and 'Argentea Variegata', and both are well-worthwhile growing.

They like a rich soil and do well in limy conditions in sun or shade. Make sure that you plant them deeply or they won't flower. They can be propagated by seed.

Lilium spp. LILY
Some of the lilies have been grown for centuries, and there's a new race of hybrids available that could well be used in modern cottage gardens. They tend to be shorter and to present their blooms upwards, creating quite a show. However, for the aficionado it's the few older species that give the real cottage garden feel.

Lilium candidum. Height: 1–1.5 m (3–5 ft). Spread: 30 cm (1 ft). Flowers: Summer. Known as the madonna lily, this is probably the oldest recorded of them all, and it was certainly grown as far back as the tenth century. It produces wonderful, scented, pure white flowers and is known as the symbol of purity. It's a bit of an odd

The newer hybrid lilies have been bred so that the flowers present themselves upwards, creating a more striking, perhaps somewhat brash effect. Nonetheless some, like 'Enchantment', are well suited to the modern cottage garden.

man out because it *must* be planted in autumn in a sunny spot and it should be covered with no more than about 2.5 cm (1 in) of soil.

L. martagon. Height: 1.2 m (4 ft). Spread: 23 cm (9 in). Flowers: Summer. Another old plant, the Turk's-cap or martagon lily has been cultivated since at least 1596. It has up to about twenty pink flowers per stem, each with reflexing petals like a turban – hence the name. There's a white form, 'Album', and a superb, almost black one, 'Dalmaticum'.

L. lancifolium or *L. tigrinum.* Height: 1.8 m (6 ft). Spread: 30 cm (1 ft). Flowers: Late in summer. A splendid plant, the tiger lily produces black-spotted, orange flowers. Unfortunately it's very prone to virus diseases.

L. pyrenaicum. Height: 60 cm–1.2 m (2–4 ft). Spread: 30 cm (1 ft). Flowers: Summer. Another old variety cultivated since the sixteenth century, the Pyrenean lily produces spikes with ten or more small, greenish yellow, Turk's-cap flowers with spots and lines. There's also an orange variety.

L. regale. Height: 1–1.8 m (3–6 ft). Spread: 30 cm (1 ft). Flowers: Summer. The regal lily is one of the best whites with a strong perfume. Each stem has up to twenty trumpets with white on the inside and purple staining on the outside. There's also a pure white variety, 'Album'.

L. auratum. Height: 2.4 m (8 ft). Spread: 30 cm (1 ft). Flowers: Late summer. Introduced from Japan in 1862, the popular golden-rayed lily produces about twenty scented flowers of ivory with a central band of yellow and purple spotting.

Most lilies should be planted in autumn or spring among herbaceous plants or shrubs where the roots will be shaded but the heads in the sun. Prepare the soil first by digging in organic matter, and on heavy soil rest the bulbs on a good layer of grit. Generally plant so that the tops of the bulbs are covered with 10–15 cm (4–6 in) of soil. They can be propagated by removing and planting 'scales' taken from the bulbs.

Ornithogalum nutans BATH ASPARAGUS
Height: 45 cm (1½ ft). Spread: 15 cm (6 in). Flowers: Early summer.
A British native, rare in the wild but widely cultivated. It was popular in the earliest cottage gardens for its panicles of green-and-white flowers and for its edible shoots. It prefers some shade and an open, well-drained soil. Propagate by division immediately after flowering.

Ornithogalum thyrsoides. Height: 45 cm (1½ ft). Spread: 15 cm (6 in). Flowers: Early summer. Known as the chincherinchee, this was introduced to Britain from South Africa in 1757. It produces attractive, creamy white flowers over a long period. Unlike the British native, this needs a sunny spot. Propagate by division after flowering.

Scilla peruviana
Height: 45 cm (1½ ft). Spread: 30 cm (1 ft). Flowers: Early summer.
Produces large heads of white or violet, star-shaped flowers. Needs a retentive soil and a sunny spot. Propagate by division.

Tulipa spp. and hybrids TULIP
Of course, there are hundreds of tulips that admirably suit the cottage garden and they're far too numerous to list here. I suggest you get hold of a specialist catalogue to choose. But bear in mind that tulips need to be baked in the sun to thrive and produce new bulbs. In a cottage garden that's not easy, because the bulbs are swamped with the foliage of surrounding plants and in almost total shade. You may therefore need to replace them every year or two.

My own experience has been that, happily, the one type to survive for a long time is the cottage tulip. So that would be my own priority, and it certainly looks best in cottage gardens. There are many varieties in all colours. Lily tulips and parrot tulips also fit in well, as does the species *Tulipa sprengeri* which has lovely, orange-red flowers and seems to seed itself around. Plant the bulbs in the autumn or early winter.

Plants for the Front of the Border

Shrubs

Cytisus kewensis BROOM
Height: 30 cm (1 ft). Spread: 60 cm (2 ft).
Flowers: Early summer.
A prostrate broom raised at Kew in 1891, this has delightful, creamy white flowers. Look out also for the variety 'Nikki' which bears yellow flowers. *Cytisus prostratus* 'Golden Carpet' is about the same size and has brilliant yellow flowers. Grow them in a sunny spot in well-drained soil and propagate by half-ripe cuttings in summer.

Genista pilosa BROOM
Height: 30 cm (1 ft). Spread: 1 m (3 ft). Flowers: Late spring/early summer.
This British native is closely related to *Cytisus* and confusingly also called broom. It forms a prostrate mat of yellow pea-like flowers. Look for the variety 'Lemon Spreader' or the slightly taller 'Goldilocks'. Grow them in any well-drained soil in full sun and propagate by softwood cuttings in summer.

Lavandula angustifolia OLD ENGLISH LAVENDER
Height: 60 cm (2 ft). Spread: 60 cm (2 ft).
Flowers: Summer.
Old English lavender has been around since 1265, but actually it's not English at all, having been brought to Britain from the Mediterranean. Of course, it's quite indispensable in the cottage

The French lavender at the front of this border displays its peculiar flowers with two 'rabbit's ears' petals protruding from the top. It goes well with a fine clump of honesty at the back.

garden. Its grey foliage and copious blue flowers are superbly perfumed and a magnet for bees. It has been used as a scent for centuries and is still one of the best air fresheners available.

There are now many different named varieties, like the white 'Alba' and the vigorous lavender-blue 'Grappenhall'. If you want to mix colours, there are also several pink varieties, such as 'Loddon Pink' and 'Hidcote Pink'. None, in my view, is as satisfactory as the traditional lavender-blue varieties.

If you want a dwarf hedge, go for 'Munstead' or the white 'Nana Alba'. The variety 'Vera' is Dutch and has large, grey leaves. French lavender (*Lavandula stoechas pedunculata*) is also worth searching out; it has strangely shaped flowers with petals protruding from the top like rabbit's ears and is very attractive, though it's for warm gardens only.

Clip over plants in the spring, removing all flower heads and cutting down to within a few centimetres of the old wood but not into it. Regular attention will ensure that the plants remain compact and bushy. Give them a sunny spot and very good drainage, and propagate by softwood cuttings in summer.

Rosa spp. and varieties
'Cécile Brunner'. Height: 75 cm (2½ ft). Spread: 60 cm (2 ft). A delicate little Polyantha rose, producing perfectly shaped, pink blooms from pointed buds.
'Emily'. Height: 75 cm (2 ½ ft). Spread: 60 cm (2 ft). An English rose with soft pink, cupped flowers and a strong fragrance.
'Kathryn Morley'. Height: 75 cm (2½ ft). Spread: 60 cm (2 ft). An appealing little English rose with numerous soft pink flowers.
'Little White Pet'. Height: 75 cm (2½ ft). Spread: 60 cm (2 ft). A cottage favourite, producing a cushion of delicate, creamy white blooms.
'Nathalie Nypels'. Height: 75 cm (2½ ft). Spread: 60 cm (2 ft). An attractive Polyantha rose with semi-double flowers of strong pink. Very free-flowering.
'Pretty Jessica'. Height: 75 cm (2½ ft). Spread: 60 cm (2 ft). A good, repeat-flowering English rose with cupped flowers of strong, deep pink.

1 *Tanacetum haradjanii*
2 *Arabis alpina* 'Flore Pleno'
3 *Ajuga reptans*
4 *Aurinia saxatilis* 'Dudley Nevill Variegated'
5 *Thymus vulgaris* 'Silver Posie'
6 *Anthemis punctata cupaniana*
7 *Myosotis*
8 *Armeria welwitschii*
9 *Phlox douglasii*
10 *Erysimum torulosum*
11 *Osteospermum* 'Langtrees'
12 *Teucrium polium*
13 *Alchemilla mollis*
14 *Lunaria annua*
15 *Lonicera nitida* 'Baggesen's Gold'

A superb cottage border in early summer,
filled with low-growing plants.

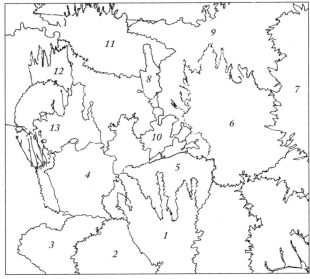

1 *Sisyrinchium californicum*

2 *Eschscholzia californica*

3 *Nemophila menziesii*

4 *Anthemis punctata cupaniana*

5 *Santolina chamaecyparissus* 'Lemon Queen'

6 *Lonicera nitida* 'Baggesen's Gold'

7 *Weigela* 'Florida Variegata'

8 *Delphinium* 'Blue Tit'

9 *Philadelphus* 'Boule d'Argent'

10 *Rosa* 'Pink Peace'

11 *Lavatera olbia*

12 *Berberis thunbergii* 'Red Pillar'

13 *Campanula persicifolia* 'Alba'

However little you may feel you know about the artistry of planting, remember that nature will always give you a helping hand. Here a little natural backlighting creates a magical effect.

Another English rose, 'The Prince', produced the longest flowering season of all in my artisan's garden.

'Pretty Jessica' is an English rose ideal for near the front of the border. It retains the lovely 'quartered' shape of the old roses while flowering continuously.

Rosa richardii. Height: 1 m (3 ft). Spread: 1.2 m (4 ft). Probably the oldest rose in cultivation. It forms a sprawling shrub with clear pink, single flowers followed by black hips. Leave unpruned.

'The Prince'. Height: 75 cm (2½ ft). Spread: 60 cm (2 ft). A superb English rose with deep crimson flowers turning deep purple. An excellent colour and free-flowering habit.

Santolina chamaecyparissus 'Nana' COTTON LAVENDER
Height: 30 cm (1 ft). Spread: 45 cm (1½ ft). Flowers: Summer.
Grown in cottage gardens since the sixteenth century, this is really a foliage plant with bright, silvery leaves which are finely divided and very

delicate. The bright yellow flowers are a bonus.

It must have a sunny and very well-drained position, so add plenty of coarse grit if your soil is very heavy. Propagate by taking cuttings in late summer.

Santolina virens is about the same size, but has green leaves which contrast well with the vivid yellow flowers.

Teucrium fruticans SHRUBBY GERMANDER
Height: 30–60 cm (1–2 ft). Spread: 60 cm (2 ft). Flowers: Summer.
A lovely, grey-leaved, evergreen shrub grown in cottage gardens since 1714. All summer long it's clothed in delicate blue flowers which contrast well with the foliage. It's considered to be tender, but I've grown it in my cold garden for years with no problems. Still, it's best to give it the protection of a south wall if you can. It must have full sun and excellent drainage. Propagate by softwood cuttings in summer.

Wall germander (*Teucrium chamaedrys*) is smaller and has a creeping rootstock, so it could need controlling. It has attractive, toothed leaves and pink flowers. Give it similar conditions as shrubby germander, or plant it in a wall pocket. Propagate by dividing the root.

Herbaceous Plants

Anemone nemorosa WOOD ANEMONE or WINDFLOWER
Height: 15 cm (6 in). Spread: 30 cm (1 ft).
Flowers: Spring.
A British native that grows in shady woodland and is ideal under shrubs. It produces dainty flowers in white or sometimes pale pink or even blue. There are several named forms in pink, lilac and blue. It runs easily, but is never intrusive. Propagate by division.

Anthemis punctata cupaniana
Height: 30 cm (1 ft). Spread: 1 m (3 ft).
Flowers: Early summer.
A lovely edging plant for a sunny spot, this produces silvery mats of foliage topped by chalk-white daisies. Propagate by division.

I would also recommend golden marguerite *(Anthemis tinctoria)* for the front of the border even though its flower heads reach 1 m (3 ft), because it will flop over the paths and make an excellent edging plant. The mats of green foliage are a fine foil to masses of brilliant yellow daisies in summer. Look out especially for the variety 'E.C. Buxton', which is lemon-yellow, and the creamy yellow 'Wargrave'.

Arabis caucasica ROCK CRESS
Height: 23 cm (9 in). Spread: 60 cm (2 ft).
Flowers: Early spring to early summer.
Introduced in 1798, this well-known and popular cottage plant is widely grown to tumble down walls and to edge paths. It forms a mat of grey/green foliage covered in snow-white flowers. There are a few pink varieties too. It must have good drainage, so work in some coarse grit before planting. Propagate by seed sown in spring in the coldframe.

Armeria maritima THRIFT or SEA PINK
Height: 10 cm (4 in). Spread: 20 cm (8 in).
Flowers: Summer.
A British native and grown in cottage gardens as edgings to paths since the sixteenth century. It makes hummocks of spiky, green foliage covered with deep pink flowers. There are also a few varieties of *Armeria juniperifolia* (or *caespitosa*) worth growing. 'Bevan's Variety' is bright pink and 'Alba' is white.

Aubrieta hybrids
Height: 15 cm (6 in). Spread: 45 cm (1½ ft).
Flowers: Spring
Introduced in the late seventeenth century, this delightful little edging or rock plant has been a favourite ever since. There are several good modern hybrids which are far superior to the old cottage plants. Look for the carmine 'Alix Brett' and the red double 'Bob Saunders'. 'Maurice Prichard' is pink and 'Red Carpet' is, of course, red. They must have a well-drained soil and sun. After flowering, cut them over with shears to keep them bushy and perhaps to restrict their spread. They can be increased by cuttings in spring in the coldframe.

Campanula carpatica BELLFLOWER
Height: 10 cm (4 in). Spread: 20 cm (8 in).
Flowers: Summer
Introduced in 1774, this is another invaluable edging plant, making mats of green foliage covered in upward-facing bells of white or blue. There are several good named varieties, all of which need a well-drained soil and a sunny spot. They love to warm themselves on path edges. Propagate by division in autumn or spring.

Cerastium tomentosum SNOW-IN-SUMMER
Height: 5 cm (2 in). Spread: 1 m (3 ft).
Flowers: Early summer.

The pinks in the front of this border flower for a long time and stand out well against the dark foliage of Berberis thunbergii *'Atropurpurea Nana' and the purple sage on the left of the picture. The planting is dominated by a hybrid lily in the centre.*

Grown since 1648, but too invasive for small gardens. For preference grow *Cerastium tomentosum columnae*, which is better behaved. It makes mats of silvery foliage topped by masses of white flowers. Grow it in sun in poorish soil and propagate by division.

Convallaria majalis LILY-OF-THE-VALLEY
Height: 23 cm (9 in). Spread: 30–60 cm (1–2 ft).
Flowers: Late spring.
Grown in gardens since the earliest times, but not without its problems. It's a rapid and rampant colonizer, so it needs regular control. However, it produces lovely, sweet-smelling white flowers in profusion. It'll grow almost anywhere in sun or shade and in any soil. A much better form is the large-flowered 'Fortin's Giant', and there's a pink one too: 'Rosea'. If you can find it (and afford it!), there's an extraordinary variety with green-and-yellow-striped leaves called 'Vic Pawlowski's Gold'. It's superb, but expensive. Propagate by either digging up a chunk and transplanting it, or setting out individual roots in autumn or early spring.

Dianthus hybrids GARDEN PINKS
Height: 25 cm (10 in). Spread: 30 cm (1 ft).
Flowers: Summer.
Grown in cottage gardens certainly since the seventeenth century, the old pinks are not to be missed. They have delightful flowers in many shades of pink, white and red, often with wonderful markings and the finest perfume in the garden. Alas, the old pinks flower, in the main, only once, but modern hybrids are perpetual. However, some have lost the old-fashioned look in the breeding and a few have even lost some of their perfume. The best bet is to grow modern

hybrids that combine the old-fashioned look and perfume with perpetual flowering. Varieties like 'Gran's Favourite', white with purple lacing; 'Becky Robinson', pink laced with red; 'Devon Cream', an unusual variety with a yellow background streaked with pink; and, of course, 'Doris' with shrimp-pink flowers with a carmine ring and a very strong perfume.

Don't miss out on the older varieties, though, such as 'Mrs Sinkins', raised in 1868 by the master of Slough workhouse and named after his wife; it has fringed white flowers and a powerful perfume. 'Bridal Veil' was raised in the seventeenth century and bears very double flowers with fringed petals and a red central zone; while 'Nonsuch', from the same period, is single and pink with red markings.

Above all, pinks must have good drainage, so on heavy soil use lots of coarse grit and give them a sunny position. Propagate by cuttings in the coldframe in mid- to late summer. They can also be grown in gritty, soil-based compost in pots.

Dodecatheon meadia SHOOTING STAR
Height: 50 cm (20 in). Spread: 23 cm (9 in).
Flowers: Early summer.

A delightful little plant which came from the USA in 1774. It produces clumps of fresh green foliage and pink, cyclamen-like flowers. It needs moist soil and semi-shade and resents disturbance. Propagate by division or seed.

Erigeron karvinskianus or *E. mucronatus*
Height: 15 cm (6 in). Spread: 15 cm (6 in).
Flowers: Summer.

A marvellous small daisy that starts white and changes to pink and then red before fading; it continues flowering all summer. It likes a sunny spot, but will also grow in shade and even seeds itself in walls. Propagate by seed sown in the coldframe in spring. Though it's a perennial, it's probably best grown as an annual.

Euphorbia myrsinites SPURGE
Height: 15 cm (6 in). Spread: 30 cm (1 ft).
Flowers: Early summer.

Introduced in 1570, this unusual plant produces straggling, prostrate stems with rosettes of evergreen, blue-tinged leaves and flowers of greenish yellow. This type of spurge likes to be grown in a sunny spot at the front of the border. It can be propagated by division.

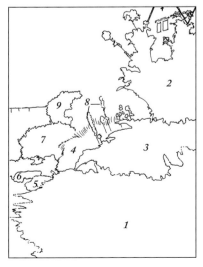

1 *Nepeta faassenii*
2 *Rosa* 'Chapeau de Napoléon'
3 *Acanthus mollis*
4 *Stipa arundinacea*
5 *Dianthus deltoides*
6 *Viola* 'Bowles' Black'
7 *Paeonia lactiflora*
8 *Aconitum* 'Bicolor'
9 *Lavatera olbia*

William Robinson's garden at Gravetye has been restored to its original splendour.

Geranium himalayense *is ideal for the front of the border. Its leaves often produce brilliant autumn colours, but it runs underground so it could need restraining. Still not to be missed.*

Geranium spp. Cranesbill

Many of the cranesbills are suitable for the front of the border, especially those that spread. See page 152.

Geum rivale Avens

Height: 30 cm (1 ft). Spread: 30 cm (1 ft).
Flowers: Early summer.
A British native for cool places. Look out for 'Leonard's Variety' with bell-shaped flowers of coppery pink flushed with orange, and 'Lionel Cox' with similar flowers in primrose-yellow.

Geum borisii is a hybrid with large, warm orange flowers, well worth growing in sun or part-shade.

G. chiloense. Height: 60 cm (2 ft). Spread: 45 cm (1½ ft). Flowers: Early summer. Taller plants with the flowering heads on longer stems and also sun-lovers. Two popular varieties are 'Mrs Bradshaw' which is bright, deep red and 'Lady Stratheden' which is deep yellow. Both can be raised from seed and are well worthwhile. Otherwise propagate by division.

The strong orange flowers of Geum borisii *are considered by some to be difficult to place. Try using them as contrast in a blue border and they really come into their own.*

Helleborus niger Christmas rose

Height: 30 cm (1 ft). Spread: 45 cm (1½ ft).
Flowers: Winter.
Pure white flowers are produced generally after Christmas, though a lot depends on the particular plant. Some will make it, most won't. If you must have them for the festive season, put a cloche over them. For cultivation details see under 'Lenten rose' on page 154.

Heuchera spp.
Heuchera americana Alum root or coral flower

Height: 45 cm (1½ ft). Spread: 30 cm (1 ft).
Flowers: Early summer.
Introduced to Britain from the USA in 1656, this species is really grown for its foliage. Its rounded

leaves are mottled green and coppery brown, and the dainty spikes of green flowers are a bonus.

H. sanguinea is the same-sized plant as the above species, but with green leaves marbled with white. It produces tall spires of bright red flowers. It has, however, been superseded by several hybrids like 'Red Spangles', the pink 'Charles Bloom' and crimson 'Gloriana'. They make excellent edging plants or ground cover and are happy in most well-drained soils in sun or part-shade. It's important to divide them every two or three years and this should be done in late summer/early autumn.

Iris chrysographes
Height: 45 cm (1½ ft). Spread: 30 cm (1 ft).
Flowers: Early summer.
Makes a clump of grassy leaves with several spikes of almost black flowers. Look for the variety 'Black Knight'. It will grow in sun or part-shade. Propagate by seed or division.

Limonium latifolium SEA LAVENDER or STATICE
Height: 30 cm (1 ft). Spread: 45 cm (1½ ft).
Flowers: Late summer.
Grown since 1791, this attractive plant produces clouds of tiny lavender-coloured flowers which are often dried for winter decoration. It likes full sun and a well-drained soil. Propagate by seed, division or root cuttings in early spring.

Liriope muscari LILYTURF
Height: 30 cm (1 ft). Spread: 45 cm (1½ ft).
Flowers: Autumn.
This old plant has long been used to edge borders in cottage gardens. It makes tufts of grassy leaves from which arise spikes of small, violet flowers. It likes sun and a well-drained soil. If, as sometimes happens, it refuses to flower, shift it to another place, at the same time dividing it. Propagate by division.

Lychnis flos-jovis FLOWER OF JOVE
Height: 45 cm (1½ ft). Spread: 45 cm (1½ ft).
Flowers: Early summer.
A close relative of the British native campion, this has been grown since 1726. From clumps of greyish, woolly foliage arise heads of typical campion-red or deep pink flowers. The variety 'Hort's Variety' is clear pink. Grow them in sunshine and ordinary soil and propagate by division.

Nepeta faassenii CATMINT
Height: 45 cm (1½ ft). Spread: 45 cm (1½ ft).
Flowers: Summer.
Introduced in 1784, this lovely plant has graced cottage gardens ever since. Its blue, lavender-like flowers are borne above attractive, greyish foliage. It's beloved of cats, which like to find a plant in the sun and lie in it, but they can be deterred by a sprig or two of holly or berberis placed in the middle of the clump. It prefers a sunny spot and well-drained soil. Propagate by division. See also *N. gigantea* on page 157.

Omphalodes cappadocica BLUE-EYED MARY or NAVELWORT
Height: 23 cm (9 in). Spread: 23 cm (9 in).
Flowers: Summer.
A delightful small plant for a shady spot. It has simple, blue flowers throughout the summer and requires retentive soil and some shade. Look out too for the 'Irish Form', whose flowers form a five-pointed cross of dark blue on a very pale blue background.

Omphalodes verna has been grown since 1633. It's slightly smaller and differs in its cobalt-blue flowers which appear in spring. Treat it in the same way. Propagate both by division in spring.

Polygonum affine (correctly now *Persicaria affinis*) KNOTWEED
Height: 23 cm (9 in). Spread: 30 cm (12 in).

Flowers: Summer/autumn.

A slowly spreading, carpeting plant that can become invasive if not controlled with a spade in spring. The variety 'Superba' is the one to grow, with pinkish white flowers turning crimson. It likes retentive soil in sun or part-shade.

Persicaria amplexicaulis grows to 1.2 m (4 ft), but the variety 'Arun Gem' will reach only 60 cm (2 ft) and is well worthwhile for its bright pink flower spikes. The variety 'Inverleith' is crimson.

All like a reasonably retentive soil and some shade.

Potentilla hybrids CINQUEFOIL

Height: 45 cm (1½ ft). Spread: 60 cm (2 ft).
Flowers: Summer.

Most of the hybrid potentillas have strong-coloured flowers which will last for a long period during summer and are ideal for the front of the border. They tend to spread and sprawl across the surface. Look out particularly for the bright red 'Gibson's Scarlet', the mahogany-and-red 'Gloire de Nancy' and the orange 'William Rollison'.

Potentilla nepalensis has much the same habit and some very good varieties too. 'Roxana' is rosy orange; 'Miss Willmott' is a good pink; while 'Master Floris' is yellow and deep pink.

All prefer good drainage and full sun and are propagated by division.

Primula spp.

Members of this large genus have been grown in cottage gardens since the earliest times. Then they would have been collected from the wild but now, of course, that's illegal. Fortunately the natives are generally not difficult to raise from seed.

Primula veris. Height 20 cm (8 in). Spread: 23 cm (9 in). Flowers: Spring. The cowslip is a well-known British native with spires of scented, yellow flowers. It prefers full sun and a limy soil.

There are many named varieties of Primula vulgaris, *our native primrose, including this one called 'Quaker's Bonnet' (now correctly called* P. vulgaris *'Lilacina Plena'. They quickly form a good clump and are best divided every other year.*

Propagate by seed sown in trays or modules in the coldframe. It can be grown in grass but is best established by growing in pots or modules and planting rather than by direct sowing.

P. vulgaris. Height: 15 cm (6 in). Spread: 15 cm (6 in). Flowers: Spring. The primrose bears characteristic, flat, yellow flowers and prefers shade and a retentive soil. Propagate by seed as for cowslips or by division. There are also many named varieties, both singles and doubles, in a wide range of colours. Look out for the superb, double pink 'Quaker's Bonnet'; the double purple, edged white 'Miss Indigo'; the deep crimson 'Roy Cope'; and the yellow 'Sunshine Suzie'. There are many, many more excellent varieties. For best results they should be divided regularly, preferably annually.

P. polyanthus. A cross between primrose and cowslip, the polyanthus forms a large group with many varieties in a huge range of colours from blue to yellow, orange, red and white. The most popular are perhaps the Pacific hybrids, but the Barnhaven strain is quite superior.

P. elatior. Height: 25 cm (10 in). Spread: 23 cm (9 in). Flowers: Spring. Another British native carrying tall stems of scented yellow flowers, the oxlip prefers a sunny spot and ordinary soil. Propagate by seed or division.

P. denticulata. Height: 30 cm (1 ft). Spread: 30 cm (1 ft). Flowers: Spring. Known as a reliable plant, the drumstick primula, introduced in 1842, produces tall stems on top of which are large, spherical flowers like drumsticks. Hybrids are available in shades of lavender, purple, pink, crimson and white. It prefers a moist soil and some shade. Propagate by seed or division.

Candelabra primroses. Height: 50 cm (20 in). Spread: 30 cm (1 ft). Flowers: Summer. Tall stems carry loose heads of flowers in shades of yellow, orange, pink, cream, red and purple. The plants prefer moist soil and some shade and should be propagated by division. Look out especially for *P. beesiana* with yellow-centred, pink flowers; *P. bulleesiana*, which has flowers in a wide range of colours; the salmon/orange 'Inverewe'; 'Miller's Crimson', with flowers of red/pink with a black eye; and 'Postford White'.

P. florindae. Height: 60 cm (2 ft). Spread: 60 cm (2 ft). Flowers: Summer. A vigorous, spreading plant producing tall stems with loose heads of yellow, drooping flowers. It prefers moisture and sun or partial shade. Propagate by seed or division.

Pulmonaria officinalis LUNGWORT
Height: 25 cm (10 in). Spread: 45 cm (1½ ft).
Flowers: Spring.
Grown since before 1597 and thought to be a cure for diseases of the lungs because the spotted leaves were said to resemble a diseased lung. Actually they're quite attractive. The plant bears pretty pink-and-blue flowers too. There are also some lungworts without spotted leaves, among which is the superb 'Sissinghurst White'.

P. angustifolia. Height: 23 cm (9 in). Spread: 45 cm (1½ ft). Flowers: Spring. Introduced in 1731, this lower-growing plant produces pink buds which open to blue, so there are always the two colours on the plant at once.

P. saccharata. Height: 30 cm (1 ft). Spread: 60 cm (2 ft). Flowers: Spring. Introduced before 1683, this handsome plant has long leaves which are spotted or completely silver/grey. The flowers are pink in bud, opening to blue.

All lungworts like a shady spot and a retentive soil, though they'll grow well under trees. Propagate by division or seed, or collect the numerous self-sown seedlings.

Pulsatilla vulgaris PASQUE FLOWER
Height: 30 cm (1 ft). Spread: 30 cm (1 ft).
Flowers: Spring.
A now rare native, this beautiful flower was certainly dug up and grown in cottage gardens. It's not difficult to raise from seed, so it's still readily available. It produces wonderful pink, purple or white flowers from a clump of silky, finely divided foliage. It prefers well-drained soil in full sun. It was once used to dye eggs green at Easter.

Saponaria ocymoides BOUNCING BET
Height: 15 cm (6 in). Spread: 30 cm (1 ft).
Flowers: Summer/autumn.
A fine plant for the front of the border, this will form spreading hummocks covered in pink flowers over a long period. It prefers sun and a well-drained soil. Propagate by seed.

Sedum spectabile ICE PLANT
Height: 45 cm (1½ ft). Spread: 45 cm (1½ ft).
Flowers: Late summer and autumn.
A clump of thick, fleshy leaves produces large,

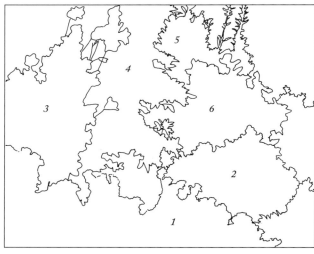

1 *Alchemilla mollis*
2 *Viola cornuta* 'Belmont
Blue'
3 *Campanula persicifolia*
4 *Choisya ternata*
'Sundance'
5 *Brachyglottis greyi*
6 *Clematis viticella* 'Etoile
Violette'

*A yellow and blue summer
border with real,
old-fashioned charm.*

flat heads of deep pink. Look for the varieties 'Brilliant', 'Autumn Joy' and 'September Glow', which are darker and more intense. They prefer a well-drained soil and full sun. The plants must be divided at least every two years or the stems flop away to leave a bare centre.

Silene dioica CAMPION
Height: 30 cm (1 ft). Spread: 30 cm (1 ft).
Flowers: Spring and early summer.
The taller red and white campions are common hedgerow weeds, but still lovely plants. I don't deliberately grow them, but if they happen to land in the border, I let them live until after flowering, when they look tatty. But I do grow the dwarf variety 'Minikin'. This forms a neat hummock of downy foliage covered with deep pink, campion flowers: well worth growing in any soil in a sunny spot. Propagate by division.

Solidago 'Golden Thumb' GOLDEN ROD
Height: 25 cm (10 in). Spread: 25 cm (10 in).
Flowers: Late summer.
A dwarfer version of golden rod (see page 141), forming a neat clump topped by bright yellow flowers. It prefers a sunny position and grows in almost any soil. Propagate by division.

Viola spp. VIOLET and PANSY
The sweet violet was first mentioned in the tenth century, so it's clear that violets have been grown in cottage gardens for many years. Indeed no cottage garden could be called genuine without them. There are many species and hybrids, most not difficult to grow. The larger-flowered pansies are very popular in modern gardens but are better grown fresh each year since they're never as good after the first season.
Viola odorata. Height: 15 cm (6 in). Spread: 15 cm (6 in). Flowers: Spring. This is the sweet violet of nosegays and a delightful little plant

producing, naturally, violet flowers with a delightful and typical perfume. There are now several named varieties worth looking out for, so get hold of a specialist catalogue. They need a shady spot in summer, and are therefore ideal under shrubs or in shade. Divide them annually if you can.
V. cornuta. Height: 30 cm (1 ft). Spread: 60 cm (2 ft). Flowers: Summer. A plant that produces masses of leaves and masses of flowers too. They're deep violet and there's a paler one, 'Lilacina', and a good white, 'Alba'. After flowering, cut the plants back with shears and water them and they'll flower again. They like a fertile soil and sun or part-shade.
V. labradorica. Height: 7.5 cm (3 in). Spread: 30 cm (1 ft). Flowers: Late spring. A rampant ground coverer, but not a problem because it's easy to pull out, and the purple leaves make it much to be desired. The flowers are light purple. It grows in any soil in sun or shade. Propagate by division.
V. tricolor. Height: 15 cm (6 in). Spread: 15 cm (6 in). Flowers: All summer. A lovely, unassuming little native with a delightful 'face' of yellow, purple, blue, cream or white, the heartsease is short-lived but will seed itself around and is always welcome. It'll grow almost anywhere, but after the first year it'll choose its own spot. Propagate by seed.
V. wittrockiana. Height: 15 cm (6 in). Spread: 15 cm (6 in). Flowers: Most of the year, depending on variety. A short-lived perennial, generally grown as a biennial.
There are hundreds of pansy varieties in every colour imaginable and there are hundreds more coming off the breeding production line every year. Sow in pots or trays in early summer for the following year. Bear in mind when germinating pansy seed that they need to be dark and not too hot, so the coldframe will be ideal.

Bulbs

Anemone blanda WINDFLOWER
Height: 15 cm (6 in). Spread: 15 cm (6 in).
Flowers: Spring.

Introduced in 1898, this easy and reliable plant produces lovely blue, white or pink flowers early in the year. Plant in large drifts in sun in rich soil. Propagate by division. There are named varieties available and recommended are 'White Splendour', the soft pink 'Charmer' and the magenta 'Radar'.

Anemone blanda *likes good drainage and sun, so it's a popular plant for the rock garden but equally at home in the front of a border. Improve heavy soil with coarse grit before planting.*

Anemone coronaria
Height: 15–30 cm (6 in–1 ft). Spread: 30 cm (1 ft). Flowers: Early spring.

Introduced in 1596, this tuberous plant produces white, red or blue flowers. It prefers good, retentive soil and semi-shade.

Crocus spp.
Height: 10–15 cm (4–6 in). Spread: 7.5 cm (3 in). Flowers: Early spring.

The Dutch yellow crocus (*Crocus aureus*) has been grown since before 1597. The Scotch crocus (*C. biflorus*) is another old one, with white flowers flushed silvery blue. They like an open, sunny situation but, because they flower early, are fine under deciduous shrubs. Propagate by division in late summer.

Cyclamen hederifolium
Height: 15 cm (6 in). Spread: 23 cm (9 in).
Flowers: Autumn.

This delightful little plant unfailingly produces pink flowers over lovely marbled leaves in green and grey. It's perfect under trees in semi-shade, where it thrives. Very similar is *Cyclamen coum*, which flowers in the early spring. Propagate both by collected seed sown as soon as it's ripe.

Cyclamen coum *flowers in the early spring and makes a very welcome splash of colour. Always buy plants and not dry corms which are rarely successful.*

Erythronium dens-canis DOG'S-TOOTH VIOLET
Height: 15 cm (6 in). Spread: 23 cm (9 in).
Flowers: Spring.

Grown since at least 1596, this has lance-shaped, spotted leaves and attractive, purple-pink flowers with reflex petals. It likes a moist, retentive soil and some shade. The name refers to the shape of the bulb, which resembles a dog's tooth. There are also excellent species available from the USA now, where the spotted leaves have won the plant the name of toad lily. *Erythronium revolutum* has taller, brighter pink flowers with a yellow centre. Look out too for the variety 'Pagoda', which can reach up to 30 cm (1 ft) and produces delightful, yellow bells.

Fritillaria meleagris SNAKE'S-HEAD FRITILLARY
Height: 38 cm (15 in). Spread: 15 cm (6 in).
Flowers: Spring.
This delightful, delicate plant produces hanging bells of chequered flowers in shades of maroon, purple, pink, grey and white. It grows well in the shade of shrubs or trees, or in grass in sun. Plant in the autumn and don't disturb the clumps. Fritillaria will spread quite encouragingly, though not rapidly.

Galanthus nivalis SNOWDROP
Height: 20 cm (8 in). Spread: 15 cm (6 in).
Flowers: Late winter.
One of the first bulbs to flower and a cheering sight. The small, white, green-tipped bells are well known and there are very attractive doubles too. Don't buy dry bulbs, which have a low chance of survival: it's better to look for plants lifted fresh after flowering. Plant them straight away in retentive soil beneath trees or shrubs where they won't be disturbed. They'll seed themselves freely and can be propagated by division.

Iris danfordiae
Height: 30 cm (1 ft). Spread: 10 cm (4 in).
Flowers: Late winter.
A delightful little bulbous iris which produces its yellow flowers before the leaves: a cheerful sight in winter. It needs a sunny spot and good drainage. Plant 10 cm (4 in) deep in an attempt to prevent the bulbs splitting up after flowering,

which will mean that there are no blooms in the following year. Otherwise, plant every year.

Iris reticulata
Height: 15 cm (6 in). Spread: 10 cm (4 in).
Flowers: Early spring.
Following on from the above is this small, blue-flowered bulb. It needs the same conditions and is available in a few interesting varieties.

Leucojum spp. SNOWFLAKE
The snowflakes have been grown in cottage gardens since the sixteenth century. They're somewhat like larger snowdrops and will grow in moist soil in shade, except for the autumn snowflake which likes sun and good drainage.
Leucojum aestivum. Height: 45 cm (1½ ft). Spread: 30 cm (1 ft). Flowers: Late spring/early summer. This, the summer snowflake, produces pendulous bells of white, prettily marked with green.
L. autumnale. Height: 25 cm (10 in). Spread: 15 cm (6 in). Flowers: Late summer/autumn. The autumn snowflake bears similar flowers to those of its summer cousin but pale pink.
L. vernum. Height: 20 cm (8 in). Spread: 15 cm (6 in). Flowers: Late winter/early spring. The spring snowflake has white flowers marked with green.
Like snowdrops, snowflakes are best planted freshly lifted while the leaves are still green. Propagate by division.

Muscari botryoides GRAPE HYACINTH
Height: 30 cm (1 ft). Spread: 15 cm (6 in).
Flowers: Spring.
The Elizabethans grew grape hyacinths, but this particular one was introduced in 1896 and supersedes others. It produces prolific blue or white flowers over a long period, but the foliage persists for some time, so plant later-leafing

Crocus and anemones produce a fine show in the early spring underneath deciduous trees which will not, of course, shade them from the spring sunshine.

herbaceous plants to cover the fading leaves. Plant in autumn. It likes sun and well-drained soil. Propagate by division, lifting the clump straight after the leaves have faded, and re-plant the divisions immediately to prevent drying out.

Narcissus spp. Daffodil
A tremendously varied plant, producing well-known and favourite flowers in spring. Taller varieties are not too happy in small cottage gardens since the leaves are very messy after flowering has finished. It is possible, of course, to plant to cover them, but my own preference would be to stick mainly with the smaller types at the front of the border. The flowers vary from pure white

Snowdrops (Galanthus nivalis) *are often the first flowers to appear in the new year and are a welcome reminder that spring is just around the corner. They were widely grown in monastery gardens. On 2 February, Candlemas Day, statues of the Virgin Mary were removed from altars and replaced with snowdrops for the Feast of the Purification of the Virgin.*

to orange and even pale pink. All grow well in well-drained soil in sunshine. Plant in late summer or early autumn, covering the bulbs with twice their own depth of soil: shallow planting leads to non-flowering. After flowering, allow the foliage to die down naturally so that it has time to build up the bulbs for flowers for the following year. For a wide choice of varieties, get hold of a specialist's catalogue.

Annuals and Biennials

Hardy annuals were a mainstay of old cottage gardens. The seed could be collected from year to year and, indeed, many of them will seed themselves with no encouragement whatever. Once you sow the poached egg plant (*Limnanthes*) or a few marigolds, you've got them forever. Don't be alarmed by the prospect, though, because they're very easy to pull out if they're growing in the wrong place.

They can be sown where they're to flower and they're best grown in patches between other plants. So just scratch some shallow furrows with a stick and sow into those in early spring. When they appear, they can be thinned out to the required distance. Alternatively they can be raised in plastic modules and planted out (see page 198).

Few half-hardy annuals are really cottage flowers, though I can't imagine the modern cottager being able to resist putting in a few. The best way with these is to buy plants after all danger of frost has gone and plant them, as for hardy annuals, in patches. Alternatively they can be raised on the windowsill and put out into the coldframe when the weather warms up a little.

Biennials were also very popular and no cottage garden was without its wallflowers and forget-me-nots. They're a bit more of a problem because they need to be sown in a seed bed in early

There can be few plants quite so typical of the traditional cottage garden as the English marigold. It was widely grown in pots on windowsills and was a more or less obligatory tenant of the borders outside. It was also popular in herb gardens where it was used both medicinally and in cooking. The seed is very easy to collect and sow, but it'll happily sow itself too. Not to be missed.

summer and transplanted to a nursery bed about 15 cm (6 in) apart to grow into bushy plants before being put into their flowering positions in autumn. If you have the space to do it, you'll always grow much better plants than you can buy.

Hardy Annuals

Alyssum
Height: 15 cm (6 in).
White flowers. There is a pink too, but it's not a good cottage garden plant and should be strenuously avoided.

Anchusa
Height: 23 cm (9 in).
Star-like flowers of deep blue. Good insect attractor.

Antirrhinum SNAPDRAGON
Height: 15–60 cm (6 in–2 ft).
Well-known annuals in a mixture of colours and heights. Some older varieties were subject to a rust disease but there are now resistant ones.

Bartonia
Height: 45–60 cm (1½ –2 ft).
Produces large, glistening, golden flowers.

Calendula ENGLISH MARIGOLD
Height: 30–60 cm (1–2 ft).
Well-known flowers in orange and yellow shades.

Centaurea CORNFLOWER
Height: 75 cm (2½ ft).
This bears very double flowers in deep blue. There are other colours, but not as good.

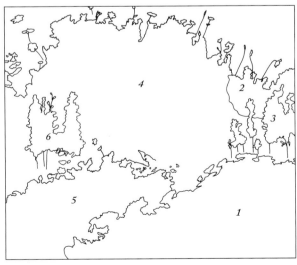

1 *Calendula* 'Fiesta Gitana'

2 *Papaver commutatum* 'Ladybird'

3 *Antirrhinum* 'Dwarf Mixed'

4 *Agrostemma* 'Milas'

5 *Gypsophila* 'Elegans'

6 *Delphinium* 'Dwarf Hyacinth-Flowered'

Hardy annuals make a brilliant border for just a few pounds and many will reappear the next year.

Clarkia

Height: 30–45 cm (1–1½ ft).

A great cottage favourite with semi-double flowers in pink, purple and white.

Convolvulus minor

Height: 30 cm (1 ft).

An eye-catching plant with bells of pink, blue and white with contrasting centres. A good insect attractor.

Delphinium Larkspur

Height: 1–1.2 m (3–4 ft).

Produces stunning tall spikes of pink, lavender, violet and white.

Dimorphotheca

Height: 30 cm (1 ft).

White, yellow and orange daisies. A good cut flower.

Echium

Height: 30 cm (1 ft).

Blue, pink and white flowers over a long period.

Eschscholzia Californian poppy

Height: 30 cm (1 ft).

Produces silky flowers in shades of red, pink, orange and white.

Godetia

Height: 15–45 cm (6 in–1½ ft).

Another cottage favourite with azalea-like blooms of pink, lavender, lilac and white.

Gypsophila

Height: 45 cm (1½ ft).

Produces clouds of dainty, white flowers often used to mix with cut flowers. Unfortunately, it's often called 'Baby's Breath', but the flowers are none the worse for that.

Helianthus Sunflower

Height: 2–3 m (6–10 ft).

A fun plant to grow, with huge, yellow flowers, but not beautiful.

Helichrysum Strawflower

Height: 30 cm–1.2 m (1–4 ft).

Bears mainly yellow and orange blooms which are often used for drying.

A packet of mixed seeds of Helichrysum bracteatum *will provide dried flowers for winter decoration. Pick them as they're just opening.*

Iberis Candytuft

Height: 23 cm (9 in).

An edging plant in shades of pink, lavender and white.

Lathyrus Sweet pea

Height: 30 cm (1 ft).

Apart from the climbing varieties (see page 113), there are a few low-growing ones that are excellent towards the front of the border. They come in the normal range of colours.

Lavatera ANNUAL MALLOW
Height: 60 cm–1.2 m (2–4 ft).
Similar flowers to its perennial cousin, in glowing pink and white.

Leptosiphon
Height: 12–15 cm (4–6 in).
A dainty edging plant producing masses of small, star-shaped flowers in many colours.

Limnanthes POACHED EGG PLANT
Height: 15 cm (6 in)
Produces masses of yellow flowers edged with white: a real eye catcher and an excellent insect attractor.

The poached egg plant, Limnanthes douglasii, *will unfailingly reseed itself each year. It's one of the best attractors of the greenfly-eating hoverfly which feeds on its pollen before laying eggs.*

Linum SCARLET FLAX
Height: 30–45 cm (1–1½ ft).
Bears silky, open flowers of brilliant red.

Nigella LOVE-IN-A-MIST
Height: 45 cm (1½ ft).
Pretty, rounded flowers in shades of pink, blue and white.

Papaver POPPY
Height: 30 cm (1 ft).
There are some superb hardy annual poppies now. Look out for the orange, yellow and white mixture 'Summer Breeze' and especially the bright-red-and-black 'Ladybird'.

Phacelia
Height: 23 cm (9 in).
An excellent plant for edging, it has bell-shaped flowers in the deepest gentian blue.

Reseda odorata MIGNONETTE
Height: 30 cm (1 ft).
No Victorian cottage garden was ever without this. The greenish flowers are not striking, but the perfume is sweet and very strong in the evening.

Tropaeolum NASTURTIUM
Height: 23 cm (9 in).
Brilliant, trumpet-shaped flowers in red, orange, yellow and pink. It will grow in the poorest soil and flower its heart out. There are also trailing and climbing varieties.

Half-hardy Annuals

Amaranthus LOVE-LIES-BLEEDING
Height: 75 cm (2½ ft).
Mentioned by Thomas Tusser in the sixteenth century and described as a 'countrywoman's

flower', this has been grown as a windowsill plant and in cottage borders ever since. It produces drooping tassels of deep crimson. It looks best as a single specimen.

Aster
Height: 60–75 cm (2–2½ ft).
Valuable because it flowers in late summer and autumn, producing large, daisy flowers in a range of blues, pinks, yellows and white.

Centaurea
Height: 1 m (3 ft).
The annual centaurea has thistle-like flowers of lilac-pink all summer.

Cosmos COSMEA
Height: 1 m (3 ft).
Indispensable cottage garden flowers. The ferny foliage sets off large daisies like single dahlias, in pink, red and white.

Dianthus ANNUAL PINKS
Height: 30 cm (1 ft).
These have much of the charm of the you get with perennials without the difficulties. They produce typical flowers in scarlet, white, crimson and pink.

Heliotropium HELIOTROPE or CHERRY PIE
Height: 38 cm (15 in).
A well-known plant in cottage gardens for generations. It forms compact cushions of deep purple flowers.

Nicotiana FLOWERING TOBACCO
Nicotiana sylvestris grows to 1.5 m (5 ft) with large, shining, green leaves and great sprays of scented, tubular, white flowers: not to be missed. *N. langsdorffii* is a little shorter with smaller leaves and delicate green flowers.

Biennials

Bellis ENGLISH DAISY
Height: 15 cm (6 in).
Cheerful little double daisy in pink or white. It makes an excellent companion for the smaller forget-me-not.

Campanula grandiflora CANTERBURY BELL
Height: 45–75 cm (1½–2½ ft).
Produces upright spikes clothed with semi-double, cup-and-saucer-shaped flowers in pink, lavender, blue and white.

Cheiranthus WALLFLOWER
Height: 30–45 cm (1–1½ ft).
A very showy, old-fashioned plant available in all the colours of the rainbow. Shorter varieties are especially good for spring containers. Always raise them yourself from seed sown outside. Bought plants are nearly always thin and weedy and those now offered in trays at garden centres are definitely to be avoided. Remember that after planting in autumn they'll make only a small amount of growth before flowering, so strong, bushy plants are essential.

Dianthus barbatus SWEET WILLIAM
Height: 15–60 cm (6 in–2 ft).
Lovely, old-fashioned flower making a large head filled with individual florets like auriculas. However, flowering in mid-summer makes it an awkward customer, so it's now rarely grown, with the preference being for longer-flowering half-hardy bedding. If you can find room for at least a few, they're well worthwhile.

Digitalis FOXGLOVE
Height: 1–1.5 m (3–5 ft).
Grown in cottage gardens since the earliest times, this plant, bearing tall, majestic spikes of

bell-shaped flowers, is indispensable. It's available in maroon, yellow, pink, purple and white, many of the colours with attractively spotted throats. It'll grow happily in shade, and seed itself.

Lunaria HONESTY
Height: 60 cm (2 ft).
Produces strong, branching stems with spikes of pretty purple or white flowers followed by attractive seed heads suitable for drying.

Matthiola incana BROMPTON STOCK
Height: 45 cm (1 ½ ft).

Wonderfully fragrant spring bedding plant with single or double flowers in pink, crimson, lavender and mauve.

Matthiola tricuspidata EAST LOTHIAN STOCK
Height: 30 cm (1 ft).
A bushier plant than the Brompton stock but otherwise much the same. It flowers late, in early summer, so, like sweet Williams, it can be a bit difficult to fit into the scheme of things.

Myosotis FORGET-ME-NOT
Height: 15–38 cm (6–15 in).
Wonderful blue flowers in spring, the smaller

A typical cottage combination for the spring is the small English daisy or bellis planted with forget-me-nots. When they've finished, the border could be filled with hardy or half-hardy annuals.

varieties mixing well with bellis and the taller ones with tulips. It'll naturally seed itself, but when you pull out plants, shake them over areas where you want them next year, just to make sure.

Viola PANSY
Often grown as a biennial (see page 181).

Tender Perennials

Never be put off growing tender perennials because they're a bit more trouble than hardy plants. That they certainly are, but most have so many good attributes that they're well worth a little extra effort. They're very easily propagated from cuttings in late summer and over-wintered on a sunny windowsill in a cold but frost-free room. They'll grow so little during the winter that they need only low levels of light, and when they get going again in spring they can be put out into the frame. Just make sure that you keep an eye on the weather forecast and cover with a thick blanket or sacking if hard frost is forecast.

They can be planted out in late spring or early summer, generally before the half-hardy annuals but after danger of hard frost has passed. Many will flower right through the summer, especially if you dead-head the blooms that have faded.

Argyranthemum spp. MARGUERITE
Height: 45–60 cm (1½–2 ft).
This easy-to-grow plant produces large daisy flowers in the genuine cottage tradition. It's available with single or double flowers in white, yellow, pink and apricot, and is very easy to propagate from cuttings.

Dahlia varieties
Height: 45 cm–1 m (1½–3 ft).
Another plant with hundreds of varieties, so get hold of a specialist's catalogue. There are two varieties which are generally recommended for cottage gardens and both are excellent, though I would suggest that you should not let your interest remain there.

The airy, lilac-flowered *Dahlia merckii* is a graceful plant for the middle to the back of the border. There's a similar white variety too, called 'Hadspen Snowflake', which is well worthwhile.

For a really dramatic display grow the large-flowered scarlet 'Bishop of Llandaff', which has superb bronze foliage and so stands out in any

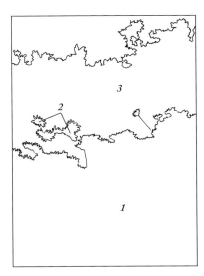

Tender perennials make a colourful show in late summer. Don't be put off growing them, because they're all easy to over-winter as cuttings on the windowsill of the spare bedroom or, with care, even in a coldframe.

1 *Osteospermum* 'Lady Leitrim'
2 *Argyranthemum* 'Jamaica Primrose'
3 *Salvia microphylla neurepia*

The marguerites, like this Argyranthemum *'Jamaica Primrose', are among the best of the tender perennials, producing a mass of superb daisy flowers right through the summer. Dead-head them regularly.*

border. It's rather subject to virus disease, though, so you might prefer 'Bednall Beauty', which is very similar.

The plants should be set out after all danger of frost has passed and supported with strong stakes. After the autumn frost has touched the foliage, dig up the tubers and box them up in garden compost with the tops just showing. In spring put them on a sunny, warm windowsill and water them, when they will produce shoots that can be used as cuttings.

Fuchsia varieties
Height: 45 cm–1 m (1½ –3 ft).
The hardy fuchsias are covered on page 143. Their half-hardy cousins are more flamboyant and will flower throughout the season. They come in a complete range of reds, pinks, blues, purples and whites, generally with two-coloured flowers. They can be grown as bushes, or single stems can be grown on over a few seasons to produce standards. This is done simply by removing all side shoots but leaving the leaves all the way up the stem. When the plant reaches the required height, the top is pinched out and the side shoots allowed to grow. They're pinched back subsequently to make a bushy head. Fuchsias are very easily propagated by cuttings taken in late summer and over-wintered on a cool windowsill or in a frost-free greenhouse. The parent plants can be lifted and kept in a just-frost-free place for the winter.

Pelargonium varieties GERANIUM
Height: 30–45 cm (1–1½ ft).
The favourite windowsill plant of cottage gardens and grown widely in all gardens in summer. It's so well known that it's hardly necessary to describe the large, ball-shaped heads of florets in a range of whites, pinks and reds, some with attractive markings on the petals. Many have two-colour zoning on the leaves too and there are also variegated varieties.

Like fuchsias, geraniums can be grown as

The perennial salvias, such as Salvia patens, *are not at all like their rather regimental-looking annual cousins. They produce a succession of intensely coloured flowers throughout late summer.*

bushes or standards. They're easily propagated by cuttings in late summer and I take cuttings from the cuttings too once they start to grow in spring, to double or quadruple the stock. The parent plants can also be lifted and stored in boxes of garden compost in a frost-free shed or garage during the winter. Keep them cold and very dry. The best way, though, is to grow young plants taken from cuttings and kept on the windowsill as described for fuchsias (see page 194). They can also be raised from seed, but this is not for us: they need to be sown in winter in a heated greenhouse and thus are very expensive to grow.

The only problem with over-wintering is a disease called black-leg. Avoid it by keeping plants very dry and airy.

Osteospermum varieties
Height: 23–60 cm (9 in–2 ft).
An attractive and showy plant from South Africa, but very much in the cottage tradition. It produces dazzling, large daisies in shades of blue, pink, purple, yellow or white. Given a sheltered, sunny spot and very good drainage, some have proved quite hardy in my cold garden, but it's still wise to take cuttings in late summer as an insurance. Again, over-winter the young plants on a cool windowsill and put them in the coldframe as soon as the danger of hard frost has passed.

Penstemon varieties
Height: 23–75 cm (9 in–2½ ft).
The hardy types are covered on page 159, but there are several that are on the borderline. Give them similar conditions to osteospermums (see above) and take cuttings in late summer.

Salvia spp.
Height: 23 cm–1.2 m (9 in–4 ft).
There are several varieties of the perennial salvia that are hardy only in the warmest gardens and many that won't even survive there. Give them sun, shelter and excellent drainage and they may last the winter. *Salvia uliginosa*, for example, has stood several very cold winters in my garden and its airy stems of blue flowers make it perfect for cottage gardens. But I always take cuttings just in case.

S. patens has never survived and doesn't come easily from cuttings. Fortunately it produces abundant seed which is collected in late summer and stored over winter in envelopes in a dry cool place. Sow in spring in a gentle heat. It has flowers of the most vivid gentian-blue and there's also a light blue and a white.

Look out too for the red-flowered *S. involucrata* 'Bethellii' with large crimson flowers. It's not difficult to propagate from cuttings.

Propagation

✤

Growing new plants from those in your garden or that of a friend is one of the most satisfying of gardening pursuits. It's also, of course, by far the cheapest way to fill your garden and it takes less time than many new gardeners might imagine.

In days gone by, nurseries were very few and far between and geared only to supplying the gentry. Cottage gardeners could ill afford to buy plants, though the real enthusiasts, and particularly those growing florist's plants, would not only walk miles to find new specimens, but would also spend much more than was wise. Of course, some of us still do that today!

On the whole, though, plants were propagated by the cottagers themselves, mainly by division – they would simply dig them from the wild or beg a piece from a friend. Many plants were distributed by monks and nuns too, and I'm sure that they would also have given seeds and cuttings to working people to take home and grow on.

Equipment was necessarily simple and techniques were sometimes quite outlandish. There are many suggestions in the first gardening manuals of, for example, practices like grafting apples on to elm or oak to change their characteristics: techniques which today we know to be biologically impossible.

In the main, rural cottage gardeners would have had no truck with such methods in any case. They were well used to the ways of nature and were no doubt expert at handling seeds and cuttings. We can learn a lot from those simple, old-fashioned techniques, all of which are just as valid today. But, of course, with modern matrials they're much easier and more successful.

PERENNIALS WITH SEEDS SUITABLE FOR COLLECTION

Acanthus	*Dierama*	*Kniphofia*	*Primula*
Achillea (but not hybrids)	*Digitalis*	*Lathyrus*	*Prunella*
Agapanthus	*Echinacea*	*Liatris*	*Rodgersia*
Alchemilla	*Echinops*	*Limonium*	*Rudbeckia*
Alstroemeria	*Erigeron*	*Linaria*	*Salvia*
Anaphalis	*Euphorbia*	*Liriope*	*Sidalcea*
Anchusa	*Festuca*	*Lychnis*	*Sisyrinchium*
Aquilegia	*Filipendula*	*Malva*	*Stipa*
Astrantia	*Gaillardia*	*Meconopsis*	*Tellima*
Campanula	*Gentiana* (some)	*Oenothera*	*Teucrium*
Catananche	*Geranium*	*Omphalodes*	*Thalictrum*
Centaurea	*Geum*	*Paeonia*	*Tiarella*
Cimicifuga	*Helleborus*	*Papaver*	*Trollius*
Coreopsis	*Hesperis*	*Phlomis*	*Veratrum*
Delphinium	*Heuchera*	*Physalis*	*Viola*
Dictamnus	*Incarvillea*	*Polemonium*	

Raising Plants from Seed

Since it's always best to use fresh seed, collect your own if you can, though bought-in seed will normally have been properly stored and will give results almost as good.

Try to collect seeds just before the plant sheds them naturally. That often means daily trips to check progress, the alternative being to wait until the seed heads turn brown and then to put a paper bag over them, tied to the stem.

It's slightly different with berries, which have to be collected before the birds strip them. However, sowing them slightly before they're ripe does no harm. Before sowing, squeeze them out of their fleshy coating.

Bring the seed heads into a dry place to clean them. It's always best to separate the seeds from the chaff, since it's there that fungus diseases lurk. I find that the best way is to separate them with the end of a knife, but if you can master the cottage skill of winnowing, so much the better. That involves tossing them up in a shallow dish to allow the breeze to blow the lighter chaff away before the seeds fall back. It takes skill and practice, which I confess I've never managed to master.

Hardy herbaceous plants, shrubs, trees and alpines should be sown straight away. Use a compost consisting of equal parts of good sieved soil, coarse grit and coir (coconut-fibre) compost in a clay pot. Water the compost and sow the seeds on top. Cover with a shallow layer of coarse grit and put the pot into the coldframe.

The seeds of herbaceous plants will be collected throughout the growing season as they mature,

If you're collecting seed, choosing the right time is probably the most difficult part of the operation. You can be sure that it's ripe if you wait until the first seed pod has released its contents naturally. Then collect the whole head into a paper bag and detach it from the plant for further drying.

and some of the earlier collections could be sown direct in shallow drills in the soil of a nursery bed. Sowing in pots, though, does give more control over conditions. It's certainly the best bet for later-maturing seeds.

They, together with the seeds of trees, shrubs and alpines, can stay in the coldframe over winter without protection from frost. The frame serves simply to keep them from becoming water-logged. The natural cold spell will trigger germination and they'll normally start to grow in the spring.

Tender perennials and annuals are somewhat different. A genuine cottage garden will contain few modern F1 hybrids, but it's worth remembering that there's no point in collecting the seeds from these since the new plants won't resemble the parent. The chances of them being worth having are remote in the extreme.

All hardy annuals and the non-F1 hybrid half-hardies are worth collecting. Take them from the plants and clean them (see page 197), but this time store them over winter and sow them in spring. They must be stored in airtight containers (film canisters are ideal) in a dry, cold place.

Sowing Hardy Annuals

Hardy annuals can be sown direct in the soil outside in early spring, in shallow drills in well-prepared but unfertilized soil. They need little in the way of nutrients and will flower better if they're a bit hungry.

Even though you'll almost certainly want to grow them in an informal drift, it's still best to sow them in rows within the required area. Weeds will also germinate at the same time as the annuals, and it's much easier to differentiate the latter if they're in straight lines. Later they can be thinned out to the required distances and transplanted if required.

Many plants can be easily raised from seed sown direct into plastic modules, though avoid the type with very small cells that growers use. Sow a tiny pinch of seed per cell, then cover with a little silver sand.

To get an earlier show, or if your soil is cold and wet, you can also sow in modules. These are plastic trays divided into many separate cells and I'd bet that the old cottagers would have killed for them.

In late winter fill them with coir compost and sow a tiny pinch of seed to each cell. Put them in the coldframe if you have room, but if not they'll germinate perfectly well outside. I grow mine on a paved area, but first I put down a piece of old sacking or felt carpet underlay to act as an absorbent base. This is kept wet so that the plants can draw up water as and when needed. Plant out as soon as the plants have formed enough roots to hold the root ball together. This is also a good way to raise hardy herbaceous plants.

Sowing Half-hardy Annuals

Half-hardy annuals need heat to germinate, so they'll have to be raised inside. Germination is

Half-hardy annuals like these tobacco plants will have to be raised inside. In the gentleman's greenhouse there's no problem, but artisans can also succeed growing them on the windowsill.

easy either over a radiator or, much better, in a small electric propagator.

There are actually very few seeds that need darkness to germinate, so I have a rule-of-thumb method for all except those that the seed packet tells me need to be kept dark. I sow on the surface of moist coir compost and cover with vermiculite. Then I cover the seed trays or pots with clear plastic and place them over the heat source. If,

like pansies, for example, they must have darkness, I cover them with black polythene.

It's when they germinate that the problems begin, because there's simply not enough light, even on a bright windowsill, to produce strong, bushy seedlings. One solution is to make a light box by cutting the front out of a strong cardboard box and painting the inside with white gloss to reflect all available light round the seedlings.

A better answer is to make a portable coldframe by again painting a strong box gloss white inside and outside. Cover the top with a piece of rigid polythene and fix some string handles to the sides. Then, whenever the temperature is high enough, the seedlings can be conveniently taken outside in the morning and brought back in when it gets colder in the late afternoon. It works very well, provided sowing is delayed until early spring. That's plenty early enough anyway.

Sowing Herbaceous Perennials and Biennials

The easiest way to raise new herbaceous perennials and biennials from seed is to sow outside and the method is the same for both kinds of plants. Sow in late May or early June in shallow drills in a seed bed outside. Cover the seeds and tamp down with the back of a rake. When the seedlings germinate and have grown big enough to handle, transplant them about 15 cm (6 in) apart in a nursery bed to grow on. Plant them in their final positions in the early autumn and they'll flower fully the following year.

Taking Cuttings

SOFTWOOD CUTTINGS

Softwood cuttings of shrubs and herbaceous perennials can be taken at any time between early and late summer. Look for soft shoot tips that have grown in the current year and cut them off about 7.5 cm (3 in) long. Put them into a polythene bag straight away and keep them out of the sun.

As soon as you get them back to your work bench, trim the cuttings below a leaf joint and remove the lower leaves with a sharp knife. It's hard to be precise about exactly how many leaves to leave on, but generally two would suffice. In fact, if the remaining leaves are very big, there's no reason why they shouldn't be cut in half to reduce moisture loss from the cutting.

Dip the whole cutting into a fungicide solution

In the artisan's garden I use a portable potting bench on the toolbox-cum-workbench to take the cuttings which are put into pots, covered with polythene and then put straight in the coldframe.

like copper fungicide (old cottage gardeners would probably have called it Bordeaux mixture) to ensure complete protection and then dip the end into hormone rooting powder or liquid. Dibble the cuttings into a pot of compost consisting of equal parts of coir seed-and-cuttings compost and vermiculite. Then water in with the fungicide solution. Cover the cuttings with a very thin, clear polythene sheet so that it's actually touching the leaves and tuck it in underneath or secure it with an elastic band. The aim is to make an airtight seal to eliminate moisture loss.

The pots can then go into the coldframe, which should be kept shaded with netting. If you have the time to put two layers of netting over the frame on very bright days, one layer on fairly bright days and none at all on dull days, you'll have even greater success, though it's not absolutely necessary. The cuttings should root in six to twelve weeks.

Tender perennials like argyranthemums and geraniums are treated in the same way except that the cuttings should be taken in late summer and there's no need for the polythene cover. Put them on a dull windowsill, out of direct sunlight.

Half-ripe Cuttings

If you fail with shrubs from softwood cuttings, you get another chance in late summer with half-ripe cuttings. Look for shoots about 7.5 cm (3 in) long that have grown in the current year. Instead of cutting them, pull them off the main stem, taking a little sliver of bark with the shoot. Again, put them in a polythene bag until you get to your work bench.

Then trim the sliver of bark to leave a very short stub and remove the lower leaves. Dip the cuttings into fungicide and rooting powder or liquid as for softwood cuttings and put them into pots of the same 50/50 compost, but this time dispense with the polythene. Place them in the coldframe and close it up. They should take about eight to twelve weeks to root.

If you want to take a lot of cuttings, as you would, for example, when you're building up enough box plants to plant a knot garden, you can dispense with the pots and put the cuttings straight into a bed of compost in the coldframe. Here the compost consists of equal parts of coir and sharp sand. Never use builder's sand.

Hardwood Cuttings

Hardwood cuttings are the easiest type to use for propagation and no doubt were the most common among the earlier cottagers. Many shrubs and roses and a few trees will respond well.

The best time to take hardwood cuttings is autumn, when the soil is still warm from the summer sun. Look for shoots about 23 cm (9 in)

long that have grown during the current year and take them preferably from near the base of the plant. Cut them off as close to the main stem as possible. Trim off the soft top just above a leaf joint and trim the bottom just below one.

Dip the cuttings into hormone rooting powder or, better still, liquid and then cut a trench in a corner of the garden by pushing in the spade and pulling it backwards and forwards. Line the bottom with sharp sand and put in the cuttings 7.5 cm (3 in) apart so that only the top 7.5 cm (3 in) is above ground. Push the soil back into the trench and firm with your boot.

The cuttings will take all year to root, so simply leave them there, weed from time to time and lift them the following autumn for planting in their permanent positions.

Division

The simplest and most commonly practised way of increasing your stock of herbaceous perennials is to divide the roots in autumn or spring. In fact, division can start late in summer and continue through until early winter when the soil will still be warm, but after that, if the plant is anything but completely hardy, vigorous and reliable, it's best to wait until spring.

Then simply lift the whole plant and remove the stronger, younger outside pieces, either by pulling them off or cutting with a sharp knife. In the case of tough roots like those of hostas, it's easiest to use an old bread knife to saw them into pieces.

Most herbaceous perennials respond well to this treatment and prefer to be divided and re-planted in this way every three to five years. In the process you can make many more plants. If you decide to re-plant in the same place, make sure that you dig out all the old root and revitalize the soil with plenty of organic matter.

In autumn or spring most herbaceous perennials can be lifted and divided. It should be possible to split them by pulling the root system apart with your fingers. Wash off excess soil first.

Sometimes the roots are too tough for this and you'll have to attack them with a knife. That's no problem as long as you can see that you're taking a bud or some leaves with each piece.

Topiary

As well as clipping and training shrubs and trees growing in the garden into pleasing shapes, you can use topiary to great effect on container-grown plants to make architectural features that are interesting and attractive all year round. Box, bay and holly are suitable subjects.

Training simple shapes, like cones, cubes or balls, is largely a matter of clipping slowly with secateurs, simply by eye. This can be a daunting task, since one slip can take some time to grow back again. The secret is to trim the plants little but often, perhaps even as frequently as every

Crowded cottage garden borders have immense charm and are not difficult to achieve. Of course, you'll make mistakes, but if you master the skills of propagating your own plants, it doesn't really matter a lot if you lose the odd one or two.

three to four weeks. And you have the consolation of knowing that, if you do make a mistake, it will eventually grow back again.

With some shapes, like cones and pyramids, for example, you can make up a template with canes to act as a guide.

The attractive spirals cut into cylindrical box and yew plants are first lined out with a piece of rope twisted round the plant. A shallow cut is then made into the foliage, the rope removed and the cut deepened to the main stem. Then the foliage is carefully trimmed to round the edges of the corkscrew shape.

Creating elaborate sculptures is more complicated. Here it's best to make up a design first of all, using thick wire. The shape is placed over the young plant and supple young growths are tied into it at regular intervals. The design is finished off by clipping. Again, do it little but often.

SECTION THREE

*A Cottage
Economy*

*T*HE ORIGINAL COTTAGE GARDENS were there for only one purpose. They were essential to feed the working man's family. Until the Black Death in 1348, labourers worked for their masters on a feudal basis, exchanging their labour for the rent of their cottages and perhaps some food. Mostly they had to be self-sufficient, growing what they could, keeping livestock, and hunting and gathering from the wild. Anything they 'bought' was obtained by the age-old barter system.

However, the scourge of bubonic plague wiped out about a third of the population, so suddenly labour was hard to come by and the serfs found themselves in a seller's market. Many of them were able to negotiate wages to buy some of their essentials. Still, it wasn't much, and the cottage garden and surrounding common land were always vital to their existence.

Conditions for the modern cottage gardener are, thankfully, very different. But while there's no physical need to grow your own, there are still enormous advantages. As ever, raising the food to feed your family will improve the quality of your life greatly.

First there's the fact that you'll be confident that you know exactly what chemicals did or did not go on to your crops. Of course, it may be that there's absolutely nothing to worry about, but I'd just like to know why the tractor driver has to get himself all dressed up like a spaceman before he sprays my lettuces. No thanks. Growing plants organically is the natural way in a cottage garden and it's much cheaper too.

There's also a tremendous difference in the quality of good, home-grown fruit and vegetables. I'm not convinced that organic gardening improves flavour and I'm not at all sure that, asked to taste the difference, I'd be able to pick out the chemically grown produce from the real McCoy. But the difference in home-grown flavour because of its *freshness* is very easy to detect. Just try it with early potatoes or peas and I know you'll agree.

Above all, there's a primeval satisfaction in growing your own produce. I suppose it's those hunter-gatherer genes talking to us, but I know that I get a very warm feeling when the shed's full to overflowing with winter roots and I know my family will eat this winter. Yes, I *know* I could go to the supermarket and buy all I wanted, but the satisfaction's still there.

PAGES 204-5 *Don't let anyone ever tell you that fruit and vegetables have no aesthetic value. In a cottage garden they look very beautiful.*

OPPOSITE *Even the artifacts used in the vegetable plot have a country appeal.*

RIGHT *Growing food was the original reason for the cottage garden and is just as important today.*

Vegetables

❀

Cultivation Methods

After Enclosure gathered pace, cottage gardeners had to make use of every bit of space that was left to them and, for different reasons, we need to do the same. Most modern gardens are small and our priorities are different. Without the absolute necessity of growing our own food, most of us prefer to devote the lion's share of the space to ornamental plants. These days they're just as important to our mental well-being as food was to the early cottagers' physical health. Whatever space is left over must therefore be used to maximum effect. There are two approaches.

The Bed System

After all my years of gardening, I've come to the conclusion that there's no better way to make use of small spaces than to grow vegetables on 1.2 m (4 ft) wide beds.

The idea is to raise the fertility to a very high level with annual applications of good compost or manure. That, coupled with the fact that all the work is done from the side paths and the soil is trodden on only once a year when it's dug, makes the best possible environment for rapid growth and massive crops.

The organic matter supplies plant nutrients, improves drainage and water-holding capacity and also provides a home for billions of beneficial bacteria. The raising of the soil resulting from its addition improves drainage and makes the bed much warmer. The fact that the bed is never

I decided to grow my vegetables in small beds in both the gentleman's and the artisan's garden. Here in the gentleman's I edged the beds with Victorian tiles to add a decorative touch.

In the artisan's garden I used tanalized timber for the edgings, then double-dug and planted up a tiny salad area. There's very little space, but enough for at least a few really fresh veg.

walked on increases the air space between soil particles and prevents compaction, giving the roots a free run and increasing the area from which they can draw food.

Ideally the beds should initially be dug two spades deep, but that's not essential. After the first year, single digging is all that's needed.

When sowing or planting, do so in blocks rather than in rows. In other words you many plant, say, six rows of lettuce 15 cm (6 in) apart each way to form a large block, without any need for access paths in between. So, by growing on the space that would, under the conventional system, be used for access paths, you straight away double productivity. Add to that the well-known fact that high fertility equals bigger yields and you can expect bumper harvests every year.

Growing in the Borders

Some gardens, of course, don't have room for even the smallest vegetable bed, but that needn't stop you growing vegetables. The answer is to grow them, just like the old cottagers did, in among the flowers in the borders.

This is another method I investigated thoroughly for my book *The Ornamental Kitchen Garden*, but I can claim no credit for the idea. That goes to an unknown cottager some time back in the Dark Ages.

The fact is that vegetables were *always* grown in patches among flowers and herbs. It was only when Turnip Townsend invented the horse-drawn seed drill that we began to grow in rows. Up to that time even the farmer broadcast seed by hand in random fashion. When the drill and the horse-hoe were invented, they were, of course, of immense value to farmers, so gardeners copied the trick of growing in long, straight rows in the mistaken idea that it must be good for them too. Nothing could be further from the truth.

First, growing vegetables in patches among flowers dispenses at a stroke with the farmer's biggest problem – monoculture. If we can hide our vegetables away, they're much less likely to be attacked by pests or diseases. And if pests do seek them out, the balanced environment of the flower borders will have attracted a colony of other wildlife that includes the enemies of those pests. Nature will do the job for us.

There's also something very enjoyable about growing in small patches, because it's much less daunting. You can come home from work and, before you sit down to eat, you can have dug over a small patch and sown it with the next crop of fresh veg.

The technique is very simple. Leave a few patches in the front of the border where you can get at them. They can be almost any size, because you can grow two or three patches of one vegetable if you need more. To keep the fertility high put on a 5 cm (2 in) layer of compost every time you sow or plant, add a little organic fertilizer and fork it all in with a small border fork. Deep digging is unnecessary and will disturb the roots of neighbouring plants. Then firm the soil a little by tamping it down with the back of the fork.

If you're sowing, simply scratch shallow furrows in the soil at the required distances apart, sow thinly into them, cover by scuffling some soil over the drills with your hand and pat them down.

For bigger seed like broad beans, sow individually in a circle. When the beans come up, they make an attractive column and can be supported by a single cane in the middle.

It's a very simple, very productive method and, most importantly, the vegetables and flowers mix quite happily together. They look good and produce high yields which don't need any spraying, and the tool kit needed is a fork, bucket and a stick. This is *real* cottage gardening.

The Victorian gentry came up with the peculiar idea that
vegetables were ugly and should therefore be hidden away in a
separate vegetable plot lest delicate young 'gels', setting eyes
upon them, should have an attack of the vapours.
Cottage gardeners at the time fortunately never experienced
the dubious advantage of such high-born nonsense and
continued to grow their vegetables in among the flowers.
Few could deny that, grown this way as a part of the whole
garden, they add a great deal and will certainly improve
the lot of the gardener in every way.

Old Methods

Vegetable-growing techniques for gardeners have hardly changed since those early days when cottagers *had* to produce most of their food from their gardens. It's still sensible to add manure to the soil if possible, or to substitute compost where it's difficult to obtain. The soil still needs fertilizer and, though we would rarely think of using the contents of the privy and there's often not room for even a few chickens, we can certainly put on much the same kind of plant food in the form of organic fertilizer bought by the bag. We still hoe and plant, harvest and sow in much the same way. Indeed the best cultivator of all, the spade, was brought here by the Romans and has hardly changed in design since.

But there are many ways in which we can improve on the results of the cottagers of old. While old vegetable varieties have a certain charm, there's no doubt that, if you're after flavour, quality and disease resistance, the newer ones are far better. So it would be folly to become stuck in the past for purely romantic reasons. Get a modern seed catalogue and grow the new varieties that the old cottage gardeners would have loved to have planted.

GLOBE ARTICHOKE

This delicious vegetable flower has been grown in Britain since the middle of the sixteenth century, but I can't imagine early cottage gardeners eating it. It was certainly grown by Victorian cottagers, though, and is a valuable ornamental plant, so I include it here.

It can be raised from seed sown in early spring inside and planted out in late spring 45 cm (1½ ft) square. If you have the space, you can prolong the season by leaving in every other plant to crop again much earlier the next year while another planting of seed-raised plants produces a later harvest.

JERUSALEM ARTICHOKE

The root vegetable equivalent of the globe artichoke was certainly grown by cottage gardeners and was recommended by Thomas Tusser in 1557. It's a permanent crop which takes up quite a lot of space and is not very decorative, so you'll need a big vegetable plot. Plant the tubers 30 cm (1 ft) apart in early spring and dig them the following winter. Those you leave in the soil will re-appear, so further planting is unnecessary.

The globe artichoke is something of an acquired taste but generally considered a delicacy by more sophisticated and better-travelled modern cottage gardeners. It's easily raised from seed.

BROAD BEAN

An extremely ancient plant, almost certainly eaten by Neolithic man and always one of the staples of the cottager's diet. It's a valuable source of protein, and the roots of the plant enrich the soil with nitrogen.

Sow outside in early spring in double rows, setting two seeds together 15 cm (6 in) apart in 10-cm- (4-in)-deep drills set 30 cm (1 ft) apart. If both seeds germinate, pull out the weaker seedling. They can also be grown in a circle in the borders.

FRENCH BEAN

Cultivated in North America as early as 5000 BC, this bean arrived in Europe in the sixteenth century. At first cottage gardeners seem to have cultivated only the climbing varieties, which are grown just like runner beans.

Bush types were here by the early eighteenth century and Cobbett suggests that they could be had in flower only ten days after germination. That must have been under glass and even then a pretty prodigious feat of horticulture.

Sow them outside, two seeds together, in late spring, setting them 30 cm (1 ft) square. Again, if both germinate, remove the weaker seedling. At the end of the season it's a good idea to leave some pods to go brown so that the beans can be dried and stored in airtight jars for use in winter.

RUNNER BEAN

Thought to have been introduced by John Tradescant in 1633, the runner bean was first grown as a purely decorative plant, trained over arbours and pergolas where the red or white flowers were much admired. It was not until the eighteenth century that the beans themselves were eaten. From then, of course, they became more or less obligatory in cottage gardens and allotments everywhere. In small gardens in particular they're a real asset, producing huge crops from a quite small area, as well as being of tremendous decorative value. Set up a row or wigwam of 2.4-m (8-ft) canes 30 cm (1 ft) apart and sow two seeds at the base of each in late spring. When they emerge, thin to one seedling.

They may need some help to start up the right cane, but after that they should look after themselves. Pick the beans regularly to ensure that you have a continuous supply.

Runner beans take up little space for the huge crops they produce.
I like to grow mine up hazel rods rather than canes to create
a more rural effect – they're still available from coppiced
woodland, but you'll need to search out a supply.

BEETROOT

It's likely that the beets mentioned by writers like Thomas Tusser in the sixteenth century were either swedes or turnips or both, because he mentions in his list 'Bleets or beets, white or yellow'. Red beet was certainly cultivated by the Romans in England, but many of the Roman vegetables went out of favour after the occupation. However, there is mention of 'Roman Beet' in 1557, so I'm not sure. Certainly they were grown by later cottage gardeners and were valued not only for their roots but for the leaves too. If you haven't tried the leaves, cook and serve them like spinach.

Sow beetroot in succession from mid-spring until mid-summer, setting the seed clusters 5 cm (2 in) apart. If more than one seedling appears, thin to leave the strongest. Beetroot can be stored through the winter in boxes of garden compost or sand in a frost-free place.

Beetroot can be grown in succession all summer and will store well over the winter. One variety will serve both purposes.

BROCCOLI

Introduced into England during the sixteenth century, this was one of the cottage gardeners' 'worts' that were so important to them. It produces delicious, flowering heads in late winter, and I have no doubt that the leaves were boiled, and boiled and boiled and eaten: they're not recommended now, though. Sow in a seed bed in mid-spring and transplant 60 cm (2 ft) apart each way when the seedlings are big enough to handle. Harvest the young shoots regularly.

BRUSSELS SPROUTS

Very popular with Victorian cottage gardeners and up to this day, but not introduced into Britain until the nineteenth century. They had been grown in Europe since about 1750. Cobbett suggests that 'the large leaves are broken down in the month of August to give the little cabbages room to grow' – advice to be studiously ignored.

This is one crop where it is probably best to choose the old-fashioned varieties. The F1 hybrids now produced for farmers and sold to gardeners are bred to crop all at once for machine harvesting: just the opposite of what we want. The old ones have a stronger flavour too.

Sow in a seed bed in mid-spring and plant out 60 cm (2 ft) apart when the plants are large enough to handle comfortably. Ideally intercrop a fast vegetable like lettuce in between.

CABBAGE

Certainly one of the most important of all cottage vegetables. John Claudius Loudon, for example, suggested that the cottager with a family of five needed a 20 rod or 505 sq. m (605 sq. yd) garden and that he should devote 3 rods or 76 sq. m (90 sq. yd) to cabbages producing, he reckoned, 525 cabbages annually. That's 100 cabbages a year *each*, which I'm sure most of us would now consider a bit of an overdose!

Spring cabbage is always one of the most welcome of vegetables early in the year. It can be eaten as 'greens' or left to heart up later – or both.

Cabbage was probably a native plant and so has been eaten in Britain since pre-history. Even the red cabbage was here in the fourteenth century, and Gerard grew Savoys in 1597. Modern varieties are generally a great advance on the old ones.

Start summer cabbage in the coldframe in late winter and plant out in early spring 23 cm (9 in) square. Follow this by sowing in early spring and transplanting to the same distances.

Sow autumn and winter cabbages in a seed bed in mid-spring and transplant them 60 cm (2 ft) apart, just as Thomas Hill recommended in the sixteenth century: 'cabbadges may be removed when they are a handfull high'. It's still good advice.

Sow spring cabbages in a seed bed in late summer and, again, transplant them when they're large enough to handle. Set them about 15 cm (6 in) apart with a view to removing every other one for spring greens and leaving the others to heart up later.

CARROT

Carrots were on Thomas Tusser's list of pot herbs and were grown in medieval times, but they were very different from the roots we know today. Pretty certainly they were much-branched and yellow, orange or, the most popular, purple. Red carrots came in during the eighteenth century and ousted all the rest.

The seeds were used medicinally and Thomas Hill claims that they 'removeth the venereall act, procureth Urine and asswageth the Chollerick, sendeth down the termes in Women and profiteth the Melanchollicke'. He also suggests that 'the wearing of this root is profitable', though he doesn't explain how or why.

Mostly the roots were used as pot herbs in the ubiquitous soups that poorer cottagers seemed to live on.

Early sowings of a quick-maturing variety can be grown in the soil of a coldframe in late winter, and the first sowings outside can be made in early spring in rows 15 cm (6 in) apart. The seedlings should be thinned to the same distance.

Continue sowing one of the later varieties until mid-summer, though these larger roots will need more room and should be sown 23 cm (9 in) apart and thinned to 15 cm (6 in). Late sowings will store in slightly moist compost or sand throughout the winter.

CAULIFLOWER

The cauliflower was not really an early cottage garden vegetable. Though probably introduced in the sixteenth century, it didn't achieve popularity here until the seventeenth. Gerard called it 'Cole flowery' and was very enthusiastic. It's probably the most demanding and difficult of our

OPPOSITE Even on the allotment it's a good idea to allow a few flowers to creep in. They help to attract beneficial insects and to lift the spirits.

Some of the newer varieties of self-blanching celery, like 'Celebrity', have very white stems and are much less stringy than the older ones.

Cauliflowers are certainly the most challenging of vegetables to grow. The secret is to get them started and to keep them growing steadily with never a check.

vegetables to grow, but has been enthusiastically produced in cottage gardens certainly since the eighteenth century.

Start early varieties in seed trays in the cold-frame in early spring and plant out 23 cm (9 in) square in mid-spring. Continue successional sowings of the same varieties outside in a seed bed until late spring.

Sow autumn and winter varieties outside in a seed bed in mid-spring and plant them out 60 cm (2 ft) apart. Never let the seedlings get too big before transplanting and don't let them dry out or they'll produce tiny, premature curds.

CELERY and SMALLAGE

Celery is a native and has been eaten since the earliest times, but probably only the leaves were used. It's likely that the early plants grown were like the wild celery, or smallage, which has

feathery leaves with a celery flavour and is used to flavour food and in soups. The plant with the fleshy stem we all know was introduced from Italy in the seventeenth century.

New self-blanching types are easy to grow and, provided they have sufficient water, produce good, succulent stems. Sow in trays or modules in the coldframe in early spring and plant out 23 cm (9 in) square in late spring.

COURGETTE and MARROW

The vegetable marrow came from the Americas to Europe probably in the sixteenth century, but didn't reach Britain until the eighteenth century. Loudon thought it came from Persia, but it's likely that, by that time, it was fairly widely distributed anyway. Later cottagers enthusiastically adopted it, not just to eat but again, to show off their gardening skills by growing huge specimens, though these were, of course, eaten too.

The courgette is a very recent introduction and

is simply a small marrow. Start seeds off in the coldframe in late spring in individual pots, setting two seeds per pot and removing the weaker seedlings. Plant out bush varieties about 60 cm (2 ft) square only after all danger of frost has passed. Trailing types are too vigorous for small gardens unless you grow them over an archway, pergola or even an arbour. The large fruits will need support, with a string around the neck, but they make quite a talking point.

Cut courgettes regularly to encourage further production, but leave a few marrows to harden in the sun in late summer and store them in nets in a cool place until the end of the year.

CUCUMBER

Grown and introduced by the Romans, the cucumber was such a favourite of the Emperor Tiberius that he ordered that he should have one every day. Thomas Hill, in the sixteenth century, waxed lyrical about 'Cowcumbers', suggesting that they should be covered with sheets during thunderstorms because they 'much feare the thunder and lightning' and that bowls of water under the fruits would stretch and straighten them as they reached for the moisture.

They were always grown outside by cottagers, mostly too poor to own greenhouses, and these would have been trailing types, allowed to wander over the ground. There are still many good trailing varieties of what we now call 'ridge' cucumbers and they can be grown up a wigwam of canes or hazel poles to save space. Alternatively there are now bush varieties which produce excellent crops and take up much less room.

Cultivate them as for courgettes and marrows.

KALE

Grown since at least the sixteenth century, kale was considered very much a working man's vegetable, if not fit only for cattle. Cottage gardeners also grew perennial kinds which could be easily propagated by cuttings. Modern varieties are tasty and certainly not to be scoffed at. Being very hardy, they're particularly useful in colder areas. Sow in a seed bed in mid-spring and transplant 60 cm (2 ft) apart each way.

LAMB'S LETTUCE

A native used widely by cottage gardeners as a winter salad, lamb's lettuce fell from favour in the eighteenth century to be replaced by lettuce. Cobbett reviled it as a common weed and it's rarely offered in seed catalogues now. I think Cobbett was right.

Lettuce, an extremely valuable garden crop, is much better when picked fresh and eaten straight away. By using cloches and some hardier varieties in winter, it's possible to get a long succession for harvesting.

LEEK

The leek is a native of Europe and mentioned by Chaucer, so is certainly very old. The cultivated form was possibly brought to Britain by the Romans and its adoption by the Welsh as the national emblem may be connected with a victory over the Saxons in the sixth century. Thomas Hill suggested that leeks stuffed into mole tunnels would drive them away or even kill them. Thomas Tusser gives us an idea of how cottagers in the sixteenth century relied on them:

Now leekes are in season for pottage full good,
and spareth the milchcow and purgeth the blood.
These having, with peason for pottage in Lent,
thou sparest both otemell and bread to be spent.

Sow them in a seed bed in mid-spring and, when they're large enough to handle comfortably, transplant by making holes with a dibber 15 cm (6 in) apart and 15 cm (6 in) deep and dropping them in. Don't refill the hole, but water them in.

Lettuce

Cos lettuce is a very ancient vegetable and was brought to Britain by the Romans, but cabbage types seem to be a sixteenth-century introduction. Certainly they have been grown in cottage gardens since then and have long been the most important salad vegetable. As with many other vegetables, their flavour can be improved, according to sixteenth-century advice, by steeping the seeds in rose water. Modern varieties need no such treatment.

Sow quick-maturing varieties in trays on the windowsill in late winter and transfer to the coldframe or under cloches three weeks to a month later. Start the main sowing in early spring outside, thinning seedlings to 20 cm (8 in) square. Some of the row can also be transplanted to give a later crop. Continue sowing once a fortnight until late summer. Winter-hardy varieties can be sown in late summer to mature in spring, but the quality will be much improved if they can be covered with cloches.

Onion

Though introduced by the Romans and used by wealthier gardeners, the onion doesn't seem to have found favour with cottage gardeners until quite late, probably the late eighteenth or early nineteenth century. They used to grow scallions or shallots (or perhaps Welsh onions) and garlic. Later the onion became a mainstay of the cottager's diet and it's still one of the most useful vegetables in the kitchen.

Onions can be raised from seed sown thinly in early spring outside in rows 23 cm (9 in) apart and thinned to 7.5 cm (3 in) between plants. Alternatively use sets (small bulbs), planted at the same spacings in late winter. Sets are particularly useful if you're gardening on very heavy soil and it's now possible to buy a good range of varieties, some of which will mature very early in the season. Put them in shallow drills so that the top of each set is just covered. Lift them in late summer and ripen them in the sun, then store in ropes or nets.

Shallots are grown like onion sets except that they're put in with 15 cm (6 in) between the sets. While the onion set simply grows to form a single, much larger bulb, the shallot will produce a clump of bulbs from each set and should be harvested in June or July. Save some of the sets for re-planting.

Orage or orach

This was the name given to the plant *Atriplex hortensis*, which was grown before the advent of spinach (or spinedge) in the mid-sixteenth century. The name was also given to the weed fat hen, and the leaves of both were boiled and used in pottage. I've never seen the seeds offered in today's vegetable lists, but the purple type is available as an ornamental and worth growing in the border for both decorative and culinary purposes. Sow in early spring.

This cottage garden in Suffolk grows a large crop of onions every year. After harvesting they're laid out on the soil to dry for a few days, then cleaned up and stored in strings hung in the shed. They last all winter. Each year a few are transplanted into a corner of the garden, together with a few leeks, and these are left to produce seed. In late summer it's collected and stored ready to be sown in spring. The onions, and many other vegetables too in this garden, cost nothing to grow.

Purple orach is grown as an ornamental. It's a hardy annual but seeds itself about freely. Well worth growing in the borders.

Parsnip

The parsnip is woody and almost inedible in its wild form, but better types were bred as early as the Middle Ages. It was a staple of cottage gardens and used to make beer, wine and even bread and cakes. Strangely Thomas Hill recommends that 'The gardener which would posess faire and big roots ought to pluck away the leaves often times and to cover light earth on the heads ...'

My own advice would be to sow in early spring in rows 23 cm (9 in) apart, setting two seeds at stations 10 cm (4 in) apart. They take some time to germinate, so sow a few radish seeds in the same drill to mark the row. Thin to one seedling and harvest after they've had a frosting. They can be left in all winter, though harvesting and storing in moist sand or compost is preferred. Grow Hamburg parsley in exactly the same way.

Peas

Introduced by the Romans, 'peason' were one of the great mainstays of the cottager's diet and a valuable source of protein. They were originally mostly of the round type and eaten dried in soups. By the eighteenth century many varieties existed and work began on breeding the sweeter, wrinkled peas.

Nowadays many of the varieties that are being offered to gardeners have been bred for farmers and designed to mature together for combine-harvesting, so you'll have to be careful to pick varieties that will mature over a longer period.

Sow them in broad drills about 5 cm (2 in) deep made with a spade. Start in early spring, setting the seeds about 5 cm (2 in) apart in the drill to make a double row. Continue at about three-weekly intervals until mid-summer. You'll need to provide support with twiggy pea sticks or with netting, which will soon be hidden by the plants. Pick regularly, and after harvesting cut down the haulm and compost it but leave the roots in the ground to release their nitrogen for other crops.

Later cottage gardeners also used to grow asparagus peas, which are eaten complete with pod. They have the disadvantage that they soon go stringy, so it's best to stick to modern sugar-pod varieties. If you want the old-fashioned dried 'peason', allow some pods to go brown in the sun and store in airtight jars.

Potato

Though this most valuable of all root crops arrived in Europe in the sixteenth century or perhaps even before, it was not enthusiastically espoused by cottage gardeners until the eighteenth century. It's not really clear why, because it *was* grown earlier in Ireland, where over-planting was later to result in the disaster of potato blight and a mass exodus.

It was also grown keenly in Lancashire in the seventeenth century, but it's not really clear why it became regionalized. When it was finally universally accepted, it rapidly became essential to the poor cottage gardener's diet. Even so, in the nineteenth century, William Cobbett

Potatoes have become a real staple in the modern cottager's diet and you'd have to go a long way to find a more nutritious, healthy food. They have the advantage that they can be stored right through the winter, and maincrop varieties will last until the next crop is ready – just. Lift them, dry them on the soil for an hour or two and store in a frost-free shed in paper (not polythene) bags.

claimed never to eat it, preferring bread.

In small gardens, maincrop varieties take up too much room to make them a realistic crop. However, every garden should try to grow a few early varieties for their exquisite flavour. Buy the seed tubers in late winter and set them up in a box in the light and in a cool but frost-free place to 'sprout'. This will greatly increase the yield. Plant them in early spring about 15 cm (6 in) deep and 30 cm (1 ft) apart in rows 60 cm (2 ft) apart. If you have no room for that, plant single tubers with a trowel in the borders. They'll make an attractive mound of foliage and produce heavy crops. If you have room for maincrop varieties, plant in early to mid-spring, setting them 38 cm (15 in) apart in rows 75 cm (2½ ft) apart.

Protect the haulm from threatened frost by drawing up soil over the leaves if necessary. Dig early varieties in early summer and the late crop in late summer or early autumn.

Radish

A very ancient root vegetable, probably developed by selection from the wild radish. Before the sixteenth century there seem to have been many different varieties ranging from small, as we know them today, to very large indeed. The illustrations in Gerard's *Herball* of 1597 show very large roots more like beetroot, some long and others round. The larger-rooted types appear to have died out after the sixteenth century and are only now coming back into fashion. Today it's possible to get varieties as big as a cricket ball and with a fine, nutty flavour.

The more common, smaller varieties are the quickest of all vegetables to mature and should be sown in short rows regularly. Start in early spring and continue at fortnightly intervals until autumn. Sow in wide drills, scattering the seed thinly and, instead of thinning out, harvest selectively to give the remaining plants more room.

Seakale

A European native, often seen growing near the sea, seakale was eaten by cottage gardeners, though until the late eighteenth century it seems to have been gathered from the wild rather than cultivated. Being a maritime plant, it needs a well-drained, sandy soil. It's now generally bought as crowns which are planted about 45 cm (1½ ft) apart each way in spring.

Seakale is at its best when forced: put a special terracotta forcer (or a bucket) over the top in early spring. For the earliest crop the forcers are put on in late winter and covered with fresh manure to warm them up.

Seakale has attractive, grey foliage and can be used to advantage in the borders. I edged my gentleman's garden herb plot with it, interspersed with flowering plants, and it looked very handsome indeed. The forced young shoots are a real delicacy.

SHALLOT

See under 'Onion' (page 218).

SPINACH

An important leaf crop for cottage gardeners, spinach was introduced in the mid-sixteenth century. It's in Tusser's list and Hill mentions it for both culinary and medicinal purposes. He also suggests that the older the seed, the faster will be the germination, but I'd take that with a pinch of salt.

The first crops can be raised in pots or modules in the coldframe from an early spring sowing and planted out in mid-spring. Also sow direct in mid-spring, sowing thinly in rows 30 cm (1 ft) apart. Thin to leave single plants 15 cm (6 in) apart.

A newer introduction is Swiss chard, which is like spinach but with a fleshy mid-rib, much sought after by gourmet cooks. Indeed it's often suggested that the leaves should be removed and only the mid-rib eaten. In true, thrifty, cottager fashion I eat both and find them delicious. They're grown just like spinach, though they're hardier, so a winter crop can also be sown.

SWEDE

The swede was introduced from Sweden in the late eighteenth century and used by cottage gardeners both for their beasts and themselves. In those days there was no distinction between varieties and they must have made a pretty uninteresting dish. Modern varieties are far, far better and, after being touched by frost, have a sweetness that makes them highly desirable. Delay sowing until early summer to avoid the risk of mildew, and then scatter the seed thinly down drills 23 cm (9 in) apart. Thin to 23 cm (9 in) apart. Swedes can be left in the ground all winter or, better, lifted after a week of frost and stored in damp compost or sand.

TOMATO

Introduced to Europe from the Americas in the sixteenth century, the tomato was at first grown only decoratively. It was thought to have aphrodisiac properties, hence its common name of 'love-apple'. It wasn't until the nineteenth century that it became universally accepted as a food crop and was then taken up by cottage gardeners in a big way. Today there are few gardens that don't grow a few and any gardener with a small greenhouse always seems to produce enough to feed a large extended family. Tomatoes are a very satisfying crop to grow.

The plants can be raised on a windowsill, but a better bet is to buy them from a nursery since they require good light conditions to make them short and bushy. They can be planted out 60 cm (2 ft) square in late spring under cloches or in the open in early summer when all danger of frost has passed.

Older cottage gardeners would have grown only upright varieties which have to be staked, tied and side-shooted throughout the season. Newer bush types can be planted and, apart from watering, forgotten until harvest time.

TURNIP

The turnip was a real cottage garden staple. It's an ancient native plant, used to feed beasts and man alike. Some types were grown for their roots and others for their tops. Today the same type is used for both purposes, and the tops are delicious provided they are picked quite young. In the eighteenth century turnips were used a lot on an agricultural scale for grazing sheep and cattle in winter and the practice remains today.

The first crop can be raised in the coldframe: select an early variety and sow in late winter. Sow direct outside in early spring in rows 23 cm (9 in) apart. Thin to 15 cm (6 in) and harvest when the roots are quite young and tender.

Herbs

❀

Herbs were the early cottage gardener's medicine chest and were very important to all families both for healing and in the kitchen. Modern cottagers may not know much about the medicinal properties of herbs, but they are quite knowledgeable about their culinary uses. The increase in travel has broadened our experience of foreign cooking, for which a wider range of herbs is essential, so a well-stocked herb garden is still important.

Herbs are also desirable as decorative plants, of course, and can be used to freshen the air far more effectively and pleasantly than those ghastly chemical aerosols which smell worse than the odours you want to banish. Strewing herbs were used to take away the much stronger smells that no doubt pervaded early cottages and to deter lice and all kinds of other creepy-crawlies. Again, that's hardly necessary today, but a bowl of pot-pourri made from herbs and flowers collected from the garden will certainly fill your rooms with the fresh smell of the countryside.

Cultivation

Most herbs need a sunny spot and a well-drained soil. So, if yours is heavy, prepare the area with plenty of coarse grit and add as much compost or manure as you can. If you can raise the soil in this way, it'll improve the drainage and warm the soil too.

You could make a special place for herbs and I've allowed for a small herb garden in both the artisan's and the gentleman's gardens. If you can make the garden near the back door, where the cook won't have to brave the elements for a sprig of parsley, so much the better.

Both my herb gardens are small, and it's therefore vital to choose the plants very carefully. Some, like lovage and angelica, make huge plants up to 3 m (10 ft) tall and are obviously not to be grown in a small plot. Many others, like mint, will run through the soil or spread to cover and choke out other herbs. The way to control the growth of those that are only a bit too exuberant is to harvest them regularly. Pinching out the growing tips provides fresh herbs and prunes the plants too. However, at times when you don't need the herbs you'll still have to do the pinching job or the more vigorous will take over.

Other than that, once they're planted, there's very little cultivation to do. Obviously keep the garden weed-free and feed only if the plants look as though they're suffering.

A small herb garden is essential for the modern cottager, so I planted one in both gardens. Here in the artisan's garden, it was sited outside the 'back door' where it would be convenient for the cook and next to the sitting area to take advantage of the pleasant aromas.

If space is limited, you can grow herbs in pots where they look very decorative indeed. Choose terracotta pots if you can and fill with a compost consisting of equal parts of good garden soil, coir compost or really good garden compost, and coarse grit. Add a handful of pelleted chicken manure fertilizer or some other organic feed to each bucketful of compost.

Allium sativum GARLIC
Height: 30 cm (1 ft).
A venerable herb that has been cultivated in Britain since Roman times and probably naturalized itself too. It has been credited with many remarkable medicinal properties, including increasing energy, protecting against plague and deterring vampires. Even today it's still widely

ABOVE *Garlic has become one of the most sought-after herbs for the modern cottager's kitchen. I've found it best to stick to English varieties, having had little success growing from bulbs brought back from France.*

OPPOSITE *It's important to find out about the plants before planning a small herb garden. Taller species like fennel, lovage and angelica will have to be grown in the borders where they'll look very decorative.*

used as a general tonic and, of course, to discourage greenfly, though regrettably that has never worked for me.

In the kitchen garlic is widely used to flavour meat dishes, salads, vegetables – in fact almost any savoury dish.

It needs a sunny and well-drained spot. Plant the separate cloves in late autumn or in early spring, though autumn planting produces much better results. Lift in late summer, dry the bulbs in the sun and store in boxes.

Allium schoenoprasum CHIVES
Height: 20 cm (8 in).
This mildly flavoured onion was first recorded in Britain in 1375, but was probably collected from the wild before that. Its leaves were widely used in soups and salads and mixed with cheeses as they are today.

It wants a sunny spot and a rich, moist soil for the best leaves, though it flowers better on poorer soil. It makes a very fine border plant with its ball-shaped, deep pink flowers and was widely used in cottage gardens to edge vegetable beds. Chives can be propagated by dividing the bulbs in spring or autumn.

Anethum graveolens DILL
Height: 60 cm–1.5 m (2–5 ft).
During the Middle Ages dill was prescribed as a protection against witchcraft and as an aid to digestion. It's still used for the latter purpose for young children.

It has a subtle flavour of caraway with a refreshing sharpness and the leaves are used in pickling. The seeds are also useful in soups and fish and vegetable dishes as well as in cakes and bread.

It needs a sunny, protected position and a rich soil. Sow it where it's to grow from mid-spring to mid-summer. Keep it away from fennel, with which it cross-pollinates.

Anthriscus cerefolium CHERVIL

Height: 38 cm (15 in).

Grown in Britain since Roman times, chervil has a refined, parsley-like flavour. It was traditionally eaten on Maundy Thursday as a restorative and the roots were eaten with vinaigrette. It's used – generously because of its mildness – in salads and many other dishes, including those containing chicken and fish. The sprays of white flowers are very dainty and beautiful in the borders.

Chervil is an annual and will run to seed in dry soil, so add plenty of compost or manure before planting and grow it in semi-shade. Sow outside where it's to grow in early spring, and, because of its habit of running to seed, again in mid- and late summer. Cover with cloches if you want a supply during winter.

Armoracia rusticana HORSERADISH

Height: 60 cm (2 ft).

Another plant that was probably introduced to Britain by the Romans and used originally mainly as medicine. It served in the prevention of scurvy and to relieve rheumatism and chilblains. In the sixteenth century it was used to make the sauce we know today, but it was generally eaten with fish rather than meat.

Horseradish is not an easy plant to grow – or rather it's *too* easy. If you plant a tiny piece of root in a border, it'll soon take hold and then you'll never eradicate it. I think it's best grown in a bed of soil on a concrete path where it can be lifted and re-planted each year. Better still, collect it from the hedgerows like the old cottagers did.

Artemisia dracunculus TARRAGON

Height: 60 cm (2 ft).

There are two types of tarragon – the French and the Russian. The latter, however, is a rank-flavoured herb, so the French type is much to be preferred. It seems to have arrived in Britain in the late sixteenth century, when it soon became used to flavour vinegars, salads and roast meat in particular. It's still used for the same purposes.

It prefers a sunny spot and must have a well-drained soil. It's best to buy a plant to start with, or take a half-ripe cutting in autumn. In winter it's safest to protect the plants with a cloche. Lift and divide the plants every four or five years, but take care when untangling the tortuous roots.

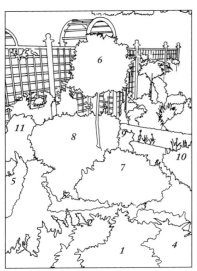

1 *Salvia officinalis* (sage)

2 *Salvia officinalis* 'Icterina' (gold variegated sage)

3 *Salvia officinalis* 'Purpurascens Variegata' (purple variegated sage)

4 *Salvia officinalis* 'Purpurascens' (purple sage)

5 *Buxus sempervirens* (box)

6 *Laurus nobilis* (bay)

7 *Artemisia dracunculus* (French tarragon)

8 *Monarda didyma* 'Croftway Pink' (bergamot)

9 *Borago pygmaea* (creeping borage)

10 *Petroselinum crispum* (parsley)

11 *Mentha piperita*

The herb plot in the gentleman's garden was planted in formal fashion in the form of a knot garden or parterre with beds surrounded by low box hedging.

Borago officinalis BORAGE

Height: 30–60 cm (1–2 ft).

Grown in Britain since the thirteenth century, borage is undoubtedly the best herb for lifting the spirits. Gerard recommended that it be drunk with wine, when 'it makes men and women glad and merry, driving away all sadness and dullness' (though this could *just* have been the effect of the wine!).

The leaf can be cooked like spinach, but its main use is as an addition to summer drinks. It was widely used in cordials until about the early twentieth century and was generally stocked by chemists. Now, of course, the flowers and leaves are used to garnish the drink Pimm's, but that's hardly a cottage garden tradition! You can preserve the herb by freezing it into ice cubes.

Borage is an easy and decorative plant which greatly brightens up the borders even if you don't use it. Give it a sunny spot, since it won't do at all well in shade. Sow it where it's to grow in mid-spring. Ever after it'll seed itself where it wants to grow, but it's easy to remove.

Campanula rapunculus RAMPION

Height: 60 cm–1 m (2–3 ft).

This biennial salad herb was a commonly grown plant in cottage gardens in the sixteenth century, but is now almost unavailable. I have found it in only one specialist seedsman's catalogue. It was grown for its leaves and roots, both of which were cooked in soups and also used in winter salads. It's a decorative plant too, with small blue or white, bell-shaped flowers.

Mix the fine seed with sand and sow in shallow drills in early summer. Thin to 10 cm (4 in) apart.

Claytonia perfoliata and *Portulaca oleracea*
PURSLANE

Height: 15–23 cm (6–9 in).

Claytonia, called both 'winter purslane' and 'miner's lettuce', is a hardy annual; portulaca or 'summer purslane' is half-hardy. Both were cultivated widely in cottage gardens during the sixteenth century for their succulent leaves, which were eaten raw in salads. William Cobbett thought little of purslane, writing that it was 'eaten by Frenchmen and pigs when they can get nothing else'. But then he didn't rate potatoes very highly either, so try it yourself. I like it.

Sow winter purslane in late summer and protect it in winter with a cloche, if you can, to produce a much better quality crop. Summer purslane should be sown in well-drained soil in sun about every month during the season.

Coriandrum sativum CORIANDER

Height: 60 cm (2 ft).

Probably introduced to Britain by the Romans, this hardy annual was used during the Middle Ages as an aphrodisiac and against scrofula. It also found a use in the kitchen to flavour roast meat in particular and is used today in curries and stews.

It needs a sunny spot and a deep, rich soil. Sow it in mid-spring where it's to grow.

Eruca vesicaria ROCKET

Height: 23 cm (9 in).

Another salad herb grown widely in old cottage gardens, rocket was probably introduced by the Romans who used it medicinally as well as in the salad bowl, where a few leaves will give a refreshing tang. The leaves can also be cooked like spinach. The boiled root was thought to draw out bone splinters from wounds.

Sow in a sunny spot in mid-spring and thin to 15 cm (6 in) apart. Repeat the sowings monthly.

Foeniculum vulgare FENNEL

Height: 2.1 m (7 ft).

An ancient perennial herb, probably native to

A fine herb bed dominated by the vivid scarlet of bergamot (see page 156). This is used in the kitchen to flavour salads, jams, jellies and even milk. It's also used to make a soothing herb tea.

Britain, and a favourite of the Romans who ate it to keep in good health and prevent obesity. It was considered by the Anglo-Saxons to be protective against evil, to increase the flow of mothers' milk and to 'make the fat grow gaunt and lank'. It was used in the kitchen by cottagers in medieval times in much the same way as today, to flavour fish in particular and their all too common soups.

In small gardens fennel's much too big for the herb garden, but it makes a very attractive plant in the border. It's probably best to buy a plant or to beg a division from a friend, but it can also be raised from seed sown in mid-spring.

Hyssopus officinalis Hyssop
Height: 45 cm–1 m (1½–3 ft).
This hardy shrub was recorded in Britain in the thirteenth century and possibly brought here by Benedictine monks who used it to flavour liqueurs. It was popular with cottage gardeners

because it's attractive, a good bee plant and useful against ailments of the mouth and throat. Now it's used in salads and particularly with fatty foods. The flowers and leaves are added to pot-pourri.

Give it a well-drained, sunny spot and buy a plant or obtain a softwood cutting from a friend in mid-summer.

Laurus nobilis BAY
Height: Depends on pruning.
Bay was used extensively in cottage gardens and often made into topiary, though it was more popular for this purpose in the grander gardens. Though a mediterranean plant, it was grown in England in the eleventh century.

It's a tender plant, so only to be grown outside all year round in the warmest areas. Elsewhere it

Bay is widely used in the kitchen and makes an attractive feature plant in the herb garden. In colder areas it must be grown in a pot.

must be grown in a pot and brought inside in winter: a porch or a cold room will do.

Bay is used to flavour lots of different cooked dishes, especially soups, stews and casseroles. The leaf is removed before serving. Bay leaves can be dried and stored in airtight jars.

You'd need to buy a plant to start with, or take a cutting from a friend's plant. Softwood cuttings root quite easily in summer. Pot into the equal-parts mixture and bring inside in late autumn. Naturally container-grown bay will need watering and feeding during the growing season.

Melissa officinalis BALM
Height: 1 m (3 ft).
Cottagers used the lemon-flavoured leaves as a nerve tonic and a heart stimulant. In the kitchen it was added to salads, to fruit and vegetables before cooking and as an infusion especially to reduce temperatures.

It also found a use as an excellent bee plant and the leaves were rubbed on hives to encourage the bees to stay. It was thought to be effective against bee stings too.

Balm prefers semi-shade and a moist soil, so it's probably best to select a spot in the border. Keep harvesting regularly and cut the whole plant back hard in autumn to retain its bushy habit. Propagate by division or seed sown in mid-spring outside.

Mentha spp. MINT, PEPPERMINT and PENNYROYAL
Height: 60 cm–1 m (2–3 ft).
Many different types of mint have been grown in Britain since at least the ninth century. They were used widely to purify water and air and to rid a room of fleas and lice, to cure headaches and mad dog bites and as strewing herbs.

In the kitchen mint was used, just as it is today, to flavour lamb in particular, with vegetables, in pea soup and to make a pleasant infusion.

In the garden the problem is its running roots. It cannot be grown in the herb garden or the borders or it'll take over. If you have a small bed surrounded by lawn, you can control it by cutting off the new young shoots when you mow the grass, but the easiest way to grow it is in a pot. Use an equal-parts mixture of soil, compost and coarse grit and take the plant out of its pot each autumn, split it up and re-plant a few roots in fresh compost.

Ocimum basilicum BASIL
Height: 45 cm (1½ ft).

This invaluable herb was used to settle the stomach, especially after excess alcohol, and was thought to relieve snake bites. It has a pungent flavour, is sprinkled on many dishes as a garnish, and is used in tomato dishes, egg dishes, soups and pesto sauce. The dried leaves are used in potpourri.

Basil is a tender herb, so it needs full sun and shelter from wind. Sow it on a windowsill in early spring and transfer the pots to the coldframe in mid-spring. Don't set it outside until all danger of frost has gone. Pinch off the flower buds as they appear and, in autumn, lift a few plants, pot them and cut them back. If you put them on the windowsill inside, they'll produce another crop of leaves. The leaves can be frozen or dried.

Origanum onites, Origanum majorana and *Origanum vulgare* MARJORAM and OREGANO
Height: 15–60 cm (6 in–2 ft).

First recorded in Britain in the tenth century, this ancient herb had many medicinal purposes from curing dropsy to toothache, rheumatism to hayfever. It was also used as a strewing herb, especially to spread on the floor of the bridal chamber. Elizabethan cottagers used it to flavour meat dishes, in salads and as an infusion just as we do today. Oregano has a somewhat stronger, peppery flavour than the two marjorams.

All do best on a sunny site, though the golden marjoram (*Origanum vulgare* 'Aureum') can scorch in strong sunshine so may need a little shade. All can be sown in mid-spring, but germination is slow and erratic. A better method of propagation is by stem cuttings or simple division. Note that sweet marjoram (*O. majorana*) is half-hardy, so will need replacing each year in cold areas.

Petroselinum crispum PARSLEY
Height: 15 cm (6 in).

This has been the most popular herb in Britain since the seventeenth century, but before then it was considered poisonous and a probable cause of epilepsy. None the less, it was used in the sixteenth century to 'cast forth strong venome or poyson', so it seems that opinions were divided. Today, of course, it's used as a garnish, in salads and sandwiches, in a superb fish sauce and, chopped with shallots, as persillade.

It's said to be difficult to germinate, but the foolproof method is to raise it on the windowsill in plastic modules in early spring. Alternatively wait until mid-spring and pour boiling water down the seed drill before sowing.

Rosmarinus officinalis ROSEMARY
Height: 1–2 m (3–6 ft).

A Mediterranean shrub, first recorded in Britain in 1340, though probably introduced by the Romans and long used by cottagers to add flavour to meats, especially lamb, rabbit and poultry. There are many folklore stories attached to rosemary. It improves the memory and is good for the head generally. Made into 'rosset sweetcakes', it makes the heart merry, it's an effective hair restorer and cures bubonic plague and bad eyesight. It's still looked upon today as a plant of

Parsley is often difficult to germinate. The seed responds to sharp changes in temperature, so the secret is to pour boiling water down the drills before sowing.

remembrance, so it's often planted on graves and in gardens in memory of the dead.

It's best to start off by buying a plant or taking a softwood or a half-ripe cutting from a friend either in early summer or autumn. It's essential to give it a well-drained, sunny spot in the garden and, because it grows tall, to harvest it regularly to keep it in shape. It will produce attractive, mauve or blue flowers if allowed to, but it's very important to trim it back in the spring after it's finished flowering to keep it neat.

Rumex acetosa SORREL
Height: 23 cm (9 in).
A native to Britain and used widely for medicinal purposes and in the kitchen, sorrel was prescribed for ulcers, as a laxative, to fix teeth in the gums, for the liver and even to restore the lost voices of singing birds. In the kitchen it was, and still is, boiled or steamed like spinach, used in the famous sorrel soup and added, in moderation, to salads.

It needs a rich, well-drained soil and will grow in sun or part-shade. Sow in mid-spring in patches with about 23 cm (9 in) between plants – you won't need a lot. It tends to run to seed in summer, when it should be cut right down to the ground, after which it'll soon produce another crop of leaves. For a winter supply of sorrel, cover the plants with cloches.

Salvia officinalis SAGE
Height: 30–60 cm (1–2 ft).
A native of southern Europe, sage was first recorded in Britain in the tenth century and was probably used before then. It was credited with the power of longevity and, even to this day, country people insist on their daily intake of sage to prolong their lives. It's still recommended to relieve indigestion, but it should be taken for this purpose only after professional advice. In the kitchen it's now used to flavour fatty meat and, of course, to make the famous sage and onion stuffing.

There are several varieties of sage with different and very attractive leaf colours including purple, variegated purple and cream, and a slightly less hardy variety with leaves splashed green, pink and white. All the coloured varieties are as useful in the kitchen as the green ones. A hardy shrub, it has purple/blue flowers and there is also a white variety.

Grow it in well-drained soil in full sun and cut it back quite hard after flowering to encourage new young shoots. Propagate by taking softwood cuttings in early summer or half-ripe cuttings in autumn.

Satureja montana WINTER SAVORY
Height: 38 cm (15 in).
This hardy shrub was first recorded in Britain in the tenth century, but was eaten well before. It was used medicinally to ease flatulence, so it was often included in dishes containing quantities of beans and peas. It's still used today for gastric complaints.

It has a peppery taste and its main use in the kitchen is still to flavour pea and bean dishes.

Herbs, like the purple sage growing here, can be used for purely decorative purposes in the borders. Because most revel in good drainage and poorish soil, they thrive in the competitive environment.

It has quite attractive small, pink flowers in summer.

It prefers full sun and a well-drained soil and can be raised from seed sown in autumn or, much better, from softwood cuttings in early summer.

Thymus spp. THYME
Height: 7.5–38 cm (3–15 in).
Thyme was almost certainly introduced by the Romans and quickly naturalized itself here. It was thought, in the Middle Ages, to enable the partaker to see fairies, and it was used to relieve the 'meloncholicke and troubled in spirit and mind'. It induced sleep and today is still incorporated in the stuffing of herb pillows.

In the kitchen thyme is used in stuffings and soups and with fatty meat. It's also made into an infusion to relieve headaches and hangovers. Common thyme (*Thymus vulgaris*) is generally best in the kitchen, though lemon thyme (*T. citriodorus*) is also used in chicken, fish and vegetable dishes, while the prostrate caraway thyme (*T. herba-barona*) is used with beef.

It must have full sun and good drainage. In the artisan's garden it grows well in the herb table, and in the gentleman's garden in planting holes in the brick paving where it spreads to form an attractive mat. Cut back any straggling plants to encourage them to form bushy growth. Propagate by half-ripe cuttings in autumn.

Tropaeolum majus NASTURTIUM
Height: 30 cm (1 ft).
Brought to Britain from the Americas, this hardy annual was grown mainly for its flowers which it produces in a range of reds, yellows and oranges throughout the spring and summer. The leaves were used to add a pleasant tang to salads, and the seeds can be chopped and used like horseradish or pickled as a substitute for capers.

Nasturtiums are very easy to grow in a sunny spot in poor soil. Sow in early spring and thin to about 20 cm (8 in) apart.

Tree Fruit

❊

If you have the room for an orchard of big, bush or standard fruit trees, or even for two or three in your garden, praise the Lord and plant them. Nothing invokes the rural idyll more than gnarled old apple trees, bearing full pink-and-white blossom in spring or groaning under a crop of red, yellow or orange fruit in late summer and autumn. Under-sow with grass and wildflowers, add a few sheep, a duck and a goose or two and you won't be far from heaven.

It's still possible to buy old varieties too, and to get them grafted on replicas of the old-fashioned rootstocks to give large trees.

If you fancy apples like 'Broad Eyed Pippin' from about 1650, 'Catshead' from 1600, 'Old Pearmain' produced as far back as 1200, or the 'Bloody Ploughman' from 1883, they're still all available. And remember that, according to sixteenth-century writers, if the grafting wood is

You can grow plenty of fruit even in a tiny garden. This 'step-over' apple is no more than 30 cm (1 ft) high, yet it produces a fine crop of 'Bountiful' cooking apples without fail every year while taking up no more than 15 cm (6 in) of space along the edge of the path.

Apples are among the most decorative of trees with fresh pink-and-white blossom in spring, followed by bright red, yellow or green fruits in autumn.

soaked in pike's blood before being grafted on to the rootstock, the apples will always be red.

Alas, few of us new cottage gardeners have room for that kind of luxury, but we can still grow plenty of tree fruit, even in the smallest plot. The answer is to grow trained trees against the house wall or the fence. And if you have a hedge round the plot, grow them trained to canes fixed to a post-and-wire support.

Tree Shapes and Training

The best shapes to grow in small cottage gardens are fans, where the branches radiate out like the ribs of a fan: this method is suitable for apples, pears, plums, peaches, nectarines, apricots and cherries. Espaliers, where the branches run horizontally and then rise in tiers of probably four, five or six branches, are an alternative way of growing apples and pears. Step-over trees are also a good idea to edge paths: these are simply single-tier espaliers.

Initial training is not difficult, but it's far better to leave that to the nurseryman and buy the trees ready-trained. Then the pruning is very simple indeed.

Apples and pears are pruned in late summer or early autumn. You simply look for shoots that arise directly from the main stems and cut them back to 7.5 cm (3 in), cutting back to just above a bud. Then look for side shoots that have come from these shoots during the year and cut them back to 2.5 cm (1 in). And that's it.

Cherries, plums and apricots are pruned in spring just as they start to grow. Simply reduce to two or three buds any shoots that are growing out from the wall, are overcrowded or not needed to increase the size of the tree. Figs can be pruned in the same way.

Fan-trained fruit trees are tied in to canes fixed to horizontal wires. This is a method that can be used for all trees you're likely to want to grow, and all will look very decorative as well as producing good crops in virtually no garden space at all.

Peaches and nectarines are a little more diffi-cult, but not if you remember that the fruit is borne on wood made the year before. So, in the winter, cut out shoots that bore fruit the previous season and tie in a replacement shoot below, made last season. That shoot is pinched back when it has made five leaves and will bear fruit. Pinch out any other shoots that grow, except one, which you allow to grow as your replacement shoot for the next year.

Medlars and mulberries need no pruning except to remove old and overcrowded wood in winter. Try to keep the head open and well shaped because both these trees are attractive ornamentals too. Most of the fruit of medlars will be borne on two-year-old wood while mulberries fruit on new wood too.

Pollination and Harvesting

Most fruit trees need to be pollinated to produce a full crop. Where this is not so, you can get away with one, self-fertile variety, but normally you need at least two trees of different varieties. The important point to note is that they must both flower at the same time.

Usually that's enough, but there is one small complication. Some trees are triploids, which means that they won't pollinate anything else. The 'Bramley's Seedling' apple is a good exam-ple, and if you grew that you'd need at least three trees: one to pollinate the 'Bramley' and another to pollinate the pollinator.

However, though trees flower at the same time, they don't necessarily fruit at the same time, so it's

While apples can be grown against more or less any wall or fence, it's best to reserve a south- or west-facing position for the fussier pears, especially if your garden is in an exposed situation. Against a south fence they produce superb crops of high quality and flavour.

possible to choose varieties to give you a longer period of harvesting.

With apples, for instance, you could start in late summer, taking and eating apples from early varieties (which don't store well), and go right through to those harvested in early winter (which can be eaten from the tree and also stored). So it's actually possible to be eating home-grown apples in Britain from late summer through to early spring the following year.

And the beauty with space-saving, trained trees is that you can grow several even in a small garden. There's another, more fascinating advance too, but let me explain about restricting and encouraging growth first.

If a branch is growing vertically, it tends to put all its energies into making strong growth, without really bothering to produce fruit. But if you pull the branch down to the horizontal or near to it, growth is restricted and fruit formation is encouraged.

In the early years of training fans and espaliers, therefore, when you want rapid growth, you tie the branches in about 45 degrees to the vertical. Later on you pull all espalier branches down to the horizontal and some of the fan's branches too.

Now for the new development. As far as I can see, the early French fruit growers, who were the undisputed masters of grafting and training trees, never thought of this and I wonder why. I bet cottage gardeners of old would have been ecstatic at the prospect.

Modern growers are now producing 'family fans'. This means that there are three different varieties grafted on to the one rootstock. So the pollination problem and the extended period of harvesting are all achieved at a stroke and on the same tree.

The big disadvantage with family trees, however, is that it's virtually impossible exactly to match the vigour of varieties, so the strongest variety eventually takes over. Yet, with a cunning the French would be proud of, British fruit tree growers graft the strongest varieties on the bottom of the fan where they'll be pulled down and restricted, leaving the more vertical, weaker ones to grow away happily. In fact, it should be possible to match the vigour of all the branches exactly just by moving them up or down.

Rootstocks

All fruit trees are grafted or budded on to a special rootstock that determines their eventual size and how quickly in their lives they produce a full crop of fruit. The rule of thumb is that the more the rootstock reduces the size of the tree, the sooner in its life it will produce a full crop. With apples, for example, the most dwarfing rootstock will produce a good crop in two years. Much development has gone on in this field, so we are no longer stuck with the large trees that old cottage gardeners would have had to grow.

With apples, for example, you can now buy trees grafted on to dwarfing, semi-dwarfing or vigorous rootstocks. And the more the stock dwarfs the tree, the quicker it'll come into bearing a full crop.

When you buy trees, therefore, ask for varieties on dwarfing stocks. This is not so important with apples and pears, because most are usually done that way these days, but with plums and cherries it's essential.

Apples

Rootstock M27 is very dwarfing and used for trees in containers; M9 is a little bigger for small trees on good soil; both need staking all their lives. MM106 is bigger and recommended for most situations. M111 is vigorous and only for large bush or standard trees.

A very decorative way of growing apples and pears is the 'double U', but trees like this are a bit hard to find and relatively expensive.

Espaliers are easier to locate and make attractive trees which crop well. They can be bought ready-trained, and developing extra tiers is not difficult.

Pears

All today are on EMLA Quince A and generally certified virus-free.

Plums

St Julien A is the most vigorous used today and produces big trees. Pixy is dwarfing.

Cherries

Most trees are budded on to Colt, which is semi-dwarfing. There is no really satisfactory dwarfing stock at present.

Peaches, Nectarines and Apricots

Generally St Julien A is used since Pixy is not satisfactory. St Julien is fine for fan-trained trees.

Recommended Varieties

Apples
Modern varieties

Variety	Harvest	Introduced
'Discovery'	Aug.	1955
'Katy'	Sept.	1947
'Fiesta'	Oct.	1972
'Sunset'	Nov.–Dec.	1933
'Rubinette'	Oct.–Jan.	1966
'Bountiful' (cooker)	Oct.–Feb.	1984

All the above varieties will pollinate each other.

Old varieties easily available

Variety	Harvest	Introduced
'Early Victoria' or 'Emneth Early' (cooker)	Jul.	1899
'Beauty of Bath'	Aug.	1864
'Charles Ross'	Sept.	1890
'Blenheim Orange'	Oct.–Nov.	1740
'Golden Delicious'	Nov.–Feb.	1890
'Sturmer Pippin'	Nov.–Apr.	1831

All the above varieties will pollinate each other.

Very old varieties obtainable from a specialist

Variety	Harvest	Introduced	Remarks
'Court Pendu Plat'	Dec.	1200	Flowers very late, so needs another late flowerer
'Ashmead's Kernel'	Dec.	1700	Flowers late
'Ribston Pippin'	Nov.	1700	Flowers early
'D'Arcy Spice'	Dec.	1785	Flowers late
'Egremont Russet'	Oct.	1872	Flowers early
'Orleans Reinette'	Dec.	1776	Flowers late
'Bramley's Seedling' (cooker)	Nov.	1813	Triploid

Crab apples

The only variety suitable for jams and jellies is 'John Downie'. For ornamental varieties see page 105. Grow them like apples.

Pears

Modern varieties

Variety	Harvest	Introduced	Remarks
'Beth'	Aug.–Sept.	1938	Flowers mid-season
'Concorde'	Oct.–Nov.	1985	Flowers mid-season

Old varieties easily available

Variety	Harvest	Introduced	Remarks
'Conference'	Oct.–Nov.	1885	Flowers mid-season
'Doyenné du Comice'	Nov.–Dec.	1849	Flowers late
'Williams' Bon Chrétien'	Sept.	1770	Flowers mid-season
'Beurre Hardy'	Oct.	1830	Flowers mid-season
'Fertility'	Sept.	1875	Flowers mid-season
'Gorham'	Aug.–Sept.	1910	Flowers mid-season
'Louis Bonne de Jersey'	Oct.	1780	Flowers early
'Pitmaston Duchess'	Sept.–Oct.	1841	Flowers late
'Old Warden'	Feb.	1575	Flowers mid-season

Probably the most popular variety of pear is 'Conference', which is one of the easiest to grow. It's also partially self-fertile, though without a pollinator yields are slightly less and the fruit tends to be elongated.

Quinces

Variety	Harvest	Introduced	Remarks
'Vranja'	Oct.	*c.*1920	Self-fertile
'Meech's Prolific'	Sept.	1850	Self-fertile

Grow quinces like pears.

Plums

Modern varieties

Variety	Harvest	Introduced	Remarks
'Avalon'	Aug.	1985	Partly self-fertile
'Cambridge Gage'	Aug.–Sept.	1927	Partly self-fertile
'Opal'	Jul.–Aug.	1925	Self-fertile

All the above varieties will pollinate each other. If you have room for only one, choose a self-fertile variety.

Old varieties

Variety	Harvest	Introduced	Remarks
'Denniston's Superb'	Aug.	1790	
'Marjorie's Seedling'	Sept.–Oct.	1912	
'Victoria'	Aug.–Sept.	1840	
'Czar'	Jul.–Aug.	1871	All self-fertile
'Giant Prune'	Sept.	1893	
'Oullin's Gage'	Aug.	1856	
'Purple Pershore'	Aug.	1877	
'Transparent Gage'	Sept.–Oct.	1838	
'Shropshire Damson'	Sept.–Oct.	16th cent.	

Peaches

Variety	Harvest	Introduced	Remarks
'Duke of York'	Jul.	1902	
'Peregrine'	Aug.	1906	All self-fertile
'Rochester'	Aug.	1900	
'Amsden June'	Jul.	1865	
'Bellegarde'	Sept.	1732	

Nectarines

Variety	Harvest	Introduced	Remarks
'Lord Napier'	Aug.	1869	Self-fertile
'Early Rivers'	Jul.	1893	Self-fertile

Figs

Variety	Harvest	Introduced	Remarks
'Brown Turkey'	Aug. onwards		Both self-fertile and grown on their own roots
'Brunswick'	Aug. onwards		

Figs were brought to this country by the Romans and have been grown here ever since. While wealthier gardeners force huge crops in greenhouses, it's not difficult to grow varieties like 'Brown Turkey' outside.

Medlar

Variety	Harvest	Introduced	Remarks
'Nottingham'	Oct.–Nov.	995	Self-fertile and grown on its own roots as a standard tree

Mulberry

Variety	Harvest	Introduced	Remarks
'Black Mulberry'	Aug.	About 1150, but possibly introduced to Britain by the Romans	Self-fertile and grown on its own roots as a standard tree

Grown in the open, figs take two seasons to ripen. Fruits that are formed at the end of the year are subject to frost damage and only the very small ones will escape. Larger figs will often remain on the tree only to fall off the following spring.

However, in my own quite cold garden I still manage to produce an excellent crop from a tree trained against a west-facing wall. But even without fruit, the superb foliage makes it well worthwhile.

Soft Fruit

❀

Soft fruit formed an important part of the diet of the cottager and was certainly grown in gardens by the sixteenth century as well as being collected from the wild. People have been blackberrying since Neolithic times and we probably still collect fruit from descendants of the same plants. Many fruits were used medicinally and to make wine, as well as being eaten fresh and cooked. They were, and indeed still are, a rich and important source of vitamins.

In old gardens, soft fruit bushes would often form part of the hedge, which would contain plants like elder for their berries, and brambles, blackcurrants and gooseberries, valued for their prickles. As well as the favourites we know and still value today, old cottage gardeners ate many fruits which we would now shun, like barberries from the berberis plant and the small berries from the amelanchier tree, which were used like raisins. It's hardly worthwhile growing them for their fruit now, except out of interest, but many ancient fruits still survive and have been much improved by breeding.

All bush fruits do best in a sunny position. They can be grown in shade, though this will reduce the crop slightly and make it a week or two later.

BLACKBERRY
A native of Britain and grown in hedgerows everywhere. There are several cultivated varieties, but few taste as good as the wild one and all take up too much room to be worthwhile growing in small gardens. However, if you're lucky enough to have a quickthorn or a mixed hedge that you can allow to over-grow a bit during the summer, it's ideal as a support for a blackberry.

If you want to do the job properly, layer the tip of a wild plant by digging a shallow hole, putting in the growing point of a briar and covering with soil. It'll soon root and produce a new plant. Otherwise grow the variety 'Ashton Cross', a new one that gets nearest to the real flavour.

If you have room, grow blackberries up a post-and-wire structure 1.8 m (6 ft) high. Plant in autumn and cut the plant right down. The following season, shoots will grow and should be trained in a half-fan shape to one side of the plant. The following year they'll fruit while new shoots are growing. The new shoots are trained into the other side of the fan and the fruited shoots are cut out. Repeat the process annually.

You might like to try an ancient cottage garden recipe that involved peeling young shoots and putting them in salads.

Blackberries really taste best when they're picked from the wild, but some cultivated varieties are quite acceptable. This new one, 'Loch Ness', has the great advantage of being thornless, so is very easy to handle when you're tying it in.

LOGANBERRY

This is a modern plant introduced from the USA. It's a cross between a blackberry and a raspberry and has the characteristics of both parents. It produces large succulent fruits ideal for eating raw or for cooking. The only worthwhile variety is called 'L654' and has never been named. Grow it just like a blackberry.

BLACKCURRANT

The blackcurrant is another native that must have been collected from the wild in ancient times. It seems to have been grown in cottage gardens since about the fifteenth or sixteenth century.

It has the disadvantage in small gardens that it's quite vigorous, needing at least 1.5 m (5 ft) between plants. I have seen them trained on a wall as fans, but the plants were straggly and not very successful. There is, however, a new variety available called 'Ben Sarek' which is more compact and can be planted about 1–1.2 m (3–4 ft) apart. Blackcurrants can be grown as individual bushes in the border too. I can find no varieties

for sale older than twentieth-century ones.

After planting, cut the shoots down to the ground. The following year there's no pruning to do, but subsequently cut all fruited branches right out each autumn. Propagate by hardwood cuttings in autumn.

REDCURRANT AND WHITECURRANT

Also natives of Britain and collected from the wild from the earliest times. They were grown in gardens a little in the sixteenth century, but did not become very popular until the seventeenth, when many new varieties were introduced. Few remain today.

'Laxton's No. 1', introduced in 1925, is the most common redcurrant now available. For a whitecurrant look for 'White Versailles', which dates from 1843.

They can both be grown as cordons against a fence or wall. Buy trained trees or prune a bush to have three shoots in a trident shape. Set three

Blackcurrants are a bit space-consuming for small gardens, but are nonetheless among the best of the soft fruits. They produce heavy crops of delicious fruits packed with vitamin C and they bottle well and can be frozen.

The whitecurrant is not as widely grown now, but it has a very pleasant flavour, especially when cooked, so you may consider it worthwhile. 'White Versailles' is the most popular variety.

canes 30 cm (1 ft) apart on wires on the fence and plant the bush at the centre cane. Then train the shoots up the three canes by tying them in regularly. In late summer, prune all the side shoots to about three buds and any shoots that come from those side shoots to one bud, just as for trained apples and pears.

If you want to grow free-standing bushes, plant them 1.2 m (4 ft) apart and prune back the tips of the new shoots to leave five buds in winter, removing crossing or crowded branches and any that are growing towards the centre of the bush. Propagate by hardwood cuttings in autumn.

GOOSBERRY

The gooseberry was a great cottage garden plant and hundreds of varieties were bred for competition, possibly springing from French ones brought to England in 1276. Gooseberry clubs were numerous in the nineteenth century, especially in the industrial centres of the North, and some of them still flourish and hold annual competitions. Varieties like 'Crown Bob', 'Wonderful', 'London' and 'Garibaldi' appear time and again in winners' lists and you might still be able to beg a cutting or two from a gooseberry enthusiast. Old varieties available now from nurseries include 'Leveller' from 1885, 'Careless' from 1860 and 'Whitesmith' from the early 1800s.

All the old varieties are, unfortunately, a bit prone to mildew attack, so new cottage gardeners would be well advised to stick with the resistant 'Invicta' or 'Jubilee'.

As well as in free-standing bush form, gooseberries can be grown as cordons like redcurrants.

The recent gooseberry variety 'Invicta' produces huge crops of tasty berries and is resistant to gooseberry mildew. This one is grown as a standard on a tall stem, so it can be underplanted, therefore taking up no garden space at all.

There's also another advance that doesn't seem to have been available to cottage gardeners of old: you can now buy plants on standard stems about 1.2 m (4 ft) tall. The latter are ideal for small gardens since you can grow other plants underneath. However, as gooseberries hate root disturbance, it's best to under-plant with permanent plants such as low-growing shrubs. Prune standards like bush redcurrants and propagate by hardwood cuttings in early autumn.

Raspberry

The raspberry is native to Europe and was mentioned by Roman writers in the fourth century. It seems likely that its domestication didn't occur in Britain on a wide scale until the latter part of the sixteenth century. By the seventeenth century there were many different types, including some with white and yellow fruits, and breeding has continued until this day. Modern varieties are a great improvement, and newly bought canes will also be free from virus disease, so older ones have all but disappeared.

My recommendations now would be for 'Glen Moy' for an early variety, followed by 'Glen Prosen'. They'll give you picking from early to late summer.

Autumn-fruiting varieties have been known since the seventeenth century, but it wasn't until the twentieth that breeders achieved real improvements. By far the best variety is 'Autumn Bliss'.

One of the problems with growing summer-fruiting raspberries in a small garden is that a row takes up a lot of space. If you have room, grow them on a 1.8-m (6-ft) post-and-wire structure, planting in autumn and cutting them down to the ground afterwards. New shoots will grow during the following season and these should be tied in at 10 cm (4 in) spacings on the wires. In the following year the tied-in canes will fruit, while

The new varieties of raspberry now available are far better than the old ones and new cottage gardeners should certainly take advantage of them. 'Glen Prosen' is a heavy-cropping late variety with a fine flavour.

new ones grow from the bottom. After fruiting, remove the old canes and tie in the strongest of the new ones to replace them.

If you have no room for a row, grow them in a column. Fix two cross-pieces of wood to a tall stake and run wires round them to take the canes. Plant one plant either side of the stake and, when the new shoots grow, tie them into the canes to form a pillar. They crop very well and look attractive too.

Autumn-fruiting varieties also take up quite a lot of space, but they need no support. Plant in autumn and cut the plants to the ground. They'll produce new shoots and fruit the following autumn. Subsequently prune down to ground level every spring.

Propagate in winter by digging up canes that have strayed into paths.

GRAPES

The grape vine is, of course, a very old plant, grown by the ancients and is still an important crop today. In Britain vineyards were common in medieval times and, indeed, before the dissolution the monasteries made vast quantities of wine and even exported it to Europe.

Wine-growing is not really successful in colder areas where, in bad years, no harvestable crop is produced at all, so it's worth attempting only in warmer parts. However, grape vines are widely grown as decorative climbers and will sometimes produce small bunches of wine grapes when they're grown in that way. If yours do, it's important to prune them back during the season to limit the size of the plant or the grapes will be too small to use.

Grapes can be grown in Britain to produce, in good years, excellent crops and very drinkable wine. However, it's not always possible to guarantee a crop every year, so if space is limited it's probably better to stick to growing them as ornamentals.

For wine grapes, choose the varieties 'Madeleine Angevine' (introduced in 1863) or 'Seyve Villard' (introduced in 1930) to produce white and 'Triomphe d'Alsace', a more modern variety, to make red. For a crop of wine grapes, with perhaps a few for eating in a good year, plant vines 1.5 m (5 ft) apart on a post-and-wire structure 1.2 m (4 ft) high. Prune back to leave three strong buds. In the first year allow three shoots to grow and take them up a central cane.

In the following spring pull two of the branches down horizontally and tie them to the bottom wire. Prune the third to three buds to provide the three shoots for the following year. They are again grown up the central cane.

The two fruiting shoots will produce side shoots which should be grown vertically and tied in to the wires. When they reach the top wire, pinch out the tops.

The fruit will be borne on these side shoots, after which they're cut right out and two of those growing up the cane are brought down and tied in their place. Once again, the third shoot is pruned back to three buds.

Propagate by hardwood cuttings in autumn.

STRAWBERRY

The verdant fields and woodlands of Britain would have yielded many wild strawberries for early cottagers to gather, including the small-fruited alpine strawberries, which were first mentioned in the tenth century. The woodland varieties were reputed to have the finest flavour.

These relatively small-fruited varieties were, however, replaced by the larger types from America by the sixteenth century and were widely grown in the seventeenth. The biggest breeding programme was carried out by the British breeder T. A. Knight, who produced hundreds of new varieties in the nineteenth century.

Unfortunately many of those old varieties were

Strawberries produce fine crops even in colder areas and no cottage garden should be without them. The maincrop variety 'Elsanta' gives heavy yields of good-quality fruit.

plagued by virus diseases and even the favourite British strawberry, 'Royal Sovereign', introduced in 1892, was almost lost, one lone survivor, free from virus, being found on an Irish bog to save the variety for modern gardeners. Now cleaned of virus, but still susceptible, it's again available.

It's best, though, to stick to modern varieties. For a succession of harvesting I'd recommend 'Honeoye', 'Elsanta' and the autumn-fruiting

Since strawberries are so decorative, with white flowers in spring followed by the attractive red berries and good foliage too, they can be planted in the borders. In the gentleman's garden they edge the vegetable plot.

In the artisan's garden rhubarb is forced under a (second-hand) terracotta forcer to produce blanched shoots of excellent flavour and greatly reduced acidity. The harvest is also earlier and, for the first fruit of the year, that's very welcome.

'Aromel'. Plant them in late summer 60 cm (2 ft) apart each way. When the fruit starts to colour, mulch with straw underneath to keep it clean and away from slugs. After harvesting, cut back the foliage to just above the crown of new leaves in the centre of the plant and remove them together with the straw.

To propagate strawberries, root a few of the small plants that grow on the ends of runners, either fixing them to the soil with a wire staple or in pots of compost. When they've rooted, detach them from the parent, dig them up and re-plant.

Strawberries are sometimes affected by virus diseases which are spread by greenfly. So, though it may go against the cottage garden ethos, it's worthwhile buying new plants when the time comes to replace the old. Commercial strawberry growers take great pains to ensure that their plants are free from insect attack and should be able to guarantee their plants. For this reason, it's also wise to buy from a specialist grower.

However, in the gentleman's garden which has the facility of a greenhouse, there's another very good reason to propagate each year. The young plants can be rooted into 7.5 cm (3 in) pots and later repotted into 12.5 cm (5 in) pots for forcing in the late winter.

Keep the pots outside until they have been subjected to a spell of frosty weather. They can then be brought into the greenhouse and grown in gentle heat to produce the earliest crop of the season. After forcing the plants will be exhausted so it's best to throw them away.

RHUBARB

In the sixteenth century rhubarb was used only medicinally and it was not until the eighteenth that it was eaten.

'Timperley Early' and 'Hawke's Champagne' are both old, early varieties suitable for forcing. The best main-crop variety is 'Cawood Delight'; if you have room for only one root, choose this and force it too. It's possible to buy container-grown plants now, so planting can be done at any time. The plants are very decorative and would look good planted in the border. If you grow more than one plant, set them 1 m (3 ft) apart.

In late winter cover a root with a terracotta forcer or a large bucket and harvest in early spring. The shoots will be paler, but much less acid and with a delicious flavour. Propagate by division in early spring, splitting the crowns with a sharp spade.

Cottage Garden Plants through History

❋

Anglo-Saxon Plants (Eighth Century)

Almond, beet, box, cherry, chervil, chestnut, coriander, cornel, cumin, elm, fennel, feverfew, fig, gladden (iris), hemp, kale, laurel, leek, lettuce, lily, linseed, lovage, mallow, mint, mulberry, mustard, onion, parsley, peach, pear, plum, poppy, radish, rose, rue, turnip, yellow rattle, vine.

Twelfth-century Garden Plants Recommended by the Abbot of Cirencester

The garden should be adorned with roses, lilies, turnsole, violets and mandrake; there you should have parsley and cost, and fennel, and southernwood and coriander, sage, savory, hyssop, mint, rue, dittany, smallage, pellitory, lettuce, garden cress, peonies. There should also be planted beds with onions, leeks, garlick, pumpkins, and shalots; cucumber, poppy, daffodil and acanthus ought to be in a good garden. There should also be pottage herbs such as beets, herb mercury, orach, sorrel and mallows.

Traditional cottage garden plants have been improved by the plant breeders so we can make even better gardens now than the originators could have dreamed of.

Garden Plants Recommended by Ion the Gardener in the Fifteenth Century

Adderstongue fern, agrimony, alexanders, apple, artemisia, ash, avens, betony, borage, bugle, cabbage, calamint, wild celery, centaury, chamomile, clary, comfrey, coriander, cowslip, cress, daffodil, daisy, dittander, elecampane, fennel, field gentian, foxglove, garlic, goosefoot, gromwell, groundsel, hartstongue, hawthorn, hazel, henbane, herb robert, herb walter, hollyhock, honeysuckle, horehound, hyndshall, hyssop, iris, lavender, leek, lettuce, lily, liverwort, lychnis, mint, mouse-ear hawksweed, mugwort, mustard, nepeta, onion, orpine, parsley, pear, pellitory, periwinkle, polypody, primrose, radish, ratstail plantain, ribwort plantain, rose, rue, ryegrass, saffron crocus, sage, St John's wort, salad burnet, sanicle, savory, scabious, southernwood, spearwort, spinach, stitchwort, strawberry, sweet woodruff, tansy, teasle, thyme, tutsan, valerian, vervain, vine, violet, viper's bugloss, wallpepper, water lily, wood sorrel, yarrow.

The organized chaos of ornamental plants and herbs evokes the true image of the English country cottage garden. It can be reproduced in the garden of a new house as well as an old one, and in the town as well as the country – just as it has been for hundreds of years. Step into the process of evolution and make your garden part of the true cottage tradition.

Garden Plants* Recommended by Thomas Tusser in his Five Hundred Points of Good Husbandry *in 1573*

Seeds and Herbes for the Kitchen

Avens, beet, betony, bloodwort, borage, bugloss, burnet, cabbage, clary, colewort, cress, endive, English saffron, fennel, French mallow, French saffron, leeks, lettuce, liverwort, lungwort, marigold, mercury, mint, onion, orach, parsley, patience, pennyroyal, primrose, rosemary, sage, sorrel, spinach, succory, summer savory, tansy, thyme, violet, winter savoury.

Herbes and Rootes for Sallets and Sauce

Alexanders, artichoke, asparagus, blessed thistle, cress, cucumber, endive, mint, musk mullion, mustard, purslane, radish, rampions, rocket, sage, sea-holly, skirrets, sorrel, spinach, succory, tarragon, violet. (He also suggested that the housewife should buy: capers, lemons, olives, oranges, rice and samphire.)

Herbes and Rootes to Boile or to Butter

Beans, cabbage, carrot, gourd, parsnip, pumpkin, rape, rouncival peas, swede, turnip.

Strowing Herbes of All Sortes

Balm, basil, camomile, costmary, cowslips, daisies, germander, hop, lavender, marjoram, maudlin, pennyroyal, red mint, rose, sage, santolina, sweet fennel, tansy, violet, winter savory.

Herbes, Branches and Flowers for Windowes and Pots

Bachelor's buttons, bay, campion, carnations, columbine, cowslips, daffodils, eglantine, feverfew, French marigold, hollyhocks, iris, larkspur, lavender, lily, love-lies-bleeding, marigold, nigella, ornithogalum, pansy, pinks, rosemary, roses, snapdragons, stock, sweet rocket, sweet Williams, violet, wallflower, white narcissus.

Herbes to Still in Sommer

Betony, blessed thistle, dill, endive, eyebright, fennel, fumitory, hop, mint, plantain, raspberry, roses, saxifrage, sorrel, strawberry, succory, woodruff.

Necessary Herbes to Growe in the Garden for Physick, not Rehearsed Before

Anise, archangel, betony, celery, chervil, cinquefoil, cumin, dittander, gromwell, hartstongue, honeysuckle, horehound, liquorice, lovage, mandrake, mugwort, plantain, poppy, rhubarb, rue, saxifrage, stitchwort, valerian.

Thus ends in breefe,
Of herbes the cheefe,
To get more skill,
Read whom ye will,
Such mo to have,
Of field go crave.

*I have modernized some of the names a little for today's readers: for example, 'peneriall' becomes 'pennyroyal'

Picture Credits

BBC Books would like to thank the following for providing photographs and for permission to reproduce copyright material. While every effort has been made to trace and acknowledge all copyright holders, we would like to apologize should there have been any errors or omissions.

Page 17 British Museum; 18 Victoria and Albert Museum/ET Archive; 19 *top* ET Archive, *bottom* frontispiece from *The Florist, Fruitist and Garden Miscellany* 1851; 24 Manchester City Art Gallery/Bridgeman Art Library; 28 courtesy Christopher Wood Gallery; 29 *top* Royal Horticultural Society, Lindley Library; 31 David Secombe/Garden Picture Library; 32 Henk Dijkman/Garden Picture Library; 48, 49 & 54 *top* Photos Horticultural; 56 *top* Elizabeth Whiting & Assoc.; 81 John Glover/Garden Picture Library; 90 Jerry Harpur; 101 Harry Smith Horticultural Photos; 110 John Glover/Garden Picture Library; 121 Linda Burgess/Garden Picture Library; 125 Brian Carter/Garden Picture Library; 132 Brigitte Thomas/Garden Picture Library; 143 Harry Smith Horticultural Photos; 161 & 169 Photos Horticultural; 171 John Glover/Garden Picture Library; 176, 184, 185, 189, 193, 195 & 219 Photos Horticultural; 242 *left* John Glover/Garden Picture Library, *right* Michael Howes/Garden Picture Library; 245 Photos Horticultural.

All remaining photographs are by Stephen Hamilton.

Useful Addresses

COTTAGE GARDEN SOCIETY
c/o Clive Lane
Brandon
Ravenshall
Betley
Cheshire CW3 9BH

MUSEUM OF GARDEN HISTORY
The Tradescant Trust
Lambeth Palace Road
London SE1 7LB

BRICK PAVIORS
The York Handmade Brick Company Ltd
Forest Lane
Alne
Yorks YO6 2LU

VICTORIAN EDGING TILES
The Bulmer Brick and Tile Co. Ltd
Bulmer
Nr Sudbury
Suffolk CO10 7EF

PAVING
Bradstone Garden Products
Okus
Swindon
Wilts SN1 4JJ

TRELLIS
Stuart Garden Architecture
Burrow Hill Farm
Wiveliscombe
Somerset TA4 2RN

OCTAGONAL GREENHOUSE
Parklines
Gala House
3 Raglan Rd
Edgebaston
Birmingham B5 7RA

LOVE SEAT
Woodworks
7 North Street West
Uppingham
Rutland
LE15 9SF

WILLOW OBELISK AND WATTLE FENCING
English Basket and Hurdle Centre
Curload,
Stoke St Gregory
Taunton
Somerset TA3 6SR

WOOD STAIN
Sadolin (UK) Ltd
Sadolin House

Meadow Lane
St Ives
Cambs PE17 4UY

CHICKEN COOP
George Carter
Silverstone Farm
North Elmham
Norfolk NR2 5EX

GALVANIZED FLOWER BUCKETS
Terrace and Garden
Orchard House
Patmore End
Ugley
Bishops Stortford
Herts CM22 6JA

LARGE CLAY POTS
Whichford Pottery
Whichford
Shipston-on-Stour
Warks CV36 5PG

SMALL CLAY POTS
The Potting Shed
Lee Valley Forge
Wharf Road
Wormley
Herts EN10 6HF

Index

❀